JOURNAL FOR THE STUDY OF THE OLD TESTAMENT SUPPLEMENT SERIES
161

Editors
David J.A. Clines
Philip R. Davies

Editorial Board
Richard J. Coggins, Alan Cooper, Tamara C. Eskenazi,
J. Cheryl Exum, Robert P. Gordon, Norman K. Gottwald,
Andrew D.H. Mayes, Carol Meyers, Patrick D. Miller

JSOT Press
Sheffield

The Moses Tradition

George W. Coats

Journal for the Study of the Old Testament
Supplement Series 161

BS
580
.M6
C62
1993

Copyright © 1993 Sheffield Academic Press

Published by JSOT Press
JSOT Press is an imprint of
Sheffield Academic Press Ltd
343 Fulwood Road
Sheffield S10 3BP
England

Typeset by Sheffield Academic Press
and
Printed on acid-free paper in Great Britain
by Biddles Ltd
Guildford

British Library Cataloguing in Publication Data

Coats, George W.
    Moses Tradition. - (JSOT Supplement
  Series, ISSN 0309-0787; No. 161)
  I. Title II. Series
  221

ISBN 1-85075-410-1

Contents

Foreword	7
Acknowledgments	9
Abbreviations	11
Chapter 1 I WILL BE WITH YOU	13
Chapter 2 MOSES IN MIDIAN	22
Chapter 3 MOSES VERSUS AMALEK: AETIOLOGY AND LEGEND IN EXODUS 17.8-16	32
Chapter 4 HISTORY AND THEOLOGY IN THE SEA TRADITION	45
Chapter 5 THE KING'S LOYAL OPPOSITION: OBEDIENCE AND AUTHORITY IN EXODUS 32–34	57
Chapter 6 LEGENDARY MOTIFS IN THE MOSES DEATH REPORTS	76
Chapter 7 HUMILITY AND HONOR: A MOSES LEGEND IN NUMBERS 12	88
Chapter 8 *METANOIA* IN ANCIENT ISRAEL: CLUES FOR UNITY AND CHANGE	99

Chapter 9
MOSES AS A MODEL FOR MINISTRY: AN EXEGESIS OF
    EXODUS 2.11-22   104

Chapter 10
THE FAILURE OF THE HERO: MOSES AS A MODEL FOR
    MINISTRY   115

Chapter 11
THE GOLDEN CALF IN PSALM 22   125

Chapter 12
HEALING AND THE MOSES TRADITIONS   135

Chapter 13
STRIFE AND BROKEN INTIMACY: GENESIS 1–3:
    PROLEGOMENA TO A BIBLICAL THEOLOGY   151

Chapter 14
VIOLENCE IN THE HEROIC TRADITION: A CHARACTERISTIC
    MOTIF IN BIBLICAL SAGAS   170

Chapter 15
THE UNITY OF ISAIAH: AN EXERCISE IN CANON CRITICISM   182

Chapter 16
SCOPE AND STRUCTURE FOR THE YAHWIST: WHERE DOES
    IT END?   190

Index of References   196
Index of Authors   202

Foreword

These sixteen essays—four of which are published for the first time—share a commitment to form-critical and traditio-historical exegetical concerns and demonstrate the theological power of these methods. 'I Will Be With You' sets a specific context for interpreting Exod. 3.14 which leads to a view of the name of Yahweh as the sign of Yahweh's presence with Israel—whether for good or for ill. 'Moses in Midian' seeks to identify the tradition of Moses' marriage to the Midianite woman, Zipporah, as the root of the tradition of Moses, sojourn in Midian. 'Moses versus Amalek' argues that Exod. 17.8-16 belongs to the genre of heroic legend which leads Coats to consider the theological context for the heroic elements of the Moses saga. 'History and Theology in the Sea Tradition' explores problems of historical reconstruction and its relation to a theological understanding and significance of the tradition. 'The King's Loyal Opposition' explores Moses' intercession during the golden calf incident as it relates to issues of obedience and authority. 'Legendary Motifs in the Moses Death Reports' isolates and explores several heroic motifs in the texts of the death of Moses. 'Humility and Honor' makes a case for the form-critical integrity of Num. 12.1-15 and argues that Num. 12.3 should read 'The man Moses was the most honorable of all persons who are on the face of the earth', thus fitting the heroic nature of the Moses saga. 'Metanoia in Ancient Israel' portrays Moses as a model for leadership, a model which is adapted, resisted, and adapted again throughout Israel's history. 'Moses as a Model for Ministry' offers a concise exemplification of the form-critical method using Exod. 2.11-22 as the text base. 'The Failure of the Hero' explores the interpretation of texts about the failure of Moses as a leader. 'The Golden Calf in Psalm 22' offers an interpretation of the golden calf incident (the calf as the throne of Yahweh) based on Psalm 22 in which the calf symbolizes Yahweh's presence and power. 'Healing and the Moses Traditions' explores several texts in which healing plays a predominant role.

'Strife and Broken Intimacy' affirms the primeval story as a story of broken intimacy whose reconciliation leads from Abraham to Isaac to Jacob and Moses to Joshua and finally to David. 'Violence in the Heroic Tradition' explores the characteristic violence of acts of heroic deliverance and asks about the role of compassion for the enemy. 'The Unity of Isaiah' offers a canonical interpretation of the book of Isaiah in which changing views of the messiah play a crucial role. 'Scope and Structure for the Yahwist' prepares Joshua 24 as the final chapter of the Yahwist narrative in analogy with the Gilgamesh Epic.

Dr George Coats is widely known and respected for his book-length contributions to Old Testament scholarship, including *Narrative Genres in Old Testament Literature* and *Heroic Man, Man of God!* (both published by Sheffield Academic Press) and his commentary on Genesis. As one colleague recently put it, 'Anyone in this generation who reads the Moses or Joseph stories has George Coats for a companion'. These essays reaffirm that reputation.

Health problems forced Dr Coats to retire from classroom teaching at the end of 1991. The idea of honoring his outstanding career as scholar and teacher by compiling a collection of his essays was initiated by Dr Sharyn Dowd, Professor of New Testament at Lexington Theological Seminary. Editing, generally kept to a minimum, was done by Dr Henry Sun, Associate Professor of Old Testament at the Seminary. Thanks go to these two colleagues for all of their efforts in bringing this project to completion.

I also acknowledge with thanks our editor at Sheffield Academic Press, Alison Bogle, for her assistance with this project; and Ms Barbara Miller and Ms Shannon Cloyd, who assisted in the compilation of the indices.

Michael Kinnamon
Lexington Theological Seminary

Acknowledgments

Chapters 1–12 originally appeared as follows:

Chapter 1
'I Will Be With You', *Lexington Theological Quarterly* 7 (1972), pp. 77-85.

Chapter 2
'Moses in Midian', *JBL* 92 (1973), pp. 3-10.

Chapter 3
'Moses Versus Amalek: Aetiology and Legend in Exod. xvii 8-16' in *Congress Volume Edinburgh* (VTSup, 28; Leiden: Brill, 1975), pp. 29-41.

Chapter 4
'History and Theology in the Sea Tradition', *Studia Theologica* 29 (1975), pp. 53-62.

Chapter 5
'The King's Loyal Opposition: Obedience and Authority in Exodus 32–34', in G.W. Coats and B.O. Long (eds.), *Canon and Authority in the Old Testament* (Festschrift W. Zimmerli; Philadelphia: Fortress Press, 1977), pp. 91-109. Copyright © Fortress Press. Used by permission of Augsburg Fortress.

Chapter 6
'Legendary Motifs in the Moses Death Reports', *CBQ* 39 (1977), pp. 34-44.

Chapter 7
'Humility and Honor: A Moses Legend in Numbers 12', in *Art and Meaning: Rhetoric in Biblical Literature* (JSOTSup, 19; Sheffield: JSOT Press, 1982), pp. 97-107.

Chapter 8
'*Metanoia* in Ancient Israel: Clues for Unity and Change', *Midstream* 23 (1984), pp. 185-88.

Chapter 9
'Moses as a Model for Ministry: An Exegesis of Exod. 2.11-22', *Faith and Mission* 3 (1986), pp. 49-57.

Chapter 10
'The Failure of the Hero: Moses as a Model for Ministry', *Asbury Theological Quarterly* 41 (1986), pp. 15-22.

Chapter 11
'The Golden Calf in Psalm 22', *HBT Theology* 9 (1987), pp. 1-12.

Chapter 12
'Healing and the Moses Traditions', in G.H. Tucker, D.L. Peterson and R.R. Wilson (eds.), *Canon, Theology, and Old Testament Interpretation* (Festschrift B. Childs; Philadelphia: Fortress Press, 1988), pp. 131-46. Copyright © 1988 Fortress Press. Used by permission of Augsburg Fortress.

Every effort has been made to trace the copyright owners of the above articles. The publishers would be grateful to be informed of any errors or omissions.

ABBREVIATIONS

BASOR	*Bulletin of the American Schools of Oriental Research*
BFCT	Beiträge zur Förderung christlicher Theologie
BGBE	Beiträge zur Geschichte der biblischen Exegese
Bib	*Biblica*
BKAT	Biblischer Kommentar: Altes Testament
BR	*Biblical Research*
BZAW	Beihefte zur ZAW
CBQ	*Catholic Biblical Quarterly*
CBQMS	*Catholic Biblical Quarterly*, Monograph Series
EncJud	*Encyclopaedia Judaica*
EvT	*Evangelische Theologie*
FOTL	The Forms of the Old Testament Literature
FRLANT	Forschungen zur Religion und Literatur des Alten und Neuen Testaments
HAR	*Hebrew Annual Review*
HBT	*Horizons in Biblical Theology*
HKAT	Handkommentar zum Alten Testament
HUCA	*Hebrew Union College Annual*
Int	*Interpretation*
JAAR	*Journal of the American Academy of Religion*
JBL	*Journal of Biblical Literature*
JR	*Journal of Religion*
JSOTSup	*Journal for the Study of the Old Testament*, Supplement Series
LTQ	*Lexington Theological Quarterly*
NCB	New Century Bible
OTL	Old Testament Library
OTS	*Oudtestamentische Studiën*
SBLDS	SBL Dissertation Series
SBT	Studies in Biblical Theology
SJT	*Scottish Journal of Theology*
ST	*Studia theologica*
TLZ	*Theologischer Literaturzeitung*
VT	*Vetus Testamentum*
VTSup	*Vetus Testamentum*, Supplements
WMANT	Wissenschaftliche Monographien zum Alten und Neuen Testament
ZAW	*Zeitschrift für die alttestamentliche Wissenschaft*
ZTK	*Zeitschrift für Theologie und Kirche*

Chapter 1

I WILL BE WITH YOU

What's in a name? 'That which we call a rose by any other word would smell as sweet.' Or so Juliet hoped. But suppose that red American beauty were labeled wild onion? To be sure, if we knew nothing of any other onion—or nothing of any other rose, we might respond as warmly to an American beauty wild onion as to an American beauty rose. Suppose Spiro Agnew were really named Benedict Arnold. If the name were neutral, if we knew nothing of Benedict Arnold, and nothing of Spiro Agnew, the man might still be the hero of our frustrated, nameless, silent majority. But we do know what a wild onion is. And a rose would just not be a rose if it were called American beauty wild onion. We do know who Benedict Arnold was. And who Spiro Agnew is. And Spiro Agnew would not be quite the same if he were called American beauty wild onion.

Juliet's torment lies in a name. But a name is not as easy to ignore as Juliet wishes. Romeo's name is not John Smith. Romeo could not be Juliet's desire, he could not be the world's ideal lover if he were not Romeo. Romeo's name could have been Romeo Puccini. And life for Juliet would have been simpler. But Romeo Puccini is not Juliet's lover. 'His name is Romeo, and a Montague'. His name is more than hand or foot or arm or face or any other part belonging to a man. His name is his history. *Montague.* How could one man, one lover be both Romeo and Montague? Both lover and enemy. What cruel irony! What terrible reality! In a name lies the upheaval of generations' hatred and the tragedy of a generation's fateful love. In a name, Romeo and a Montague, lies the entire tragic story of a pair of star-crossed lovers, all they hoped for, all they lost.

A neutral name, a name with no history, that would have been Juliet's salvation. Yet, when is a name ever neutral? If a botanist discovers a new, previously unanticipated plant, he might give it a neutral name. 'This plant shall be called X-1!' But alas, the neutral term loses its neutrality as soon as it lands on an object. Whether X-1, or wild onion, or Spiro Agnew, once the label is given, both label and object combine. Moreover, it is only by means of a name that an object can become a subject for action. The unnamed plant with a repugnant, pungent odor demands attention. But it remains a 'What's that?' until it has a name. With a name, however, it vaults out of obscurity. The plant and the name become one. Both become household terms.

For the OT a name is just as important. It is never neutral. It is full of reality. It is one with the object that carries it. Consider one of Hosea's unfortunate children. Lying without name in a crib, the child would be only an object. No personality! No history! But when he receives a name, he receives his fate, his history, his terrible destiny. '*Lo Ammi*'. 'Not my people'. And when the prophet announces that in that day his name will no longer be '*Lo Ammi*', but rather '*Ammi*', 'my people', the child's whole outlook, his history, that stuff that makes him what he really is, changes.

I

Little wonder, then, that the OT exhibits an intense concern for the name of God. The name is not just a meaningless symbol that might just as well have been wild onion, or Spiro Agnew, or dog spelled backwards. God by any other name would not be God. The name is crucial, so crucial that Israel would take special pain to safeguard it. The third commandment intends much more than a warning to little boys that they should not say 'God Damn'! It reminds the pious Israelite that even to utter the name of God is an act of higher worship.

Out of this context the story of Moses' confrontation with God in Exodus 3 and 4 must be interpreted. A theophany, a burning bush unconsumed by fire, and a nameless God arrest Moses.[1] But the show is not just for Moses' amusement. This unknown God lays rather a heavy burden of responsibility on his unsuspecting audience. 'Go. I

---

1. Source divisions confront any interpreter of this story immediately. The verses discussed in this essay belong, according to most scholars, to E. Cf. W. Richter, *Die sogenannte vorprophetische Berufungsberichte* (FRLANT, 101; Göttingen: Vandenhoeck & Ruprecht, 1970), pp. 58-72.

shall send you to the Pharaoh, and you shall bring my people Israel out of Egypt'. But how can Moses obey without having a name to respond to? That would be like responding to a wild onion without knowing what its name is. It would be like a frustrated, nameless, silent majority, surging, threatening, mysterious, a little unreal, yet frightening for any hapless Democrat.

So Moses asks for this god's name. And then comes perhaps the most enigmatic text in the OT. 'I am who I am'. *'Ehyeh 'ᵃšer 'ehyeh*. He continues: 'Thus shall you say to the Israelites: "*'Ehyeh* sent me to you"'. God said again to Moses, 'Thus shall you say to the Israelites, "Yahweh, the God of your fathers, the God of Abraham, the God of Isaac, the God of Jacob sent me to you. This is his name and this is his memorial for all generations."' What does the cryptic sentence mean: 'I am who I am'? It obviously has something to do with the name 'Yahweh', as the parallel sentences following it show clearly: ' "I am" sent me to you'. 'Yahweh the God of your fathers...sent me to you.' But what does it do? The first use of the name Yahweh in answer to Moses' question binds the name to a history. 'Yahweh, the God of your fathers...' But it is Yahweh, not *'Ehyeh* that carries the history. Yahweh is not a neutral name, even here. It needs no primary definition. The cryptic sentence, indeed, the word *'ehyeh*, does not define the name. To the contrary, it comments on the name. It is an effort, not to define, but to interpret.

If we could crack the cryptic sentence, we would thus theoretically have an insight into an OT concept of God, an early interpretation of the significance in God's name. Unfortunately this sentence, perhaps more than any other single text in the OT, has provoked a maze of scholarly suggestions. There can be no doubt that the text intends a word play between Yahweh, the name for God given to Moses, and the Hebrew verb, 'to be', *hāyâ*. The first person form of the verb, *'ehyeh,* 'I am', sounds a little like the third person form of the same verb, *yihyeh*. And the name 'Yahweh' can be seen as a form of that third person verb.[1] But even if that kind of etymology is accurate, what does it mean for this text? What kind of comment about Yahweh does the word play intend?

---

1. M. Noth, *Exodus: A Commentary* (OTL; Philadelphia: Westminster, 1962), p. 43.

16   *The Moses Tradition*

Form critical analysis of the Moses vocation account provides a control for evaluating the crucial sentence in its larger context.[1] The first task is not to lift a verse or verses out of the unit and ask what they might mean, but rather to place the verse under consideration in its proper position as a part of a larger whole. After the burning bush exposition in vv. 1-6, the narration develops around a rather long speech from Yahweh in vv. 7-10 (perhaps more properly designated vv. 9-10, since these verses, along with the crucial sentence in vv. 12-14, belong to the Elohist). Following the speech, no description of event can be seen. The text cannot thus be described as an arc of tension, a crisis leading finally to conclusion. Rather, the unit develops its basic point in the exchange of conversation between Yahweh and Moses and thus must be categorized simply as dialogue, a theological commentary.[2]

In that dialogue lies the crucial assertion. The conversation is ordered around a scheme that belongs to various vocation units. The opening speech from Yahweh commissions Moses for a particular responsibility. The conversation then centers around Moses' objections to the commission and Yahweh's response to the objection. The focal point of the unit, at least for the Elohist, lies in Moses' request for a name, structurally an objection to the commission, and Yahweh's response. Indeed, there are three separate responses to the request. And it is just here that the cryptic sentence appears. No interpretation of the sentence that ignores its structural position in the unit, its response to Moses' question, to Moses' implied objection to the commission, can be considered adequate.

Since the sentence stands in the position of response to an objection, and the response normally functions as a reassurance to the objector, we may assume that the sentence has something to do with Yahweh's reassurance. One of the characteristic elements of reassurance in vocation units throughout the OT is a stereotyped formula of assistance, 'I will be with you'.[3] The formula can appear either as a nominal sentence, $'^a n\hat{\imath}\ 'imm^e k\bar{a}$, or as a verbal sentence, $'ehyeh$

---

1. Cf. Richter, *Berufungsberichte*, pp. 57-134, for the most recent and thorough form-critical analysis of this text. Other works of importance include N. Habel, 'The Form and Significance of the Call Narratives', *ZAW* 77 (1965), pp. 297-323, and E. Kutsch, 'Gideons Berufung und Altarbau, Jdc 6.11-24', *TLZ* 81 (1956), pp. 75-84.
2. So, Richter, *Berufungsberichte*, p. 116.
3. H.D. Preuss, 'ich will mit dir sein!' *ZAW* 80 (1968), pp. 158-59.

'*immāk*. In v. 12 of the Moses vocation story, Yahweh's response to Moses' first objection employs the verbal form of the assistance formula, *'ehyeh 'immāk*. The most striking element of the response in just this text, however, is that it carries the same verbal form which appears twice in the cryptic sentence. 'I am with you'. 'I am who I am'. The text must intend some kind of correspondence between the assistance formula and the cryptic sentence commentary on the name of Yahweh.[1] A definition of the correspondence lies ready at hand: The cryptogram does work with a word play between the name 'Yahweh' and the verb 'to be'. But it does not intend to say that Yahweh is the one who essentially exists or the one who calls other things into existence. To the contrary, it intends to say that Yahweh is the one who guarantees his presence to his people. The name itself becomes a sign for the guarantee, a promise for Yahweh's presence. The name is the presence of God with his people (cf. Exod. 33.12-23).[2]

II

God's presence does not necessarily mean salvation. His presence can judge. It can destroy. Thus, God's speech to Moses in Exod. 33.1-3 judges the people for their involvement with the Golden Calf. The judgment does not prohibit the people from continuing the wilderness journey. But it does announce that the people must do so *without* God's presence. For if God should be present among his people, he would consume them. God's presence destroys those who rebel against him.[3]

Job knew the name. For Job, at least at the beginning, the name was full of hope and promise for the future. Obey the law and life under the name will prosper. In fact, the name guarantees the presence of a defender. But what happens when life under the law no longer fits into a meaningful pattern? The day looks like day. The people speak the

---

1. Cf. Richter, *Berufungsberichte*, p. 133.
2. This point of view is developed fully by M. Buber, *Moses: The Revelation and the Covenant* (New York: Harper & Row, 1958), pp. 39-55. Note Buber's emphasis on the parallel between Exod. 3.14 and 33.19 (p. 52).
3. This unit is completed in 33.19 by a new play on God's name, followed by a sentence set in syntactical pattern reminiscent of Exod. 3.14. The thrust of the play, obviously on graciousness and mercy, falls in the total unit on God's presence with his people. Cf. 33.16.

same language, use the same worn words. But none of it makes any sense. What happens when life under the law no longer prospers? For Job, the name remains, guaranteeing the presence of a defender. Only now the defender looks more like an accuser. Now the promise of presence looks more like a curse of unending judgment. 'I am with you'. 'What is man that you make so much of him, that you set your mind on him, visit him every morning, test him every moment. How long will you not look away from me, nor let me alone till I swallow my spittle?'

Whether for good or for ill, whether for salvation or for judgment, God is present. Emmanuel. For Deuteronomy, life is much simpler. God is present among his people in reasonable and ordered form. Obey the law 'that your days may be prolonged, and that it may go well with you in the land which the Lord your God gives you'. And in the midst of the people is Yahweh, the defender. Emmanuel. God with us. Deuteronomy develops the presence of God in a distinctive way. The vehicle for his presence is his name, the guarantee of his promise. That circumlocution allows Deuteronomy to preserve the necessary distance between God and his people, yet to show visible, tangible evidence of his presence.[1]

The name is attached to a place. And the place is reserved for worship. 'You shall seek the place which the Lord your God will choose out of all your tribes to put his name and make his habitation there. There you shall go and there you shall bring your burned offerings and sacrifice.' The name shares the reality of God himself. In the name, God is present with his people, in a place, at a time. And to the name the people can go to worship. God remains free, a step removed. But his name, the seal of his reputation, the symbol at one with himself, his name dwells among his people. Emmanuel. God with us.

The Deuteronomistic historian attaches the name to the temple in Jerusalem. In Nathan's oracle, a text that bears the stamp of DtrH, God promises that Solomon will 'build a house for my name'. And subsequently, in the prayer of dedication for the temple, the same tie can be seen. In the first couplet of the prayer, there is a break in the symbol of the name for God's presence. 'The Lord has set the sun in the heavens but has said he would dwell in thick darkness. I have built

---

1. G. von Rad, *Studies in Deuteronomy* (SBT, 9; London: SCM Press, 1953), pp. 37-44.

you an exalted house, a place for you to dwell forever'. In this perhaps very early fragment of a dedication prayer, God himself lives in the temple, in darkness, unprotected by the distance of a symbol, protected only by the darkness, the holy tabu of the holy of holies. But the text moves quickly from the immediacy of God's presence, perhaps dominated by Canaanite categories, to the Deuteronomistic circumlocution. 'I have built the house for the name of Yahweh, the God of Israel.' Indeed, the implication of the opening couplet is expressly denied at a later stage in the prayer:

> Will God dwell on the earth? Behold, heaven and the highest heaven cannot contain you. How much less this house which I have built. Yet, have regard to the prayer of your servant...that your eyes may be open night and day toward this house, the place of which you said, 'My name shall be there'.

As long as the temple stands, God's name will dwell there. It is as secure as the foundations of the earth. Emmanuel. God with us.

But what happens when the place where the name dwells is destroyed. Isaiah moves in a different direction. The name will be attached to a person. 'A young woman shall conceive, and bear a son, and shall call his name Emmanuel.' The same relationship between symbol and reality appears here. God remains free. He maintains his distance from man. Yet, in the name he guarantees his presence among men. But now the name is not at home simply in a place of worship. Now the name is at home in a person. The name belongs to Israel's leader, to her king, to the messiah. The messiah becomes the symbol for God's presence, the name, the seal of God himself. The messiah, the name and God, are one. The messiah is God-with-us. Emmanuel.

It is more than a little significant that the Gospel of Matthew uses the Isaiah text in the birth story of Jesus. New Testament Christology cannot be subsumed under one category. But no treatment of New Testament Christology can be deemed adequate unless it deals seriously with the tradition that places Jesus in line with the Emmanu'el child. For Matthew's Gospel, Jesus is Emmanuel, God-with-us. Just as the name symbolizes God's presence among his people and becomes a sign to guarantee his presence, his assistance, so Jesus guarantees God's presence among his people. Jesus is the name. He is the Lord, *Kyrios*. And the name and God become one.

But now the name does not dwell in a place. The people of God do not come to the name to worship, to bring sacrifices. Rather, the name comes to the people. The name dwells among the people. In a person, the name leads the people to the temple to worship. But what happens when the man who carries the name is crucified? First the temple, now the person fall the way of all creation. The day dawns, a sabbath. It looks like any other sabbath. The language sounds like any other language. But it makes no sense. The messiah is dead. Crucified. For the disciples the world of hope brought by Jesus turned to a world of despair. The promise of God's presence incarnate in Jesus, the Lord, Emmanuel, turned to desertion. From the cross they could hear only the words of a lonely psalm: 'My God, my God, why have you forsaken me?'.

How can one understand the resurrection? Jesus was crucified. The symbol was destroyed. A new crisis, comparable to the destruction of the temple, demands new hope. The disciples did not understand. But they had no promise for understanding. God promised only his presence. And his presence continued among them. The Lord has risen! Emmanuel! God with us! Significantly Matthew's Gospel closes with the risen Lord's promise: 'I am with you through all the days, to the close of the age'. The resurrection is crucial. It marks the beginning of a new age, a new hope.

Without the resurrection, the church would be impossible. With the resurrection, and the hope for the future it offers, the church can live. It knows the name. The sign of God's presence. Emmanuel. God with us. Yet, in a new age where does the name dwell? A resurrected Lord offers no sign of assurance to a world that does not believe. Without the church, the resurrection can make no sense to a technological world. With the church, however, the name dwells among the people, the sign of God's presence in an unbelieving, nonsensical world. Significantly, Paul understands the church as the body of Christ. We are Emmanuel. God with us.

But what does that mean, practically, for the twentieth century world? Viet Nam swims in blood. The Middle East threatens the world with Armageddon. What does the world know of the church? It knows divisions, petty jealousies. It knows famous cathedrals, filled with treasures from the ages, standing in the midst of hunger and pain. What does the world know of a sign for God's presence in a church as much in need of the Gospel as any other institution among men? What happens when the church is destroyed?

But the church is not the temple. The name does not dwell in a place, or in various places. Even Canterbury Cathedral cannot hold the name of God. Neither does the name dwell in institutions. Institutions appear, join with other institutions to form new institutions, and disappear. Buildings and institutions merely serve the church. The name dwells among his people. In the congregation, in the body of Christ, there is Emmanuel. God with us. That means that each of us *together* bears the honor, the responsibility of the name. Moses received the name, the guarantee of God's presence, as assurance for executing a commission. The name guarantees God's presence. But it is not just for the benefit of Moses' private life. The name comes to the church with a commission. Without the name, the church's commission would be impossible. With it, the commission can be embraced with vigor. The commission addresses the church with responsibility for the world, the nations (cf. Gen. 12.1-3). For the world the church stands as the sign of God's presence. For the world the congregation offers the symbol. The promise of the symbol is not submission to a meaningless life. The promise is to a life that makes sense, a world that offers opportunity to live in love and peace with our fellows. The promise we have from the name, the promise we represent to the world, is a promise for that kind of life, a life to embrace with joy and hope. We are the sign of that promise. We are Emmanuel. God with us.

Chapter 2

MOSES IN MIDIAN

The Book of Exodus narrates at least two important events that involved Moses during his exile in Midian under the protection of a Midianite priest: his marriage to a daughter of the priest, reported in Exod. 2.11-22, and his commission to lead his people out of Egypt, the subject of Exod. 3.1–4.18. M. Noth defines the relationship between the two by emphasizing a dominating role for the vocation tradition:

> This subject not only takes up the greatest amount of space within the section but must also have formed the kernel of the tradition from the beginning of its history, for no other starting point can in fact be found for an historical tradition of a stay of Moses in the land of Midian...The action taken by Moses against the unjust assault of a 'Hebrew' in Egypt which compelled him to flee from Egypt (2.11-15) is as little an independent element of tradition as the exemplary readiness to help which he displays in the scene at the well in the land of Midian (2.16-20).[1]

Yet problems in structure and tradition-history confront this conclusion. The problem in tradition-history is apparent when one compares the vocation tradition in Exod. 3.1–4.18 (JE) with the vocation tradition in Exod. 6.2–7.6 (P). The latter example of the tradition reports the events as if they occurred in Egypt, not in Midian. Noth treats this difference lightly: 'P later passed over this story [of God's theophany on the mountain of God] and unthinkingly has Moses receiving his commission in Egypt.[2] His position has a theological overtone:

> Moses experienced his first encounter with God on the mountain of God in Midian...Of course the Israelites stand under the care and protection of

---

1. M. Noth, *Exodus, A Commentary* (OTL; Philadelphia: Westminster Press, 1962), p. 30.
2. Noth, *Exodus*, p. 33.

their God even in Egypt. But this land was still not worthy of becoming the scene of a direct theophany to Israel; this takes place only in the wilderness.[1]

The problem in structure is more subtle: In P the vocation commission demands Moses' response, and a narration of its execution follows (Exod. 7.6). Indeed, the vocation account stands in immediate relationship with the sign cycle, Exod. 7.7–10.29 (11.9-10). In the JE account Moses responds to the commission. But the commission cannot be executed immediately; Moses must first return to Egypt. Thus, the vocation account ends in 4.18 without a notation of the execution of the commission. A narration of the execution does appear in JE, in Exod. 4.27-31, again in Exod. 5.1–6.1, and as in P, in the sign cycle of Exod. 7.7–10.29. But intervening between the vocation account and these texts are 4.19-23 (see the discussion of these verses below) and 4.24-26. The vocation account is, in some measure, incomplete without the narration of the execution of the commission.[2] Yet the structure of the narration (as well as a shift in setting from Midian to Egypt) holds the execution apart from the principal unit.

Noth suggests that the Sinai tradition lies behind the narration of the theophany on the mountain of God and Moses' commission as a messenger of God to the Israelites. The equation between the mountain of God and Sinai would not have been an original part of the tradition. The mountain of God was originally an unnamed mountain in Midian. But the equation was established before the tradition was fixed as it now appears in Exod. 3.1–4.18. And with its appearance, the possibility is open for a parallel between Moses' experience, his flight from Egypt to Midian, and Israel's experience, its flight from Egypt to Sinai. The parallel thus enables Noth to detect an early contact between the exodus and Sinai traditions.[3] Noth's conclusions, however, do not adequateley account for the contrasts between the JE vocation account in Exod. 3.1–4.18 and P's version of the same

---

1. Noth, *Exodus*, pp. 31-32.
2. See W. Richter, *Die sogenannten vorprophetischen Berufungsberichte: Eine literaturwissenschaftliche Studie zu 1 Sam. 9. 1-10; 16; Exod. 3f. und Ri 6.11b-17*: (FRLANT, 101; Göttingen: Vandenhoeck & Ruprecht, 1970), pp. 123-27. The well-known opinion that 4.27-31 and the point of contact in the vocation account are secondary does not affect this observation.
3. Noth, *Exodus*, pp. 32-33. Cf. also H.J. Gunneweg, 'Mose in Midian' *ZTK* 61 (1964), pp. 1-9.

tradition in Exod. 6.2–7.6. In this paper I shall focus on structure and tradition-history in the JE account. My principal goal, however, is not to compare the JE version of the vocation account with P's version of the same tradition. It is rather to determine where the kernel of tradition about Moses in Midian lies. Contrary to Noth, my thesis is that the kernel lies in the marriage story.

I

The first narration relevant to an analysis of traditions about Moses in Midian is Exod. 2.11-22. The unit breaks into three principal parts: vv. 11-14a, 14b-17 and 18-22. Verses 11-14a describe Moses' intervention when an Egyptian unjustly attacked two 'Hebrews'. It presupposes the narrative in 2.1-10 by casting Moses in a privileged position, yet aware of his relationship with the oppressed people. It thus incorporates a structural problem already present in the Moses birth-adoption story: Exod. 2.1-10 and its introduction in 1.15-22 tie into the introduction to the exodus traditions in 1.8-12 without being a necessary development from the exodus exposition. The narration in 1.15-22 provides a kind of transition from the oppression motif in 1.8-12 to the principal birth-adoption narrative in 2.1-10. But the exposition in 1.8-12 does not anticipate the exposure policy of 1.15-22 or the narration in 2.1-10. The two parts, 1.15-22 and 2.1-10, are in effect secondary in the structure of the exodus traditions.[1] Exod. 2.11-14a thus places the initial unit of tradition about Moses in Midian in a similar secondary position in the overall structure of the exodus traditions. And it functions as a transition from the birth-adoption narrative to the major portion of the narration in 2.14b-22, in much the same way that 1.15-22 functions as a transition from the exposition in 1.8-12 to the birth-adoption story.

The structure of vv. 11-14a develops by narrating Moses' response to a conflict. Moses intervenes once, then again. And in the second intervention, the crisis of the unit appears. Moses' deed is known. He had killed an Egyptian for unjustly beating the 'Hebrews'. Now two 'Hebrews' taunt Moses with his deed. Verses 14b-15a then open the second major element of the unit by marking a change in scene—the

---

1. B.S. Childs, 'The Birth of Moses', *JBL* 84 (1965), pp. 109-22. Cf. also H. Gressmann, *Mose und seine Zeit, ein Kommentar zu den Mose-Sagen* (FRLANT, 18; Göttingen: Vandenhoeck & Ruprecht, 1913), p. 17.

Pharaoh sought to kill Moses when he heard of Moses' intervention. So Moses fled to Midian. Structure in this portion nevertheless follows the same device employed in the first part. Moses intervenes in a conflict. He defends seven daughters of a Midianite priest against shepherds. But rather than leading to a threat against his life, this intervention creates a circumstance which opens a possible resolution for the Pharaoh's threat. Moses is invited to share the hospitality of the Midianite priest. And under the protection of the priest's hospitality, the Pharaoh no longer poses a problem.

In the MT Moses' flight to Midian and his marriage to the priest's daughter obviously serve as a connection between the Moses birth-adoption story in Exod. 2.1-10 and the account of Moses' commission on the mountain of God in 3.1–4.18. Behind the overall plot structure of 2.11-22, however, stands an older tradition, a tradition about marriage.[1] The stereotyped pattern of the section is easily recognizable. Moses sits by a well, has an occasion to meet the daughters of the Midianite priest, and receives an invitation from the priest after the daughters had returned home and reported to their father (cf. Gen. 24.1-67 and 29.1-30). The marriage narration ends in vv. 21-22.[2] But the principal point of the conclusion is not a presentation of Moses' new family. Verse 21b, the reference to the marriage, and v. 22, an etiology for the name of Moses' son, seem to be virtually appendixes. The point of the conclusion lies rather in v. 21a: 'Moses was content to dwell with the man'. The marriage tradition, as in Genesis 29, emphasizes the relationship between the bridegroom and his father-in-law, not the relationship between the bridegroom and his wife. In Exod. 18.1-7 the same picture can be seen. The father-in-law brings Moses' wife and sons to meet him in the wilderness. But the focal point of the reunion is between Moses and his father-in-law. The wife and children are almost humorously ignored in the description of Moses' reception for his father-in-law (cf. v. 7).[3]

---

1. Noth (*Exodus*, p. 30) recognizes the marriage tradition as an old element. But it cannot, so he argues, constitute the kernel of the Midianite tradition.
2. On vv. 23-25, see below.
3. In Exod. 18.1-7 Moses has two sons, while 2.11-22 mentions only one (cf. in contrast the plural reference in 4.20). This distinction may well represent distinct stages in the history of the marriage tradition. But it does not affect this point of my argument.

II

It is not necessary to analyze the structure of the vocation account in Exod. 3.1–4.18 in detail.[1] The first significant point in structure and tradition-history of this narration is that vv. 1-6 in Exodus 3 represent a distinct element of tradition, associated with the vocation tradition at a relatively late, though pre-JE stage.[2] This tradition carries the substance of a theophany to Moses on the mountain of God.

The mountain of God is not obviously a Midianite mountain. In Exod. 18.27, for example, Moses' father-in-law leaves the mountain of God and travels 'to his land' (*'el-'arṣô*), a distant locale. Exod. 3.1 suggests that the mountain is Horeb. But the name in this particular position is generally recognized as secondary. There is other evidence to suggest an identification between the mountain of God and Sinai (cf. Exod. 4.27; 24.13; 1 Kgs 19.8). But the identification is held in tension with an overriding distinction between the two.[3] The distinction can still be detected in the juxtaposition of Exodus 18, with its setting at the mountain of God (cf. v. 5) and Exodus 19, set at Sinai. The two units of tradition are held apart by the itinerary framework in Exod. 19.1-2. Indeed, the itinerary does not provide an opening for including the mountain of God setting of 18.5, since 19.2 notes a departure from Rephidim, the setting for Exod. 17.1-7 and 8-16. But it makes no reference to the mountain of God. Thus, unless the itinerary chain conceives the mountain of God as a site at Rephidim, not a likely possibility, it apparently excludes the mountain of God site and its tradition. Moreover, even if 19.1-2 were removed as a late framework in the midst of JE traditions, the two units in chs. 18 and 19 would not be well integrated. The one contains an independent

---

1. See Richter, *Berufungsberichte*, pp. 57-133. The purpose of this stage in my essay is not to develop an alternative hypothesis about the original setting for the vocation tradition. It is rather to show that evidence for identifying the setting as Midian is weak and inconclusive.

2. Richter, *Berufungsberichte*, pp. 72-82. Cf. also H. Gressmann, *Mose und seine Zeit*, pp. 23-50.

3. See G. von Rad, 'Beobachtungen an der Moseerzählung Exodus 1–14', *EvT* 31 (1971), pp. 579-88. Von Rad sees evidence for two distinct 'Sinai' traditions. The one, centered in Exodus 3, is fully determined by the exodus theme; the mountain of God would play a role here. The other, in Exodus 19–24, would not be so fully determined by the exodus.

tradition about juridical order in Israel, the other the beginning of a large framework narrative. But whether the two names, mountain of God and mountain of Sinai, were secondarily identified is not the primary issue. The point is that no reference to the mountain of God puts the mountain clearly in Midian (cf. Exod. 24.13; 1 Kgs 19.8). Exod. 4.27 implies that the mountain of God is away from Midian, away from the Midianite priest, in the wilderness. Thus, it seems to me that the parallel between Moses' flight *to Midian* and Israel's flight *to Sinai* rests on the weakest of foundations.

The theophany story in 3.1-6 is nevertheless constructed in the context of Midianite traditions. But the point of contact between the story and its Midianite context does not derive from location in Midian. A Midianite setting is finally irrelevant to the theophany tradition. The point of contact with the context comes from the responsibility Moses owes to his father-in-law. Exod. 3.1 describes Moses shepherding the flock of Jethro, his father-in-law, the priest of Midian. This reference to context seems to be secondary even for the theophany narration.[1] But it does suggest that in the last stage of development for the theophany-vocation tradition, the context with Moses under the protective care of his Midianite father-in-law defines the setting.

The same stage of tradition can be seen in 4.18. With this verse, the vocation narration comes to an apparent conclusion. The commission to Moses in 3.16-18 instructs Moses to go to the elders of Israel and with them to the king of Egypt (cf. also v. 10). Then Moses returns to Jethro, his father-in-law, in order to seek his permission to leave. This verse is thus in harmony with the mountain of God setting. Moses was at some distance from his father-in-law. But it also ties into the larger context of the Midianite priest father-in-law traditions. Moses must seek permission from his father-in-law to leave his house and thus his authority (cf. Gen. 31.25-32).

Yet despite this framework of Midianite tradition around the vocation account, no substantial element in the vocation itself depends on a Midianite setting. No part of the vocation narration reflects Moses' dependency on the authority of his father-in-law. Thus the following tradition-history conclusions seem to me to be in order: (1) The vocation account at its earliest stage describes the events of Moses' call

1. The theophany narration itself does not depend on Moses' responsibility to his father-in-law. Verse 1 functions, not to introduce the principal characters of the narrative, but to tie the narrative to its larger context. Cf. also Exod. 4.18.

without specifying Midian as its setting. (2) The vocation account, perhaps including some reference to an execution of the commission, was joined with the theophany report, set on the mountain of God. (3) A traditional relationship between the mountain of God and Jethro, perhaps reflected in Exodus 18 as well as the allusion to the herding of Jethro's flocks in Exod. 3.1, opens the door for attaching the vocation tradition to a Midianite context. It seems to me to be clear, moreover, that the principal point of contact at this stage is not with Midian, a geographical one, but with the Midianite priest father-in-law, a familial one.[1]

III

These conclusions about tradition-history can be sharpened by analyzing Exod. 2.23-25 and 4.19-23. Exod. 2.23aα alludes to the story in 2.11-22. But the point of contact in the allusion is the introductory connecting link in 2.11-15a, not the central core of tradition in vv. 15b-22. Moreover, the impact of the allusion is to note that the crisis in the plot of the marriage story is now completely over. Moses fled to Midian to escape the Pharaoh. Now the king of Egypt, the one who was seeking to kill Moses (4.19), is dead. With this observation the final stage of the marriage story is rounded off (cf. Exod. 1.6). Verses 23aß-25 then set the guiding motif for the vocation account. Verses 24-25 especially anticipate the speech in 3.7-8. These two elements reflect the structure and function of transitions.[2]

Exod. 4.19-23 is more problematical. Noth observes that v. 18 and vv. 19-20a stand as doublets and assigns the two to separate sources (v. 18 to E, vv. 19-20a to J).[3] But the two elements are not structural

---

1. H.J. Gunneweg ('Mose in Midian', pp. 4, 5) suggests that the principal purpose for the flight to Midian is to provide a transition between the traditions about the exodus, originally unrelated to the name of Yahweh, and the traditions about a Midianite cult of Yahweh. It provides an opening for making the exodus a Yahwistic tradition. This position fails to evaluate the weak relationship between the call account including the crucial revelation of the divine name and the Midianite tradition. In Exodus 18 the point of contact does not lie primarily with a cultic celebration associated with a Midianite Yahweh, but with the establishment of a new legal order. Cf. R. Knierim, 'Exodus 18 und die Neuordnung der mosaischen Gerichtsbarkeit', *ZAW* 73 (1961), pp. 146-71.
2. G.W. Coats, 'A Structural Transition in Exodus', *VT* 22 (1972), pp. 129-42.
3. Noth, *Exodus*, p. 34.

doublets. Verse 18 closes the vocation account with an exchange of speeches between Moses and Jethro, opening the door for Moses to fulfill the commission speech in 3.16-18. Verses 19-20, however, summarize the commission and set the stage for its execution. Moreover, vv. 21-23 anticipate the sign cycle of Exod. 7.7–10.29. Thus, again, the structure of a transition dominates the unit. And again, the transition presupposes the vocation tradition cast in its larger context with Moses in Midian (cf. v. 19, with its specification that Moses was in Midian and that the men who sought to kill Moses were dead).

Both of these transitions reflect a period of redaction in the history of the vocation tradition, a process for joining distinct elements of tradition together into a larger whole (R^{je} or R^{jep}?). Both suggest an awareness that the structural position of the vocation account is artificial, that the vocation account needs transition to make it harmonious with its context. In effect, they provide mortar for cementing the account into its present position. Yet they do not establish that the vocation acccount appears at an inappropriate point in the JE exodus narratives. Rather, they suggest that the tie between the vocation tradition and Midian, or better, the Midianite priest father-in-law is artificial. Like the birth-adoption story, the Midianite father-in-law story would be secondary in the structure of the exodus narration.

The break is heightened by the short narrative in 4.24-26. This unit is completely isolated from its context.[1] To be sure, one of the principals is Zipporah, the daughter mentioned in the marriage tradition. But the name, Zipporah, is not well rooted in 2.11-22.[2] Thus, it may be that this narrative, 4.24-26, not the marriage tradition, provides the traditio-historical root for Zipporah. At least the name does not provide a basis for labeling 4.24-26 a Midianite tradition.[3] The one point of contact with the context, a tenuous one, lies in the reference to a lodging place, v. 24 (cf. Gen. 42.27, where the word *mālôn*

---

1. B.S. Childs, *Myth and Reality in the Old Testament* (SBT, 27; London: SCM Press, 1968), pp. 59-65.
2. Noth, *Exodus*, p. 37.
3. Against H. Schmid, *Mose: Überlieferung und Geschichte* (BZAW, 110; Berlin: Töpelmann, 1968), p. 32. My point is that Zipporah is not clearly an original principal in the Midianite tradition. The marriage story notes that Moses married a daughter of the Midianite priest. Her name is incidental to that story, perhaps primarily rooted in Exod. 4.24-26.

certainly refers to a place). The shift in setting from Midian back to Egypt suggested by the transition in vv. 19-23 would provide an opening for reference to a lodging place. Moreover, this narrative describes events that occurred during the trip back to Egypt, away from Midian, at least insofar as the overall collection of traditions in 2.11–4.31 is concerned. The basic isolation of vv. 24-26, however, emphasizes this position as a structural transition as well as the artificial relationship between the vocation account and Midian.[1] The artificial relationship then comes sharply to the fore in vv. 27-31. Hardly an independent unit, these verses report a stage in Moses' execution of the commission. And it is carried out in Egypt.

IV

This argument does not prove that the vocation tradition originally cast the events of Moses' call in Egypt. But it does suggest that the vocation tradition cannot be tied originally with Midian, or even the Midianite priest. The crucial question now would be about the kernel of tradition concerned with Moses in Midian. If the primary point for Moses' exile in Midian does not lie in his initial encounter with God on a Midianite mountain, where does it lie? The answer to this question seems to me to be the marriage tradition. This narrative must be evaluated as more than an introduction to the vocation account. It has roots in an independent tradition. That tradition may be closely associated with the mountain of God, represented in 3.1-6 by the theophany report. Yet even here no kernel of tradition can be seen if the perspective is limited to geographical terms. Moses is on the mountain of God, not because the mountain is in Midian, but because he is herding the sheep of his Midianite father-in-law. But even here the relationship between the Midianite father-in-law and the theophany report does not appear to be intrinsic to either tradition. If the kernel of the marriage tradition can be seen at all, it must lie in the relationship between the father-in-law and Moses. The goal of the tradition is to explain the origin of the relationship. One might thus seek the closest point of contact for Exod. 2.11-22, not in 3.1–4.18, but in 18.1-27. There is no clear suggestion in the marriage narration that would anticipate the new juridical order described in 18.13-27. Yet this

---

1. On Exod. 12.43-49; 13.1-16 as similar units isolated at a point of structural transition, see Coats, 'A Structural Transition', pp. 140-41.

order has its roots in a positive relationship between Israel and Midian (cf. especially 18.1-12).[1] The two texts would be designed, at least in part, to justify a positive relationship between at least a portion of Israel and her traditional enemy.[2]

V

To summarize: (1) I cannot find sufficient evidence to support the thesis that the kernel of tradition about Moses in Midian lies in the Moses vocation narrative. To the contrary, the vocation story seems to have been cemented into a larger framework of narration about Moses in Midian without reference to intrinsic points of contact. (2) The kernel of tradition about Moses in Midian can be found in the narrative about Moses' marriage to a daughter of the Midianite priest. The intention of the narrative is, however, not to account for the relationship between Moses and the woman. The woman seems relatively unimportant as a principal in her own right. Rather, the intention is to account for the relationship between Moses and his Midianite father-in-law.[3]

1. See R. Knierim, 'Exodus 18', pp. 147-52.
2. Cf. H.W. Brekelmans, 'Exodus XVIII and the Origins of Yahwism in Israel', *OTS* 10 (1954), pp. 215-24. See also A. Cody, 'Exodus 18, 12: Jethro Accepts a Covenant with the Israelites', *Bib* 49 (1968), pp. 153-66.
3. This paper was completed during a research leave in Heidelberg, Germany, 15 October 1970 through 15 August 1971, supported by generous financial assistance from Lexington Theological Seminary, Lexington, Kentucky, and the Alexander von Humboldt Stiftung, Bad Godesberg, Germany.

Chapter 3

MOSES VERSUS AMALEK:
AETIOLOGY AND LEGEND IN EXOD. 17.8-16.

The narration in Exod. 17.8-16 provokes interest, not only because it reports an ancient battle between the Amalekites and Israel, with Israel on the defensive, but also because it appears to be so completely isolated from its context. It has nothing to do with the complex of stories about Israel murmuring against Moses and Yahweh, just preceding it in Exod. 14.1–17.7. It has no clear contacts with the traditions about Moses and his father-in-law, following in Exodus 18.[1] Moreover, the allusion in 17.8 to Rephidim stands in loose relationship to the narration itself and probably represents an accommodation of the pericope to the itinerary chain structuring the wilderness journey as a whole.[2] The narration thus functions as a part of the wilderness theme in the final redaction of the Pentateuch. But it fails to make use of basic motifs from the wilderness traditions. Moses makes no appeal to Yahweh for direction in the face of the Amalekite threat. Yahweh offers no instructions for meeting the crisis. There is no obvious divine protection from the enemy, no divine leadership, no

---

1. Exodus 18 is also isolated from its context, B.S. Childs, *The Book of Exodus: A Critical Theological Commentary* (OTL; Philadelphia: Westminster Press; London: SCM Press, 1974), pp. 326-29. Childs notes the shift by emphasizing that the writer slows the pace of his narrative, looking back at what has happened. 'In ch. 18 the writer returns to Moses, the man'.
2. On the function of the itinerary as a structuring device for the wilderness theme, cf. G.W. Coats, 'The Wilderness Itinerary', *CBQ* 34 (1972), pp. 135-52. On the isolation of this pericope, cf. J.H. Gronbaek, 'Juda und Amalek: Überlieferungsgeschichtliche Erwägungen zu Exodus 17.8-16', *ST* 18 (1964), p. 32. On the secondary character of the place name, cf. M. Noth, *A History of Pentateuchal Traditions* (trans. B.W. Anderson; Englewood Cliffs: Prentice-Hall, 1972), p. 120 n. 340.

divine initiative at all.¹ Indeed, neither the wilderness theme nor any of the other major structuring categories so commonly cited for analysis of the Pentateuch provide anything more than superficial context for this account.

What, then, can account for the position of this pericope at just this point in the structure of the Pentateuch? Indeed, what can most adequately account for its presence in the Pentateuch at all? This question proves more pressing when one considers the appearance of the same tradition, although not in the same form, at other places in the Old Testament (cf. particularly Deut. 25.17-19 and 1 Sam. 15.2-3). Thus the governing question: Why does the tradition appear in this particular form at just this particular place in the structure of the Pentateuch?

1. *Form-Critical Analysis*

J.P. Hyatt suggests that 'the narrative here is an aetiological story, designed to explain the origin of the perpetual hostility between Israel and Amalek, and also the origin of an altar, probably in the vicinity of Kadesh, which had the name "Yahweh is my banner"'.² In so far as the final form of the story is concerned, Hyatt's observation is accurate. Two aetiological elements appear at the end of the unit, v. 14 and vv. 15-16. And both relate to Israel's struggle with the Amalekites. Their appearance here thus casts the unit as an aetiology. Moreover, both elements point to a divine dimension in the tradition. In v. 14, the commitment to destroy the Amalekites by blotting out their remembrance 'from under the heavens' appears in a Yahweh speech to

---

1. The 'rod of God' in v. 9 carries the single reference to God in the narration of the event, apart from ther aetiological elements in vv. 14-16. The aetiological elements do not point to this particular battle, however, but to coming perpetual warfare with Amalek. It would be difficult to conclude that the event described here derives from divine intervention simply on the basis of v. 9. Cf. the discussion below.

2. J.P. Hyatt, *Exodus* (NCB; London: Oliphants, 1971), p. 183. For a similar position, cf. M. Noth, *Exodus, a Commentary* (trans. J.S. Bowden; OTL; Philadelphia: Westminster Press; London: SCM Press, 1962), p. 141. K. Möhlenbrink, 'Josua in Pentateuch', *ZAW* 59 (1942/43), pp. 16-24. Möhlenbrink agrees with this conclusion, suggesting moreover that the two aetiological elements point to two recensions in the tradition, one with its center on Moses, and the other and older with its center on Joshua. The Moses recension would have converted the original form of the tradition from its Joshua center.

Moses. And in vv. 15-16 the altar constructed by Moses carries a name which, though a bit obscure, connects with an affirmation of Yahweh's perpetual war with the Amalekites. With these elements, therefore, the impression of divine absence in the unit is softened.

Yet, the aetiological elements are clearly secondary in the unit. In both cases, the reference to Yahweh's relationship with the Amalekites develops a promise for what Yahweh is going to do, not what he has already done (cf. also Deut. 25.17-19). In v. 14 this point is clear by virtue of the verbal construction *kî māḥōh 'emḥeh*. And in v. 16, the emphasis falls, not on this particular battle, but on a war of Yahweh against Amalek which will continue throughout the generations (*middōr dōr*). B. Childs highlights this problem by observing the rough connection between this perpetual enmity and the victory described in Exodus 17.[1] Do the aetiological elements not tie more readily with that facet of this tradition that remembers a disastrous defeat inflicted by Alamek, such as it reflected in Deut. 25.17-19? Thus, it would seem to me to be clear that the aetiological elements are not rooted intrinsically in the preceding verses but stands as an appendix.[2]

The one possible exception to this point lies in the argument that the stone in v. 12 constitutes a parallel to the altar in vv. 15-16. The two would be a double explanation for an important stone at some particular locality. In that case, the second aetiological element would be rooted in an indispensable part of the story and suggest a primary function of the unit as aetiology.[3] Yet the stone itself demands no particular emphasis in the movement of the narration. And no explicit tie to the stone can be seen in the aetiological elements. The aetiological character of the pericope thus appears to me to be secondary and unessential for the narration in vv. 8-13.[4] To limit discussion of the

---

1. Childs, *Book of Exodus*, p. 313.
2. Noth, *History*, p. 120, n. 343. This point seems justified to me. To define other elements of disunity in the narrative, leading to two distinct versions of the story, is not. Against Möhlenbrink, 'Josua in Pentateuch', p. 18.
3. Noth, *Exodus*, p. 143. Hyatt, *Exodus*, p. 185, also notes some possibility for connecting the stone in v. 12 with *kēs yāh*, taking that phrase with the Vul., Sam. Pent. and Syr. as 'throne of Yahweh'. Cf. R. Smend, *Yahweh War and Tribal Confederation* (trans. M. Rogers; Nashville: Abingdon Press, 1970), pp. 79-80.
4. The tradition in this unit may have been intended originally to explain the origin of the perpetual hostility between Israel and Amalek. Other appearances of the tradition concentrate on that facet. But if that is the case, the tradition history does not

unit to its character as aetiology would thus misrepresent the basic movement of the whole.

The narration in vv. 8-13 reveals a structural design and intention quite distinct from an aetiology. The account opens in v. 8 with an announcement of the attack by the Amalekites. The body of the pericope, vv. 9-12, then focuses on *Moses'* response to the attack, not Joshua's, not even Yahweh's. That response breaks down into two major sections. The first, v. 9, is a Moses speech, unveiling his plans for defense to Joshua. The speech details two particular facets: (1) Under the commission of Moses, Joshua will select an army and head the fight with Amalek. (2) Moses will go to the top of the hill with the 'rod of God' in his hand. The second major section, vv. 10-12, reports how those plans were carried out. And the structure of the report follows the same twofold pattern of the speech: (1) v. 10a picks up Joshua's work, while (2) vv. 10b-12 describe Moses' work. The distinction in length alone points to the structural emphasis on Moses. But that is not all. The description of Joshua's work carries the primary report that a battle was fought. But no details of the battle appear. The rise and fall of the battle come in the second part, the fruits of Moses' work. For when Moses holds his hands high the tide of the battle moves to Israel. But when he lets them fall, the tide turns to the Amalekites. Indeed, the outcome of the battle depends on Moses' ability to stay at his job. There is, then, no sound of clashing armies in this battle report. There is no blood and death. There is only the weariness of the central figure.

The narration concludes in v. 13 with a report of the battle's outcome. The subject of the verb in this verse is Joshua. 'Joshua mowed down Amalek and his people with the edge of the sword'. But Joshua's position in this element does not elevate him in importance over Moses. To the contrary, his job is simple, a mopping-up action dependent on Moses' stamina and faithfulness at his post (cf. 1 Sam. 14.6-15).

It would seem to be clear, then, that structure in this unit puts central weight on Moses, with his faithfulness and stamina the source of a major victory over an enemy. Several problems, at least, confront this conclusion.

facilitate an exegesis of *this* narration very effectively. For even though the aetiological elements cast the final form of the unit as such an aetiology, the basic core in vv. 8-13 has no such interest. So, Childs, *Book of Exodus*, p. 315. Cf. B.O. Long, *The Problem of Etiological Narrative in the Old Testament* (*BZAW*, 108; Berlin: Töpelmann, 1968), for principles in evaluating the question.

First, if Moses is the central figure, with focus of the unit on his crucial role, would not Aaron and Hur blur the focus? To hold one's hands high from morning to the setting sun is a virtue of outstanding quality, even for Moses. But when his arms grow weary, Aaron and Hur provide assistance. Would not that assistance detract from a central focus on Moses? M. Noth makes the point:

> Yet here again some rivals, who are now insignificant, appear alongside of Moses, prompting one to conjecture that they have been pushed into their present subordinate position through a subsequent emergence of Moses in this particular narrative...Originally they were presumably the ones who carried out the action that was effective in granting victory...It cannot at any rate be maintained that the figure of Moses is especially firmly anchored in Exod. 17.18ff.[1]

The text itself, however, cannot support Noth's conjecture. (The tradition history behind the text may not have given Moses a role in this battle. But this narrative moves to the other extreme.) Moreover, one cannot assume from the assistance Aaron and Hur give to Moses that Moses was never the central figure. A central figure in OT tradition, particularly a warrior in the field, commonly has a companion who serves him, an armorbearer (cf. 1 Sam. 14.6-15; 31.1-7). But the armorbearer does not eclipse the role of his master.[2] The same point applies for Aaron and Hur. Their assistance emphasizes Moses' *weariness* to the very brink of his endurance. But their assistance also emphasizes his faithfulness to his task, his stamina in the face of limitations on his strength. He will do what he must do to win the battle even if it is beyond the normal limitations of his strength.

Secondly, J.H. Gronbaek argues forcefully that this tradition must be taken as holy war tradition. 'Moses supplies the Israelites with a power, and this power comes from Yahweh. Thus, the victory over the Amalekites is the victory of Yahweh. But this in no way excludes that Joshua is the one who kills the Amalekites with the sword...'[3]

---

1. Noth, *History*, p. 166. I see no evidence for reconstructing a Joshua form of the tradition as the Vorlage for the Moses tradition. The figure of Joshua is incidental in the text, always functioning as the servant of Moses, not as a primary figure in his own right. Against Möhlenbrink.

2. On the role of the assistant in medieval legends, cf. J. de Vries, *Heroic Song and Heroic Legend* (trans. B.J. Timmer; London: Oxford University Press, 1963), pp. 189-90.

3. 'Moses führt den Israeliten eine Kraft zu, und diese Kraft kommt von Jahwe.

And, one might add, this point would also not preclude the tradition's placing emphasis on the figure of Moses. But would the point not suggest that the primary focus falls, not so much on Moses, the servant of God, as on God, the source of the power for victory? Particularly if the holy war element is understood explicitly as Yahweh war, the focus of the tradition must fall, not on Moses, but on Yahweh. Verse 9b is crucial for this question: Moses announces that he will go to the top of the hill with the 'rod of God' (*ûmaṭṭēh hā'ᵃ lōhîm*) in his hand.[1] Would this designation not undergird Gronbaek's point, since the power Moses exerts is associated in some way with the rod and the rod derives finally from God (cf. Exod. 4.1-5)?

One way to resolve the problem is to consider this unique phrase as an insignificant and secondary facet of the narration since it has no function at all in the following verses.[2] Yet, the rod and the uplifted hand are parallel, as H. Gressmann suggested.[3] The parallel relationship can be substantiated by reference to the same parallel construction in Exod. 14.16.[4] Is it possible, then, that only *hā'ᵃlōhîm* is

---

So ist der Sieg über die Amalekiter der Sieg Jahwes, welches aber keineswegs ausschliesst, dass Josua es ist der Amalekiter mit dem Schwert schlägt...' (Gronbaek, 'Juda and Amalek', p. 43). Cf. also Smend, *Yahweh War*, p. 103.

1. H. Gressmann, *Mose und seine Zeit, ein Kommentar zu den Mose-Sagen* (FRLANT, 18; Göttingen: Vandenhoeck & Ruprecht, 1913), pp. 157-60. In commenting on the connection between the rod and the aetiological elements, he observes: 'Damit ist deutlich ausgesprochen, daß Jahwe mit dem Mose-Stabe identisch ist oder wenigstens aufs engste zusammengehört'.

2. Noth, *Exodus*, p. 142. Part of the problem in this verse is the designation of the rod as the rod of God, a specification that occurs rarely in the exodus or wilderness traditions (cf. also Exod. 4.20). In fact, the rod is labelled at other points in the traditions quite explicitly as Moses' rod (cf. Exod. 7.19; 8.12; 14.16).

3. Gressmann, *Mose*, p. 158.

4. Again, a textual problem arises. The parallel in Exod. 14 involves the rod without the designation 'rod of God'. But no question can be raised about whether the rod in Exod. 14 is traditio-historically the same phenomenon as the rod in Exod. 17. Of more importance, the parallel in Exod. 14 involves the rod and the hand of Moses, cast as a singular noun. In Exod. 17.8-11 the parallel is again between the rod and the *hand* of Moses, cast as a singular noun. But in v. 12 the noun shifts to a plural form. Hyatt, *Exodus*, p. 184, asks: 'Do we have here the conflation of two traditions, one emphasizing the rod in the hand of Moses, the other his lifting up of both hands alone'? Möhlenbrink, 'Josua', pp. 16-24, develops a similar position, casting the uplifted hands as an act of prayer (cf. particularly p. 19, and the commentaries he cites there). But that position is difficult to maintain (so,

secondary in this text, a pious gloss intended to give the unit a divine aura it does not otherwise have? Such an alternative can offer nothing more than speculation. The crucial point is that for both Exodus 14 and Exodus 17 the outstretched hand with its parallel in the outstretched rod is crucial for the emergence of the miraculous event. And certainly it is not possible to eliminate both elements as secondary. Moreover, the 'rod of God' does nothing more in Exodus 17 than the rod without such a qualification in Exodus 14 or, for that matter, the hand in either tradition. Whether the designation of the rod as the rod of God is secondary, or the whole phrase is secondary does not alter the basic gesture. Moses stretches out the symbol of his power. And that act effects the event. The power derives from Yahweh. There is no doubt about that. But the only reference to God in the entire section of narrative in vv. 8-13 is hardly firm affirmation for contending that a major point of the unit is recognition of Yahweh's power. That element is simply not present.

How, then, is the rod/hand parallel to be understood? Does the parallel belong to plague tradition vocabulary and thus place the Moses-Amalek tradition back into the general organization of traditions around the exodus theme?[1] That alternative seems to me to be the weakest of any. There is no reference here to oppression by an unrelenting master. The enemy is not the Egyptian hoard. This tradition stands totally outside the framework of the theological organization that dominates the exodus theme. Yet, the rod in this pericope cannot be disassociated from the rod Moses employs in his dealings with the Pharaoh (cf. Exod. 4.20). It is possible to suggest that the rod appears in this text by virtue of its proximity with the Meribah story in Exod. 17.1-7.[2] But that alternative does not seem to me to be viable. But even if one were able to show that the object enters this text as a part of the redaction bringing several stories together, he

---

Noth, *Exodus*, p. 142). Yet, the identity between the uplifted hand, with no rod at least explicitly in it, and the hands outstretched over the enemy seems strong to me. Evidence for two traditions is rather slim. Can we not more adequately explain the shift from singular to plural just in v. 12 as an effort to accommodate the story to *two* assistants who supported Moses when he grew weary?

1. Childs ('A Traditio-Historical Study of the Red Sea Tradition', *VT* 20 [1970], p. 409) observes; 'Whereas in the JE accounts the imagery associated with the plagues is entirely missing in the sea account, the reverse is true for P. Again the plague imagery returns... "Moses stretches out his hand" (14.21)'.

2. Gronbaek, 'Juda und Amalek', p. 33.

would still have the outstretched hand as a parallel that demands explanation. A more attractive alternative is to consider the rod, even the 'rod of God', and its parallel in the hand of Moses as a motif that is peculiar to neither the exodus theme nor the wilderness theme, but to traditions centering in some manner on Moses. Albeit rooted in God's power, the rod is the instrument of the wonder-worker and characteristic of Moses traditions wherever they might appear.[1]

Still, must we not attach this tradition to the general collection of traditions about Yahweh war? Is this not a holy war, with the focus of attention thus by definition not on Moses, as it would seem on the surface, but on God?[2] First, it must be admitted that holy war motifs do appear here, and even more strongly in the Exodus 14 parallel. Thus, the instructions to select men (b^ehar-$lānû$), implying a smaller band than was necessary, and the results of the battle cast as mowing down the enemy with the edge of the sword ($wayyah^alōš\ y^eh\ ôšua'\ldots l^epî$-$hāreb$) can stand in the context of holy war.[3] Secondly, the battle is for Israel clearly defensive. Moreover, the allusions to the tradition in Deut. 25.17-19 and 1 Sam. 15.2, with no reference to Moses, as well as the aetiological elements would support the point. The traditio-historical background of the unit may well be rooted in holy war tradition from the tribe of Judah. Yet, this unit shifts the focus away from the battle. The structure of the unit places the center of gravity on the main strength of a single figure. Why would a holy war story pay so little attention to the details of the war? Why would its narration shift from the scene of the battle to a single vigil above the battle? And of even more importance, how can a holy war story fail to note that it was Yahweh, not Moses, who gave the enemy into the hands of the Israelites?[4]

---

1. Childs, *Exodus*, pp. 313-15, calls attention to the parallel in Balaam's curse. 'In Exod. 17 the hands are the instruments of mediating power, as is common throughout the Ancient Near East... This amoral element of the unleashing of power through an activity or a stance is still reflected in the story'. To explore the 'magical' element in this act contributes very little more in an evaluation of the narrative.
2. So, Gronbaek, 'Juda und Amalek', p. 44.
3. The point can be supported by reference to Exod. 14.13-14, 16, 25, 27, 30; Josh. 6.1-21.
4. So, cf. Smend, *Yahweh War*, pp. 110-11. Num. 21.21-31 also fails to note such an explicit attribution of success to Yahweh (but contrast Num. 21.34). But there is a specific reason for its absence. The land of Transjordan is understood by the tradition as less than hallowed ground (cf. Josh. 22.19) and thus not derived as an

It seems clear to me, then, that this pericope cannot be adequately described as an aetiology, although the final form of the unit has been transformed into aetiology by the appendix. Nor can it be adequately understood as a battle report with its roots in holy war tradition. Nor can one say that *this unit* was originally an Aaron story or a Hur story or a Joshua story. Indeed, one cannot even say with clarity that the unit is a story. Its structure maintains no consistent point of tension, but rather relies on relatively disjointed notations in order to emphasize, not the battle as an event in God's dealings with his people, but the stamina and faithfulness of Moses to his task. The point can be seen clearly in v. 12, set in the contrast between the observation that 'the hands of Moses were weary' (*wîdê Mōšeh k^{e}bēdîm*) and the observation, 'his hands were steady' (*way^{e}hî yādāyw '^{e}mûnâ*). The key term *'^{e}mûnâ*, connotes particularly faithfulness to an official task, not necessarily a military one (cf. 2 Kgs 12.16; 22.7; 2 Chron. 34.12. Cf. also 1 Chron. 9.22). And it is that faithfulness, depicted here in physical exertion, highlighted by the extended period of time and the struggle to maintain its standards, that carries the narration. As a narration designed to emphasize such virtue, the unit (particularly in vv. 8-13) can most adequately be understood as legend.[1] Moreover, its quality as legend is specifically *heroic*, even with the assistants and the field general.[2] The stamina of one man defines the quality and stature of *the* giant from Israel's past.

2. *Structural and Theological Context*

How, then, are we to understand the context for a heroic legend in the middle of the Pentateuch? The break between the murmuring stories (Exod. 14.1–17.7) and the Sinai narrative (Exod. 19.1ff.) provides a seam in the redaction of the whole and thus a natural place to include

explicit gift from Yahweh's hand.

1. R.M. Hals, 'Legend: A Case Study in OT Form-Critical Terminology', *CBQ* 34 (1972), pp. 166-76. I cannot see that the basic character of the narrative as *legend* has been altered by the aetiological elements. Rather, the aetiological elements appear as extrinsic additions. The latest form of the narrative is thus not simply aetiology, but legend plus aetiological appendices.

2. For a definition of heroic, cf. de Vries, *Heroic Songs*, p. 180. For a slightly different approach, cf. H.M. Chadwick and N.H. Chadwick, *The Growth of Literature* (Cambridge: Cambridge University Press, 1932), pp. 1-18.

distinct tradition elements. But is there any way to account for a heroic legend, with its focus on Moses, appearing in the middle of traditions classically understood as narrations of Yahweh's initiative in saving Israel? Does the heroic legend have any antecedents? Or is it totally isolated, not only from its immediate context, but also in the overall structure of the Pentateuch.

There are other Moses traditions with heroic motifs, also somewhat roughly integrated into the structural themes centering in the exodus and the wilderness.[1] The birth story, Exodus 2, contrasts with the introduction to the exodus theme in Exodus 1, as Gressmann noted.[2] The one depicts the Pharaoh's desire to kill Hebrew male children in order to resolve the Hebrew problem and his anxiety over it. The other shows the Pharaoh attacking the Hebrew problem by heavy, oppressive labor. A combination of the two has the Pharaoh killing off his labor force, a problematic point of tension in final narration. The Moses-Jethro story, also in Exodus 2, stands over against the basic themes of the call narrative in Exodus 3, presenting Moses as a figure who by his show of strength wins his position in the household of Jethro, including one of his host's daughters as a wife.[3] Exodus 18 may perhaps appear also as a distinct tradition, structured into the Pentateuch at the redactional seam that offers position to the Moses-Amalek legend. And the narration presents Moses as the story-teller, with an impressive and successful account to tell. Finally, Deuteronomy 34 incorporates heroic motifs into the Moses death report. And the report functions as a final pinpointing of Mosaic virtues.[4] To suggest that these traditions show rough integration with the structural themes of the exodus and the wilderness is not to say that they are antithetical to those themes. To the contrary, they complement in many respects the overall pattern. The birth of Moses sets the leader in Egypt, in a position of power, ready to observe the oppressed state of his people. The Jethro tradition provides a distinctive context for the call narrative. But they can also compete with the theological interests centering in Yahweh's

---

1. The traditions derive almost entirely from J or JE. P seems to have conceived the Moses tradition in a different garb. Cf. Noth, *History*, pp. 262-76.
2. Gressmann, *Mose*, pp. 1-4.
3. Cf. Coats, 'Moses in Midian', *JBL* 92 (1973), pp. 3-10. See ch. 2 above.
4. Cf. Coats, 'Legendary Motifs in the Moses Death Reports', in *Proceedings of the Sixth World Congress of Jewish Studies* (Jerusalem: World Union of Jewish Studies, 1975). See ch. 6 below.

initiatives, as I believe to be the case in the Moses-Amalek legend. I would suggest, then, that two complementing, at points competing, structural patterns must be recognized when one attempts to control the form-critical problem of the Pentateuch or Hexateuch. One is the general system of themes, centered around Yahweh's initiative on Israel's behalf. Noth, Zimmerli and von Rad have defined the programmatic lines of these elements. The other is a system of heroic structure, centered around Moses' initiative on Israel's behalf. The two come together in the plague stories, even in the murmuring stories. Or the one can be elevated over the other (cf. Deut. 34.6; Num. 21.33-35). But in overall pattern they maintain a balance, an intricate interweaving of themes. This suggestion, incidentally, would shed some light on the Pentateuch-Hexateuch question. For the one scheme of structure would presuppose completion in Joshua, while the other would specifically prohibit continuation into Joshua.

In the final analysis, however, the most pressing difficulty regarding context for the heroic pattern in the Pentateuch is not structural but theological. God takes the initiative in promising his presence to his people. And he defends them, cares for their needs, and finally gives them the land, all in response to that promise. But where is the promise-fulfillment scheme in the heroic pattern? The description here centers in the trusted servant who by his own virtue can seize the initiative to act for his people. And that audacity receives the approval of God. It is important to note that the two spheres of theological interest are not antithetical. The promise-fulfillment scheme may not be present in the heroic pattern. But is does not deny the value of the heroic pattern. To the contrary, the Pentateuch holds the two in delicate balance.

It is at just this point that an important theological issue appears. To loose the balance between the two schemes is to distort the theology of the Pentateuch. If one should elevate the heroic beyond its limitations within the balance, the results would mythologize the tradition. The hero in effect becomes God.[1] But significantly the OT never succumbed to that temptation. Moses remained very much the flaw-filled hero, condemned to die before entry into the land. Indeed, one may wonder whether the remarkable paucity of references to Moses outside the Pentateuch reflects a reaction away from the temptation to elevate Moses farther than the tradition would allow. But to over-balance the

---

1. De Vries, *Heroic Songs*, pp. 227-41. Cf. the discussion of this point in Coats, 'Legendary Motifs in the Moses Death Reports'.

tradition in the other way is more problematic, particularly for contemporary exegesis. W. Brueggemann reflects on the problem:

> Salvation revolves around deeds of intrusion which stress discontinuities between God and culture and bear witness to an invading God. This has been the God of Israel which the Church has celebrated, with special emphasis upon the Exodus traditions...The Church has been so deeply committed to a theology of salvation that it could not affirm that man has potentiality for being able and responsible, trusted and effective in caring for the creation in which he finds himself.[1]

The tendency challenged by Brueggemann can be documented at several points. K. Barth once wrote, for example, that,

> as we can see already from the older historical records from Exod. 17.8f. on, there is no contradiction in the fact that it is God who fights for the Israelites, and that the Israelite bravely grips and wields his sword in obedience to His command and implicit trust in Him.[2]

To be sure, there is no contradiction in the balance. The heroic man can stand as an obedient servant of God. But Exod. 17.8-9 cannot really support the point. For there is no divine command here. Barth uses the Moses story to illumine the role of David. But in the illumination the problem is even more pronounced:

> These two things [God who fights and the Israelite who wields the sword] are so unified in the figure of David that in fact we can only see them together. Yet both are so related in the tradition that the whole light does not proceed from the sword of David, nor does it fall on him as the daring commander and royal general of Israel, but it proceeds from God and therefore shines on God...[3]

In Exodus 18, however, the light *does* fall on the daring commander. G. von Rad reflects the same tendency:

> Not a single one of all these stories in which Moses is the central figure, was really written about Moses. Great as was the veneration of the writers for this man to whom God had been pleased to reveal Himself, in all these stories it is not Moses himself, Moses the man, but God who is the central figure.[4]

---

1. W. Brueggemann, 'The Triumphalist Tendency in Exegetical History', *JAAR* 38 (1970), pp. 374-75.
2. K. Barth, *Church Dogmatics* (Edinburgh: T. & T. Clark, 1957), II, p. 375.
3. Barth, *Church Dogmatics*, p. 375.
4. Von Rad, *Moses* (London: Lutterworth, 1960), pp. 8-9.

But, such a conclusion does no justice to a *legend*. The *legend* is about Moses, and only through Moses is it about God.

The Pentateuch itself reveals evidence of a struggle with this balance. The oldest forms of the Sea tradition (Exod. 15) describe the event totally in terms of divine activity. But in the narrative (Exod. 14). Moses enters the description as an efficient agent. Moreover, in the plague narrative Moses and God interchange in the designations of principal agents (cf. Exod. 7.20-25). Yet despite the struggle, or perhaps precisely because of the struggle, the balance remains. And, in that balance Moses appears as

> a free adult who is given remarkable freedom. The theological foundation of the literature is the unspoken assumption that Yahweh stands by this man to whom he has committed himself, that the promise is now at the disposal of man, that man has been trusted with the promise.[1]

Brueggemann's comments refer to David. But it seems to me that the image applies also to heroic Moses, not apart from divine intervention, but balanced with it. If contemporary exegesis is to lay a solid foundation for a biblical theology, it cannot succumb to the tendency to tip that balance toward what Brueggemann labels a triumphalist position. His call to turn away from a triumphalist theology toward a more viable perception of the nature of man in wisdom tradition and its impact on Davidic formulation is justified. But the call should be expanded to include a more adequate perception of the image of man in the Pentateuch, particularly in the person of Moses. For Pentateuchal theology the balance is crucial. Moses is not simply the blind servant, dancing his minuet of obedience to the sound of an all-encompassing divine drumbeat. To the contrary, for Pentateuchal theology Moses is *both* servant of God *and* heroic giant.

---

1. Brueggemann, 'The Triumphalist Tendency', p. 372.

Chapter 4

History and Theology in the Sea Tradition*

What really happened at the Sea of Reeds? Scholars interested in history and theology in traditions about Israel's early past face unusual problems in evaluating the Sea tradition. No archaeological data clarify the OT accounts of the event. Thus conclusions about both history and theology must rest on OT texts alone. But even more grievous, the OT texts include narratives and poems that at times diverge radically in their description of the event. With pieces of evidence that appear to be contradictory, how can one attack the question about what really happened?

A brief review of the history of the tradition will illustrate the problem. The oldest allusion to the event appears in the Song of Miriam, Exod. 15.21b: 'Sing to the Lord, for he has triumphed gloriously; horses and chariotry he has thrown into the sea'. A highly mythopoeic description of the event, this couplet corresponds to an early fragment of tradition preserved by the Yahwist in Exod. 14.27b: 'Yahweh shook the Egyptians into the midst of the sea'. Yahweh disposes of his enemy as if brushing dirt from his hands. These early texts provide only one detail about the event: God destroyed an enemy in the sea. A slightly different image appears in Exod. 14.21a, again from the Yahwist: 'Yahweh drove the sea with a strong east wind all the night'. In all probability, vv. 24-25 and 27 complete this picture for the Yahwist: the chariots prove ineffective, perhaps mired in the 'dry ground' left by the east wind, and the Egyptians flee in panic to their destruction, to a sea restored to its normal bounds. The detail describing destruction of the enemy remains as the focal point of the narrative. But now an east wind, a sea temporarily out of its bounds, an enemy fleeing in panic replace the mythopoeic picture of Yahweh throwing the enemy to their destruction.

---

* This essay is a revised and expanded edition of an inaugural address to the faculty and students of Lexington Theological Seminary, delivered on Nov. 15, 1968.

The song of the Sea, Exod. 15.1b-18, employs different imagery. Verses 4-5 correspond harmoniously with the Song of Miriam: Yahweh throws his enemy into the sea. Verses 6-10, however, develop a description of a path cut through the waters:

> [6] Your right hand, Yahweh, glorious in power;
> Your right hand, Yahweh, shatters the enemy.
> [7] In the greatness of your majesty,
> You overthrow your enemy,
> You send forth your fury.
> It consumes him like chaff.
> [8] With the wind of your nostrils the waters piled up.
> The floods stood like a heap.
> The deeps congealed in the heart of the Sea.
> [9] The enemy said, 'I will pursue,
> I will overtake; I will divide spoil.
> My desire shall have its fill with him.
> I will draw my sword.
> My hand shall bring him to ruin.'
> [10] You blew with your wind.
> The Sea covered him.
> They sank like lead into the mighty waters

The wind motif plays an important role, to be sure (cf. vv. 8, 10). But the chariots are not mired in mud; the Egyptians do not flee in panic. Rather, they pursue the Israelites on a path through the sea as apparent victors moving to the spoil (v. 9), only to be covered by the waters they thought to be as firm as a wall. The new detail: a path in the sea for Israel's escape and for Egypt's destruction (cf. the P narrative in Exodus 14).

Jos. 2.10, set in a larger framework of conquest for the Deuteronomistic History, changes the picture of the Sea event even more drastically. Rahab explains her concern to help the Israelite spies: 'Because we have heard that Yahweh dried up the waters of the Reed Sea before you when you came out of Egypt'. Here, significantly all reference to destruction of the enemy drops away. In its place, the tradition now points simply to crossing the water on dry land. Secondly, Isaiah knows about a path in the sea where the enemy languishes and dies (Isa. 43.16-17). But he can also describe the same event without reference to an enemy army (Isa. 51.9-10):

> Awake, awake, put on strength
> O arm of Yahweh.
> Awake as in days of old.
> Generations of long ago
> Was it not you who cut Rahab
> Who pierced Tannin?
> Was it not you who dried up the sea,
> The waters of the great deep,
> Who made the depths of the sea a way for the redeemed to pass over?

An enemy can be recognized in this poem. But the enemy is the sea, and defeat of the enemy provides, not protection against a military threat, but a means for crossing the sea. The mythological language of this poem is an extension of the tradition that focusses on crossing the sea without reference to the Egyptian enemy. This radical change in describing the Sea event derives, not from confusion among the Israelites about whether an enemy army was in fact destroyed at the Sea, but rather from a reformulation of the Sea tradition under influence from traditions about Israel's crossing the Jordan.

The problem with the question about what really happened at the Sea of Reeds can now be focused somewhat more sharply. With this wide diversity of details, details that contradict on occasion, details that appear to be all important at one level, yet disappear altogether at another, what can be said about what really happened? How can a single event be reconstructed? Or perhaps more to the point, with this wide diversity of details, how can the tradition, or any stage in the tradition, be taken seriously? What authentication does it command?[1]

I propose three theses as tentative procedure for meeting this problem. The *first thesis* is that alternatives for determining the value of the tradition have been inadequately formulated. The alternatives appear commonly at some point on a spectrum between authentic or inauthentic tradition, realistic and understandable or fanciful and incredible, reality or falsification of reality. The event described by the tradition really happened. Or it did not really happen. There is, of course, an intermediate ground. If the description is too fanciful, then

---

1. J. de Vries, *Heroic Song and Heroic Legend* (trans. B.J. Timmer; London: Oxford University Press, 1963), p. 181. De Vries captures the nature of our problem by posing a question to Alexander the Great: 'Noble Alexander, was your Ilion really situated in layer VIIa? Are you so sure that Achilles ever lived? Perhaps you show an honourable veneration for something that is a figment of the imagination'. But cf. below, p. 50 n. 1.

the scholar must cut through the secondary accretions in order to recover the kernel of genuine tradition. And the goal of the evaluation in each case would be to provide some kind of objective reconstruction of the event.

Two considerations point to the inadequacy of these alternatives. First, to reduce critical analysis to reconstruction of the event, for all of its justification in the task of history writing, can easily interfere with an adequate exegesis of the tradition. A review of several historians' work illustrates the depth of the problem. F. Cross describes what really happened at the Sea: 'So far as we can tell, the Egyptians are cast out of barks or barges into the stormy sea; they sink in the sea like a rock or a weight and drown'.[1] But that reconstruction falls wide of an adequate exegesis of the texts at hand. Not only do the texts say nothing about a barge, a bark, a ship of any kind, but they point clearly to a far more complex picture than this reconstruction suggests. Indeed, Cross rests his proposal on a weak interpretation of the Song of the Sea, virtually ignoring the significance of v. 9 and its pursuit motif. J. Bright does not ignore the pursuit of the Egyptians in his description of the Sea event: 'It appears that Hebrews, attempting to escape, were penned between the sea and the Egyptian army and were saved when a wind drove the waters back, allowing them to pass (Exod. 14.21, 27); the pursuing Egyptians, caught by the returning flood, were drowned'.[2] The event he paints, however, comes across as an emasculated hulk in comparison to the biblical tradition. Indeed, he seems to be hung on the necessity to affirm the authenticity of the tradition without credible evidence to support the affirmation: 'The Bible's own witness is so impressive as to leave little doubt that some such remarkable deliverance took place'.[3] The weakness of the assertion is manifest, it seems to me, just like the weakness in building the same assertion on the observation that customs reflected by the tradition derive from the period claimed by the narrative. One might just as easily argue the opposite point: 'The Bible's witness is so impressive, so exaggerated, as to leave little doubt that the entire account has been manufactured out of whole cloth'. The weakness of the assertion

---

1. F.M. Cross, 'The Song of the Sea and Canaanite Myth' in *God and Christ: Existence and Province* (New York: Harper & Row, 1968), p. 17.
2. J. Bright, *A History of Israel* (Philadelphia: Westminster Press, 1972), p. 120.
3. Bright, *A History of Israel*, p. 6.

derives, however, not simply from its unsupported character but from weakness in formulation. What does it mean to say that some such event 'took place'? Are there not other categories that more adequately capture the nature of event, at least the nature of the tradition, than 'really happened'?

M. Noth's account of the event shares some of the same problem. Recognizing the varied levels of interpretations, of mutations and additions in the Sea tradition, he observes simply that 'the detachment of Egyptian chariots sank in the water owing to some unexpected disaster...The incident itself...remains veiled from our sight'.[1] Noth has often been accused of nihilism in his historical statements, of an inability to say anything very concrete, particularly in dealing with Israel's early history.[2] And here he may deserve the critique. Moreover, Noth makes an explicit allusion to the enemy motif without considering the problems posed by its disappearance at various levels of the tradition's history. If one describes the event in terms of a 'detachment of Egyptian chariots', must he not also consider why some references to the event make no use of the motif? Yet, Noth avoids painting a detailed picture of the event. And it is at this point that his presentation lacks the color of the others, the air of 'what really happened'. But surely his cautious remarks stand the test of critical evaluation far better than a more detailed description of the event based on only one level of tradition or a weak combination of details from various levels.

The most impressive reconstruction of the event at the Sea comes from the work of L. Hay.[3] He argues that the path cut in the water, or water blown by an east wind, is not at all the crucial detail about the event. Indeed, even the *crossing* motif has no substantial basis in earlier levels of the Sea tradition. Rather, the event can be most adequately depicted as 'a military encounter in which Israel defeated the pursuing chariotry of Pharaoh'. Evidence to support this position can be gleaned from various points, particularly in the narrative traditions of Exodus 14. And Hay does so in full view of the tradition's history.

1. M. Noth, *The History of Israel* (New York: Harper & Row, 1958), pp. 116-17.
2. J. Bright, *Early Israel in Recent History Writing* (SBT, 19; London: SCM Press, 1956), pp. 79-110.
3. L.S. Hay, 'What Really Happened at the Sea of Reeds?', *JBL* 83 (1964), p. 399.

Yet, precisely in this reconstruction, the problem appears most clearly. None of the texts reporting the event at the Sea describe a military conflict between two armies. The evidence for suggesting that the event really was a military conflict is impressive. And it can be drawn, at least in part, from all levels of the tradition. But the conclusion must be inferred. Israel apparently had no interest in reporting the event in that kind of detail. Indeed, when one observes that details important for early descriptions of the event are radically altered or dropped altogether at later points in the history of the tradition, he must conclude that particular details do not constitute intrinsic parts of the tradition. The significance of this conclusion cannot be appropriated simply as the difficulty historians face in isolating *bruta facta* from layers of interpretation. There can be no doubt that interpretation procedures account for the changes and mutations in the history of tradition. But loss of such a central detail as the enemy destroyed in the sea (cf. Jos. 2.10) suggests that particular facts even with their various stages of interpretation are not intrinsic for the transmission of this tradition. Is it necessary to argue, then, that history cannot be deemed the proper category for describing the significance of OT traditions? If we work with a definition of history that arises from the modern western world, from an effort to describe the events of history in concrete, positivistic terms (what really happened) we should probably admit that history is the wrong category. Disunity among the various stages of tradition leaves the impression that none of the circumstances described there can seriously be considered historical.[1] Thus, if evaluation of the text depends on a narrowly defined concept of history, the text must be dismissed as a falsification of reality or embraced in a naive assertion of its veracity. And in both cases, the exegetical task will have been derailed.

Secondly, our understanding of Israel's early history can be informed not only by bits and pieces inferred or gathered at random from the OT witness, but also by the understanding of history itself at home in the OT text. To pose the historical alternatives first is to limit the possibilities for adequate exegesis of the text and thus for adequate evaluation of the historical character of the text. Rather, the first question should be a literary one: what understanding of the event at the Sea do the various traditions reflect? Then, on the basis of that

---

1. Cf. J. Barr, 'Revelation Through History in the Old Testament and in Modern Theology' in *New Theology* I (New York: Macmillan, 1964), pp. 66-67.

question, one can ask what sense of history can be seen in these traditions. This procedure may not permit an accurate description of events as they developed. Indeed, it suggests that history for the sea tradition cannot be confined to a box of time and space, cause and effect, as if it were one among several beads on a string composing a larger whole. Rather, in the sea tradition the event demonstrates a distinct openness toward the future. It develops unique significance for each new generation, significance that can produce mutations in old details or create new details. It suggests an understanding of event that depends on a decidedly subjective appropriation of evidence. That understanding, it seems to me, must be carefully evaluated, indeed, perhaps appropriated, if one wants to talk of history or theology in the Sea tradition.

My *second thesis* is that Israel's theological understanding of event, particularly the Sea event, breaks open the stalemate in the spectrum of authentic/inauthentic analysis and should be taken seriously as a genuine historical datum in the reconstruction of Israel's history. M. Noth made the point in the introduction to his *History of Israel*.

> An element of the inexplicable is in fact present in *all* human history and is bound to be present not merely because it is not even remotely possible to embrace the whole profusion of cause and effect even in the historical present, let alone in the past, and least of all in the remote past, but above all because history is not merely a constant repetition of complicated concatenations of cause and effect if God is really active in history not simply as a πρῶτον κινοῦν but as the ever present Lord working with the superficial interplay of cause and effect. Inevitably, therefore, there is an element of mystery of the 'unhistorical' in all human history which makes its presence felt on the frontiers of all historical knowledge.[1]

But Noth himself never really takes the mystery of history as a serious element in opening the history of Israel. It seems to me nonetheless, that for historical analysis, it is crucial to determine what theological significance colors Israel's perception of the Sea event. What understanding of history shines through Israel's formulation of the Sea event? My concern here is to say, not that we should break history into two compartments, the old Geschichte/Historie dichotomy, but rather that we should recognize the constitutive element self-understanding plays in history and not eliminate it as a second-level, interpretative factor above (or below) the real history.

---

1. Noth, *The History of Israel*, pp. 1-2.

Two pitfalls threaten at this point. First, we face a temptation to transfer objectivizing pursuits from historical reconstruction to theological formulation. In the sea event we know that God is the kind of God who concerns himself for oppressed people. The proposition is true. The OT witnesses at various junctures, not just in the sea tradition, that God maintains special care for those whom others oppress. And the point comes to the fore in this tradition. But is that point the significance of the tradition? Where is God's concern for oppressed people ever in doubt? Does the Sea tradition not assume God's care for the oppressed and move on to a new point?[1] Or we might suggest that in the Sea event God affirms that he is faithful to his promises. This issue appears explicitly in some OT traditions, although not in the Sea material. In Exod. 17.1-7, for example, Israel rebels against Moses and God. And a question characterizes at least a portion of her rebellion: 'Is Yahweh among us or not'? Yahweh's act would in some measure affirm his promise to be with his people. But even in Exodus 17 the question hangs on the periphery of the unit. For the majority of the OT tradition, certainly the Sea tradition, God's faithfulness to his promise is not at issue.

Secondly, the objectivizing tendency can reduce understanding of the event to a series of propositions. 'The event occurred when the east wind blew the water back and allowed Israel to cross on dry ground.' 'Then you came to the sea; and the Egyptians pursued your fathers with chariots and horsemen to the Reed Sea. And when they cried to the Lord, he put darkness between you and the Egyptians, and made the sea come upon them and cover them; and your eyes saw what I did to Egypt, and you lived in the wilderness a long time'. But such procedure, whether oriented toward history or theology, seems to me to fall woefully short. I cannot see evidence that Israel is primarily interested in preserving traditions about the sea *simply* as a series of propositions. One has only to compare the completion of the so-called Credo in Jos. 24.14-15.

Where, then, can the theological significance, so crucial for the OT's own historical understanding, be pinpointed? The *third thesis* now follows. Israel preserves tradition about the sea event, not as a series of propositions about what really happened or what she believed about God as a result of what really happened, but as evidence of a moral

---

1. R. Knierim, 'Offenbarung im Alten Testament', *Probleme biblischer Theologie* (Festschrift G. von Rad; Munich: Chr. Kaiser Verlag, 1971), p. 211.

imperative. In the priestly account of Exodus 14, the imperative builds on the formula, 'You shall know that I am Yahweh'. Knowledge of God and particular events are crucially interrelated for the OT. But what precisely is that relationship? Zimmerli's form critical studies of the formulae in expressions about Israel's knowledge of Yahweh suggest that an event announced by a prophet, or in this case Moses, serves as a foundation for asserting, 'You shall know that I am Yahweh'.[1] The Sea event establishes the validity of the assertion; it proves to Israel that 'I am Yahweh'. That knowledge constitutes the core of the event for P's understanding of the sea tradition.

But what is the content of that knowledge? Israel does not discover through the event that Yahweh is the kind of God who acts in such and such a manner, in this case, who protects Israel from her enemy or leads her through the dangers of the wilderness. Quite the contrary, she already presupposes that God acts in her history. Neither does the knowledge imply confirmation that God lives up to his promises. God's character is not at issue.[2] Rather, the point of issue lies in some manner in the relationship between God and his people.

The crucial content of revelation for the Sea tradition lies in the assertion that 'I am Yahweh', at least for the P source (cf. v. 18). This formula functions most obviously as a self-introduction formula, to be used by someone not previously known by his addressees (cf. Gen. 45.3-13). But Israel knows Yahweh. And there is no question of some strange God competing with Yahweh for recognition in the Sea event. The P source construes the Egyptians as the subject for the formula in this case. Yet, even here there is no competition from

---

1. W. Zimmerli, 'Ich bin Jahwe', *Geschichte und altes Testament: Beiträge zur historischen Theologie* XVI (Tübingen: Mohr, 1953), pp. 179-209. Also 'Das Wort des göttlichen Selbsterweises (Erweiswort), eine prophetische Gattung', *Mélanges bibliques redigés en l'honneur de André Robert* (Paris: Blood & Gay, 1957), pp. 154-64.

2. R. Tomes ('Exodus 14: The Mighty Acts of God; an Essay in Theological Criticism', *SJT* 22 [1969], p. 475) observes: 'Slowly the exodus becomes a pointer to the conclusion that God cares for all slaves... So we may say that the significance for us of the exodus story is that God acted on behalf of an oppressed people'. I cannot see, however, that the tradition serves in any way to introduce the idea that God cares for the oppressed, as if that point were previously unknown. Nor do I see evidence suggesting that this tradition functions as one in a mosaic of traditions describing how God characteristically acts. The point of the tradition seems to me to go further, as I shall suggest below.

other deities who claim responsibility for the event. And the event is not presented as an introduction of Yahweh to the hapless Egyptians. Rather, it serves to establish Yahweh's authority over the Pharaoh and his army (v. 18b). The function of the formula in this context more nearly corresponds with the use of the formula in law codes as the foundation for obedience to Yahweh's will (Lev. 18.1ff. Cf. also Gen. 41.44).

Knowledge of God produced by the Sea event, then, does not contain various assertions about God's nature or his essence. Rather, it confesses Yahweh as lord over his subjects. Moreover, the event demands some kind of response from the people who witness it, either as eye-witnesses or as witnesses in the history of the tradition's transmission. The response must come from any witness, not just from Israel.[1] Thus, v. 18: 'The Egyptians shall know that I am Yahweh'. And Exod. 15.14-16 describes the Canaanites' response (cf. also Jos. 2.10). In J (14.31), Israel responds to the event in a similar way: 'So Israel saw the great deed which Yahweh did against the Egyptians. And they feared Yahweh and they believed in Yahweh and in Moses his servant' (cf. Isa. 43.10). Knowledge of God in the sea tradition is commitment to Yahweh as Lord. The significance of the event is that in the event Israel, or Egypt, faces God's demand for obedience: 'You shall have no other gods before me'. The traditions about this event understand history as if it carries an imperative for decision and commitment.

A footnote: the imperative is for religious commitment. 'Now therefore fear the Lord and serve him in sincerity and in faithfulness; put away the gods which your fathers served beyond the river, and in Egypt, and serve the Lord. And if you are unwilling to serve the Lord, choose this day whom you will serve'. But commitment to Yahweh is at the same time commitment to a particular moral stance vis-à-vis neighbor or stranger, the oppressed, the widow, the orphan. 'You shall not pervert justice due the sojourners or the fatherless, or take a widow's garment in pledge; but you shall remember that you were a slave in Egypt and the Lord your God redeemed you from there; therefore I command you to do this'. The event does not tell Israel

1. The notion of an objective datum, unencumbered by subjective interpretation from an eye-witness or generations of subsequent witnesses, seems as pointless as the conundrum about a tree falling in a forest with no human witnesses about. But if the response is a crucial element in the event, must it not also be taken seriously in any reconstruction?

simply that God cares for the oppressed. It tells Israel that since God cares for oppressed Israel, Israel should care for all other oppressed people.[1] If the tradition elicits a response to that imperative, if it functions from generation to generation as a tool for forming the moral fiber of the people, then it has claimed its grounds for authenticity.

Conclusions

(1) Israel's understanding of the Sea event suggests that event has a primary moral content. If history is not to be sterile, that content must be evaluated as a crucial part of the historical task. (2) History of Israel cannot be separated from Israel's law. Narrative in the Pentateuch cannot be siphoned away from the law in the Penteuch as the more interesting, the more relevant part of the OT.[2] (3) The same

---

1. Knierim,'Offenbarung im Alten Testament', p. 225, highlights the discussion about revelation in the OT by calling for consideration of not only the locus for revelation (revelation as history), but also the place (revelation in history) and the subject of revelation (God as Yahweh/Yahweh as God). This point seems to me to be crucial. My point is that revelation of God's identity, 'God is Yahweh/Yahweh is God', carries an analogue that fills a confession out with moral content. 'Yahweh is our God'. 'You shall have no other gods before me'. And that claim for absolute fidelity headlines the entire law. The same point can be made with reference to other kinds of tradition. Cf. de Vries, *Heroic Song*, pp. 181-82. In response to the questions cited in n. 1 p. 45 de Vries concludes: 'These are indeed questions that Alexander could not have answered and which would have seemed to him entirely senseless. But they are questions that we can raise only to our own shame. Reality is not what happened more than two thousand years ago in the Scamander plain, but what has lived for centuries in the memories of many generations as a precious testimony to a glorious past, and—even more important—from which these generations have come to life'. It is the power of the tradition to bring subsequent generations to life that marks its authenticity.

2. M.C. Lind, 'Paradigm of Holy War in the Old Testament', *BR* 16 (1971), pp. 25-26, develops a familiar position about unity between history and law built on a comparison with Hittite treaty forms. And this he does in spite of caution advised by the direction of current discussion about treaty and covenant. But is the issue in the first order a form-critical one at all, open to resolution by form-critical parallels in other contemporary texts? Is the issue perhaps not much more fundamental, cutting to the very basis of Israel's view of reality. It seems to me that the drive to define the unity between history and law, Sinai and exodus wilderness, would be placed on a much more secure basis if we recognise an intrinsic element of moral demand within Israel's conception of history and a springboard from that conceptualization into the entire scope of OT law.

point, it seems to me, applies for the NT. The gospel is not simply an announcement of good news, summarized in a series of Credo propositions. It carries confession of obedience to Christ as Lord and the commitment to moral responsibility that it entails. (4) The point is relevant, not only for the Sea event, not only for the events of Israel's early history, but, as Noth observes, for all of human history. Whether the war is the war at the Sea of Reeds or the war in Viet Nam, the event carries a moral dimension that must be recognized and responded to by witnesses of all generations.

Chapter 5

THE KING'S LOYAL OPPOSITION:
OBEDIENCE AND AUTHORITY IN EXODUS 32–34

To obey or not to obey seems an uncomplicated choice, at least for the framework of the Sinai tradition. In Exod. 19.5, the appeal is clear. 'Now therefore, if you will obey my voice and keep my covenant, you shall be my own possession among all peoples'. Moreover, the content of the obedience Yahweh expects from his possession is flagged by the introductory formula in v. 6b. 'These are the words which you shall speak to the children of Israel'. Yet, the choice is not always a simple one, as the traditio-historical layers in the law would suggest. It must have been necessary always to reconsider what the content of obedience might be. Indeed, the choice can raise a pressing problem. Is it not necessary on occasion to resist a command, to appeal for some new formulation of the law?[1]

The question is sharpened by the work of L.S. Ford.[2] It is of central importance to affirm that God does not coerce his creatures, but rather strives to persuade them to obey his aims for their future.[3] Yet, that image could emerge as a rather weak and inadequate tool for expressing the breadth of thought about God. In an effort to do justice to facets of theology concerned with God's sovereignty, Ford suggests appropriating imagery of God as King. It is clear that the suggestion

---

1. G.W. Coats, 'Abraham's Sacrifice of Faith: A Form-Critical Analysis of Genesis 22', *Int* 27 (1975), pp. 389-400.
2. L.S. Ford, 'Biblical Recital and Process Philosophy: Some Whiteheadian Suggestions for Old Testament Hermeneutics', *Int* 26 (1972), pp. 198-209.
3. L.S. Ford, 'The Logic of Divine Power: God as King and the Kingdom of God', MS presented to a symposium on biblical theology and process philosophy, Indianapolis, February 28–March 1, 1974.

is rooted deeply in biblical tradition.[1] But the pattern calls for some deliberation about royal 'persuasion'. In what manner can a king tolerate opposition? Everyone knows the kind of conformity that can be expected by the pope, the president, the bishop or the dean. The image of the king, though not a part of our society's categories for power structure, surely evokes an equal if not a greater response of awe and obedience, that is, conformity to the norm recognized as the king's will. And so, if we speak of God as King, do we not commit ourselves unconditionally to a stance of obedience to his demands? Does the king not persuade with force? What sense, then, is talk of opposition, particularly when the 'opposition' is qualified by the term 'loyal'? In Isa. 45.9, the prophet makes the point: 'Woe to him who strives with his maker, an earthen vessel with the potter! Does the clay say to him who fashions it, "What are you making?" or "Your work has no handles!"?'. For Second Isaiah, opposition to the king is not loyal. It is only opposition. In the kingdom of God, is not loyalty to be understood as automatic, unquestioning obedience to the God who calls for response?

Yet, remarkably, the pious faith of Israel allows for struggle with God to work out the meaning of loyal obedience. For Israel obedience to the king was not the obedience of an automaton. Jeremiah's opposition to the king (Jer. 12.1) illustrates the point: 'Righteous art thou, O Lord, when I complain to thee; yet I would plead my case before thee'. The collocation is different here from the one in Isa. 45.9. Here the preposition following the verb is *'el*; God would, in that case, be the judge for the case. Isa. 45.9, on the other hand, employs the preposition *'et*, suggesting that God is a litigant. Yet, the content of the case in Jeremiah is formulated in terms identical to those in Isaiah. In both cases, an accusing question is addressed directly to God (cf. Jer. 12.2).[2] Yet, Jeremiah is not dismissed as a rank rebel. Thus, the

---

1. See particularly N. Perrin, 'The Interpretation of a Biblical Symbol', *JR* 55 (1975), pp. 348-70.
2. On the question as accusation in a lament, see C. Westermann, 'The Role of the Lament in the Theology of the Old Testament', *Int* 28 (1974), pp. 27-28. It seems significant to me, in this context, that Genesis 32 can develop an etiology for the name 'Israel' out of a story that depicts the eponymic father struggling with God. Regardless of the original character of the story, or the original meaning of the crucial verb, the point of the etiology is that Israel is in essence, that is, in name, the one who struggles with God.

hermeneutical problem: What distinguishes a question of accusation addressed to God, or the king, as an act of loyal trust and faith from one that can be taken only as revolution or apostasy?

The problem relates to a broad range of biblical tradition. Thus, for example, in the murmuring traditions of the wilderness theme it is crucial to ask in each instance whether key questions, addressed by the Israelites to Moses constitute matters consistent with faithful obedience or matters that spell revolution. N. Lohfink is correct particularly in his observation that the pericope in Exod. 15.22-27 does not describe a rebellion.[1] The question in v. 24 involves no breach of faith; one must therefore consider whether the verb *lûn* properly connotes such a question of faith *as well as* clear acts of rebellion, or whether in v. 24 the verb wrenches the content of the story out of its original lines and forces a reinterpretation of a story originally cast as an account of a faithful request for water. If some such reinterpretation has occurred, it in itself would reflect the hermeneutical problem at stake. A thin line divides a faithful and obedient request from one that implies rejection of the status quo and revolution.

The issue is more sharply focused in Exod. 17.1-7, since here the verbs *lûn* and *rîb* are closely associated. I have argued that the question with the verb *rîb*, structured like the question in Exod. 15.24, does not imply revolution but can be understood as neutral, whereas the question with the verb *lûn* implies revolution, rejection of Moses' authority and leadership.[2] But the two acts are not always distinguishable. What appears at one point to be loyal opposition, consistent with behavior one might expect from a faithful disciple, becomes at another point disloyal rebellion. C. Westermann has captured the same problem by suggesting that the murmuring pattern reflects the influence of the

---

1. N. Lohfink, 'Die Ursünden in der priesterlichen Geschichtserzählung', *Die Zeit Jesu* (ed. G. Bornkamm, K. Rahner; Freiburg: Herder, 1970), p. 46 n. 32.

2. G.W. Coats, *Rebellion in the Wilderness: The Murmuring Motif in the Wilderness Traditions of the Old Testament* (Nashville: Abingdon Press, 1968), pp. 53-62. Lohfink (*Ursünden*, p. 46 n. 32) sees rebellion more readily connoted by the verb *rîb*. Yet, for both *lûn* and *rîb*, patterns of rebellion must be defined on the basis of evidence derived from the context, not imposed on, or developed from a reconstruction of the context. L. Dunlop develops a similar point in his 'The Intercessions of Moses: A Study of the Pentateuchal Traditions' (dissertation; Rome: Pontifical Biblical Institute, 1970), p. 171. Dunlop, however, reconstructs the key text, placing the neutral question with the verb *lûn* and the question of revolution with the verb *rîb* (see p. 176).

lament.[1] The lament question and the murmuring accusation appear in the same mould. But the one is an act of faith, the other rebellion. Must the lamenter not always be cautious, lest his lament pass over into revolution?[2]

Exegetical Focus

In order to focus on the problem in a limited context, I shall confine detailed discussion to the pericope in Exodus 32–34.[3] The golden calf episode provides a completion of the call for obedience in Exodus 19, not only in clearly picturing a people's revolution and subsequent restoration to covenant, but also in the representation of Moses. It is my conviction that a model for a genuinely loyal obedience emerges from the interaction of the two facets.

The Revolution

There can be no doubt about the fact that the pericope begins with an account of gross apostasy. In the first panel of the unit, 32.1-6, construction of the golden calf is represented as the creation of gods for the people. In the opening imperative addressed by the people to Aaron, the point is explicit not only in the collocation, '^{a}śēh-lānû '^{e}lōhîm (v. 1), but also in the formula 'ēlleh '^{e}lōhêkā yiśrā'ēl '^{a}šer he'^{e}lûkā mē'ereṣ miṣrāyim (v. 4). Thus not only by the act of creating the images, but even more by the act of creating *multiple* images, the people revolt against the loyalty they should owe to Yahweh. Moreover, they assign to those images the credit for the exodus. The act is, therefore, relatively clear. To ascribe the exodus to golden calves is revolution.

Yet, the act is *relatively* clear because the report represents a point of view which, in all probability, sets the golden calves over against the cultic center in Jerusalem (cf. 1 Kgs 12.26-33). Insofar as the present form of the text is concerned, the hermeneutical question is no

---

1. Westermann, 'Lament', pp. 29-31.
2. W. Brueggemann, 'From Hurt to Joy, from Death to Life', *Int* 28 (1974), pp. 3-19.
3. For a review of the literary critical problems in this text, see B.S. Childs, *The Book of Exodus: A Critical Theological Commentary* (Philadelphia: Westminster Press, 1974), pp. 553-624, as well as the literature cited there.

problem. To go to Dan and Bethel instead of Jerusalem, to revere the golden calves instead of Yahweh, is by definition revolution.[1] But, if the history of the tradition does reveal a stage behind the pro-Jerusalem polemic, then the construction of golden calves may not have been so clearly an act of apostasy.[2] And the appeal to the populace in 1 Kgs 12.28 would set out the weight of the question. How should the people know whether worshipping God at Dan or Bethel is better than worshipping God at Jerusalem? Perhaps the innovation of Jeroboam is a reformation promoted by genuine faith, a desire to correct the abuses in the cult in Jerusalem and thus return the people to a proper, obedient relationship with God. Must we not be cautious in concluding too quickly, with Dtr. that the innovation is in reality the nauseous and perverse crime of apostasy?

Exod. 32.1 is, however, still more subtle in its depiction of the revolution. The initial imperative to Aaron, calling for construction of the calves, casts the act as an effort to replace *Moses* rather than a direct act of rebellion against Yahweh. 'This Moses, the man who brought us up from the land of Egypt, we do not know what has become of him'.[3] One might conclude that revolution against a particular administration can be separated from loyalty to the state only with great difficulty. Refusing belief in Moses is tantamount to refusing belief in Yahweh. And apostasy is to replace one administration with another, at least from the point of view of the displaced administration. For this text, moreover, the revolution against Moses focuses attention on the office of Moses. What authority does Moses have to lead the people further when the people have found new

1. On this stage, see Childs, *Exodus*, pp. 560-61.
2. So M. Newman, *The People of the Covenant: A Study of Israel from Moses to the Monarchy* (Nashville: Abingdon Press, 1962), pp. 179-82. See also J. Dus, 'Ein richterzeitliches Stierbildheiligtum zu Bethel? Die Aufeinanderfolge der frühisraelitischen Zentralkultstätten', *ZAW* 77 (1965), pp. 268-86.
3. For a different position, see J.M. Sasson, 'Bovine Symbolism in the Exodus Narrative', *VT* 18 (1968), p. 384. Sasson concludes: 'These repeated equations between Moses, *the man who brought the Hebrews out of Egypt*, and the calf, symbol of the *deity that brought the people of Israel from bondage*, render it plausible to assume that, to the newly-freed slaves, the molten calf was a substitute for Moses... In the ancient Near East it was not uncommon for certain animals... to represent deities and highly esteemed personalities'. Yet, the narrative context does not suggest that the calf is considered a representative for Moses. The calf substitutes for Moses by replacing him.

modes of leadership? Thus, one might anticipate by the tension established in the first panel not only a fitting response to the apostasy from God, but also some confirmation of Mosaic authority within the operation of the people.

The second panel of narrative (32.7-35) develops these two points. An initial movement carries Yahweh's response to the revolution, first as a report to Moses of the people's apostasy (v. 8), and then as a judgment speech. The judgment spells the dissolution of the covenant and the destruction of the people. Moreover, Moses' authority is elevated in v. 10b by virtue of Yahweh's designation of Moses as the new elect. Thus, in contrast to the people's move to desert Moses and build new leaders out of gold, here God deserts the people and announces his plan to build a new people out of Moses. It is only the virtue of Moses' intercession that stays the total tragedy. Significantly, in the intercession no reference to the plan for Moses as founder of a new people appears. The brief allusion is simply dropped.

The double pattern of the panel is nonetheless present in the execution of the judgment. Moses responds in anger to the festival of the golden calf by breaking the tables, an act that represents the dissolution of the covenant.[1] And the destruction of the calf, with the people sentenced to drink the remains, is at least an act of hostile coercion, if not a trial by ordeal, to determine loyalty or revolution in the bowels of the people. Moreover, Moses' involvement in the ordination of the Levites also shows his authority to respond in kind to the apostasy of the people. The penalty for the crime of innovation in electing new leaders in the place of Moses is thus severe and, in a manner that stands in tension with Moses' intercession on the people's behalf, reminds any revolutionaries that one objects to the King only with fear and trembling.[2] The double motif is completed when, following a new intercession, Yahweh refuses to reinstate the people, reminds Moses that the guilty must suffer the consequences of their rebellion, and promises the judgment. The one amelioration for the judgment is a reconfirmation of Moses' task in leading the people. The promise for an angel does, to be sure, suggest some degree of divine presence. But it does not renew the covenant with the people or point to any stage along the way. The angel confirms the authority of *Moses* in v. 34: 'Now go, lead the people to the place of which I have spoken to

1. Childs, *Exodus*, p. 569.
2. See the treatment of these aspects in narrative style in Childs, *Exodus*, p. 563.

you [sing.]; behold, my angel shall go before you [sing.]. Nevertheless, in the day when I visit, I will visit their sin [plur.] upon *them*'. And the judgment follows in v. 35. Thus, despite the continuation of the journey, despite the reconfirmation of Moses as the leader of the people, the covenant is broken. God is not with his people. If the story to this point represents the interests of Jerusalem as polemic against the North, then the impact of the polemic is clear. The covenant is broken. And there stand the pieces. The picture is unfortunately all too sharp.

Intercession

The pericope in Exodus 32 develops a polar motif as a point of tension with the major focus on the revolution of the people. And the polar motif, namely, the intercession of Moses, opens a narrative line that is not completed in ch. 32. Yet, precisely in the intercession of Moses the problematic quality of the loyal subject's obedience to the King emerges.

Exodus 32. Moses' intercession on behalf of his people appears twice in 32.11-13 and 32.30-32. In both cases the intercession represents a polar contrast with the context. The first intercession follows two of Yahweh's speeches to Moses, the second of which announces the divine intention to destroy Israel and replace it with a nation drawn from the seed of Moses. The intention to destroy is expressed by reference to the hot wrath of God burning against the people *(w^{e}yiḥar-'appî bāhem wa'^{a}kallēm*, v. 10). Moses' intercession (v. 11) opens with an explicit reference to that hot wrath (*lāmâ yhwh yeḥ^{a}reh 'app^{e}kā bĕ'ammekā*). It thus connects clearly with the preceding context.[1] Moreover, this opening question appears in the form of an accusation, like the accusation of the lament or the murmuring rebellion. With second person suffixes it addresses God directly and calls into question the legitimacy of the divine act. 'O Lord, why does thy wrath burn hot against thy people?' The question alone is enough to raise the specter of rebellion around the head of the servant of the Lord, since the clay ought not to say to him who fashions it, 'What are you making'? But the specter grows in the continuation. Moses argues by citing a hypothetical response from the Egyptians, should Israel die at the

1. The intercession reflects heavy influence from Dtr. See Childs, *Exodus*, p. 559, as well as Childs's comparison with the Dtr. parallel, pp. 567-68.

hands of God in the wilderness: 'With evil intent did he bring them forth, to slay them in the mountains, and to consume them from the face of the earth' (v. 12).

The development of the argument is crucial. It is not that the Egytians would attribute an evil intention to God, and thus in order to protect his reputation he should desist. Rather, it corresponds to similar arguments in intercession (Num. 14.13-19); to pursue the intention to destroy the people would violate the previous promise to establish a covenant of loyalty with the people. It is on the basis of an appeal precisely to that promise that Moses himself labels God's intention to destroy as an evil *(hārā'â)*. The point of the argument is that, even for God, violation of the initial aim in the relationship between God and people is evil. And the intercession attempts to persuade God to pursue the initial aim, to act in consistency with his own promise. For this tradition, even God must live in the tension of the hermeneutical problem. Where is the line that distinguishes justifiable innovation from unjust rebellion against loyalty to the covenant? Thus, God does not impose the lure of loyalty as a tyrant unbound by a reciprocal commitment of loyalty. Rather, he enters a mutual commitment without appropriating his creatures as instruments of his pleasure dangling on his string. On the basis of the intercession, God is persuaded. He repents and reassesses his announced goal. But also of significance here, the tradition shows Moses as a servant who can intercede boldly for his people without himself falling under divine wrath as a rebel. Moses' intercession saves the day. It persuades God. And his persuasion, even with threats of coercion, is his responsibility as an obedient servant of God.

The polar tension between intercession and revolution continues in the following panel. In a report of Moses' descent to the people with the tables of God in his hand, the text shows no clear indication of impact from the Mosaic intercession or the divine repentance. Indeed, it has long been recognized that the report apparently presupposes that in the descent, Moses had no prior knowledge of the rebellion. And when he discovers the apostasy of the people, he responds in a fit of wrath that rivals the previous intention of God to destroy his people. He breaks the covenant, forces the people into a trial by ordeal, summons Aaron to account for the crime, and finally condemns at least a portion of the people to destruction. Where is the appeal to mercy now? To be sure, the destruction scene incorporates an ancient tradition of ordination for the Levites. But in its present form, the scene can only be taken as the occasion of Moses' wrath. Moreover, the occasion leaves the people without covenantal commitment. And without covenantal commitment, the consequence of God's concession to the intercession in v. 14 is not very clear.

The same point can be made in reference to the intercession and concession of Num. 14.13-25. Following a divine announcement of intention to destroy the whole people and establish a new people through the seed of Moses, Moses intercedes. And the basis of the intercession is the prior promise. To destroy the people would destroy the promise. Verse 20 marks the concession. But then follows a sentence that reduces the impact of the concession. If the people must die in the wilderness, with only Caleb or Caleb and Joshua heirs to the promised land, where is the impact of the concession? Yet, the display of wrath does not appear to be disruptive in the narrative. It is, on the contrary, a narrative style built from interplay of polar tensions.[1] And the polar tensions create the essential movement in this story.

The continued crisis in Exodus 32 is captured by a renewal of the intercession in vv. 31-32. In this case the intercession begins with confession. The people are, in fact, rebels. But the appeal that might correspond to the accusation in the previous intercession is broken, with only a protasis suggesting the formal structure it might have carried. The weight of the intercession is, however, carried by a contrasting protasis and its completion. 'Now, if thou wilt forgive their sin—and if not [if you will not forgive them], blot me, I pray thee, out of thy book which thou hast written'. The appeal is now a threat. And the serious quality of the appeal is clear (cf. Num. 11.11-15).

Contrary to the previous intercession, in this case the appeal of the intercession, or at least the threat, is not heeded. In a direct rejection of the threat, the response to the intercession notes that only the guilty will be blotted out. The innocent may not stand in the place of the guilty. Moses will not die. But the negotiation is stalemated. The impact of that point is made quite clear in v. 34b. The day will come when the guilty will stand their sentence (cf. Num. 14.21). Thus, the commitment is not renewed. The presence of God that defines Israel as distinctive from all people is not returned. Verse 34a emphasizes this point. Moses, not God, must lead the people. And the angel goes

---

1. So Childs, *Exodus*, p. 567.

before Moses, the seal of his leadership. Yet, a crucial point of the pericope seems to be that Moses can oppose the divine intention and not himself be counted as a rebel. In an audacious threat, Moses submits his resignation. And the divine response affirms the legitimacy of Moses' office, his struggle for his people. He has not yet persuaded God to complete the restoration. But his efforts to persuade have not been met with rejection. The future is open for Moses to continue his struggle, for the shape of the mutual commitment to be hammered out in a mutual exchange of aims between God and his servant. In this case to contend with God is the mark of the obedient servant.

Exodus 33–34. The concluding comment in 32.35 leaves the goal of the intercession unfulfilled. The covenant is broken, the people punished. And so, in a sense, the pericope is complete. Rebels will be plagued. Yet, the appeal to the prior promise, already a part of the narrative in ch. 32, remains at center stage in ch. 33. The transition to the first panel in ch. 33 is somewhat rough, pointing to the tension between the broken covenant and the intercession. Verses 1-6 repeat the movement of 32.33-34. Yahweh directs continuation of the move toward the land, and the foundation of the direction is the promise. But the movement must occur without God's presence. An angel will lead the way. But there is no indication that the angel alleviates the threat posed by God's absence. The suffixes here are still singular, as in the parallel section of ch. 32. It is not so clear here, however, that the singular suffixes refer to Moses in contrast to the people (cf. v. 3). The angel represents leadership in some degree for all the people. But even with this concession, the angel's leadership is a step removed from God's presence. Moreover, God will himself dispel the occupants of the land, But even that promise does not reduce the judgment in the directive. 'But I will not go up among you, lest I consume you in the way, for you are a stiff-necked people'. The goal of the intercession is thus as yet unfulfilled.

The role of Moses vis-à-vis the people demands some attention here. In 32.33-34 the judgment stood against the people, with Moses distinct, not guilty of his people's sin. And the angel functioned in some manner as an affirmation of his leadership. Here, there is some confusion. In v. 1 Moses receives the directive to lead the people to the land of the promise. Verse 2 might be taken as a parallel to the promise for an angel in ch. 32 since the suffixes in the judgment sentence of v. 3 as well as the central pronoun are also second person singular (contrast 32.34b). Yet, the people, not Moses alone, are intended. 'You [sing.] are a stiff-necked *people*'. Thus, the distinctive function of the angel in ch. 32 to confirm Mosaic leadership fades, and the focus falls on the punishment. The movement is repeated in vv. 4-6 with a narrative report to the people of the *bad* news (*haddābār hārā'*). The report includes in v. 5 a citation of the judgment. But in this case the division between Moses and people, apparent in 32.33-34, again emerges. The citation, a speech addressed to Moses, is introduced with a message commission formula. Thus, Moses is to address his people with an oracle of God. And the message defines the people as stiff-necked with a second person *plural* pronoun. 'You [pl.] are a stiff-necked people' (v. 5). The people stand under the judgment, whether addressed in plural or singular forms. And Moses mediates between the condemned people and the judge.[1]

With the repetition of the judgment as denial of presence for the people in their move to the land, the narrative shifts to the intercession. Verses 7-11 set the stage by describing Moses' regular office as mediator, associated intimately with the tent of meeting.[2] And central to the description is the symbol for divine presence. When anyone would seek Yahweh, he would approach the tent. Then Moses would enter the tent and the pillar of cloud would descend on it. And the conclusion stipulates Moses' unique position. 'Thus the Lord used to speak to Moses face to face, as a man speaks to his friend' (v. 11). In the face of such a general introduction to Moses' role as intercessor, the intercession in vv. 12-13 is doubly poignant. For the crisis provoking the intercession is the threat of divine absence.

The intercession begins in v. 12 with a citation. God had instructed Moses to bring the people up. 'Thou sayest to me, "Bring up this people"'. The issue is thus personal, not *simply* on behalf of the people. Verse 12aß would then appear to contradict the promise for an angel to lead the way: 'Thou hast not let me know whom thou wilt send with me'. But the issue cannot be resolved by such a circumlocution. The promise for an angel is not the same as the promise for God's own presence. And it is that promise which is at stake. Thus, with another

---

1. Various layers in the history of tradition may well account for the rough quality of this narrative element, rather than redaction of literary sources. See Childs, *Exodus*, pp. 584-86.
2. Childs, *Exodus*, p. 592.

citation, Moses develops the argument out of personal position. 'Thou hast said, "I know you by name, and you have also found favor in my sight"'. Significantly, it is out of that personal favor that the point of the argument appears in v. 13: 'Now...if I have found favor in thy sight, show me now thy ways that I may know thee, and find favor in thy sight'. But the appeal is general. It is only in the final touch of the storyteller's hand that the argument suggests the particular content of the intercession. 'Consider that this nation is *thy* people'. That point demands careful attention. It refers to the people as 'thy people' (*'amm^{e}kā*, a point which may imply the covenantal promise. But the reference does not ground the appeal Moses makes to God, at least not in the same sense as the promise tradition in 32.13.[1] The argument is not that because these people are God's people, God should show Moses his way. The argument is that because Moses enjoys favor in the sight of God, God should show his way, that is, see that the people are his people. Thus, an appeal that appears general has a subtle particularity. It is a call for a reformation of the covenant grounded in the unique relationship of trust and friendship between God and Moses.

The intercession wins a concession. 'My presence will go with you, and I will give you rest' (v. 14). But the concession is personal,[2] it is directed personally to Moses, not to the people (cf. LXX). Moses' response is thus quite in order. The concession is not yet enough. And so he continues his negotiation. It should be noted, however, that v. 15 is not limited to the personal appeal of the earlier section. It is an appeal for the people, cast in first person *plural* form. 'If thy presence will not go with me, do not bring *us* up from this place'. (The LXX reads a first person singular form. But the change violates the development of Moses' argument.) Indeed, the appeal focuses on the presence of God *for the people* as the crucial, distinctive quality that defines the people. Without the presence, there is no people. But it also focuses on the bond between Moses and his people. Without that bond, there is no leader. 'For how shall it be known that I have found favor in thy sight, *I and thy people*? Is it not in thy going with *us* so

---

1. Childs, *Exodus*, p. 594, which develops a different position. But see the comments on p. 595.
2. So Childs, *Exodus*, p. 594. See also J. Muilenburg, 'The Intercession of the Covenant Mediator (Exodus 33.1a, 12-17)', in P. Ackroyd and B. Lindars (eds.), *Words and Meanings* (Cambridge: Cambridge University Press, 1968), pp. 159-81.

that we are distinct, *I and thy people*, from all other people that are upon the face of the earth?' (v. 16).

The concession and following exchange of dialogue in vv. 17-23 again complicate the picture. In v. 17a the goal of the intercession is apparently reached. And the reason for the concession is the favor Moses holds in the eyes of God (v. 17b). But that point was never at issue. The point of the intercession is to return the people to favor. And the text apparently refuses to establish a relationship which must depend on continued grace mediated through the favor Moses has always enjoyed. Thus v. 18 carries a new appeal: 'I pray thee, show me thy glory'. The new concession establishes the name before Moses. and the name carries with it the surety of God's presence. That element is fundamental for the covenant between people and God. Traditional images define this new demonstration of presence, however.[1] The allusion to God's gracious and merciful character recalls the word play from Exod. 3.14, again an element in the promise of presence. The description of God passing by Moses recalls the scene with Elijah in 1 Kgs 19.11-14. And again, the point is that God establishes intimacy with his own.

Chapter 34 continues the narration directly. The covenant will be reformulated as the first one. And a narrative account of the theophany promised in ch. 33 brings Moses' work to fruition. The tables of stone are restored. Yahweh appears, and his name is proclaimed. But even yet Moses is not satisfied. The covenant is not yet fully established with the people. The point is perhaps implied in the stipulation for Moses to come to God alone (34.2-3). And in the stipulation the unique office of Moses can be seen. But the point is also present in the proclamation of the name. In a traditional formulation, God's mercy and grace move to the fore. But v. 7b has a counter pole. The guilty are still guilty. The renewed intercession in vv. 8-9 is thus comprehensible. Moses' appeal for the people is now explicit and unambiguous: (1) presence of God, (2) forgiveness and (3) renewed covenant. Moreover, here as in the other intercession the basis for the appeal is the favor Moses holds personally in the eyes of God. But his identification with his people lays that favor on the line. 'Go in the midst of *us*...pardon *our* iniquity and *our* sin...take *us* for thy inheritance' (v. 9).

1. See Childs, *Exodus*, pp. 595-96.

The result of the intercession is also unambiguous. The covenant will be established. And the announcement focuses on the people. In v. 10, God speaks: 'I make a covenant. Before all your [sing.] people I will do marvels, such as have not been wrought in all the earth or in any nation; and all the people among whom you are shall see the work of the Lord; for it is a terrible thing that I will do with you [sing.]'. And then follows the stipulation of the covenant, with an appropriate conclusion in vv. 27-28. The goal of the intercession has now been achieved.

The concluding panel, vv. 29-35, must be placed in the context of the intercession motif, even though the intercession itself is no longer a part of the narration. The verses connect somewhat roughly with the context. One would expect some notation that the stipulations of the covenant were accepted by the people. That element occurs, at least in symbolic form, in ch. 35. Those who were willing contributed to the tabernacle as Yahweh commanded. But not in ch. 34. The conclusion to ch. 34, then, sacrifices completion of the narrative line in order to focus on Moses as the one who intercedes.

The shining face, in 34.29-30, highlights Moses' unique position. It is possible, on the basis of the reference to the veil in vv. 33-34, to suggest that a cultic mask, a symbol of the office, lies behind the panel.[1] However, the crucial point of the text is not to explain the origin of a mask. Rather the image highlights the symbolic quality of Moses' stature and authority. The veil that must cover Moses' shining face does so, as has long been noted, when he is not functioning in his official capacity.[2] The shining face is itself the symbol of the authority the man holds.

Hab. 3.4 describes a similar pattern of images, with the veil (a different word but apparently a similar image) functioning to emphasize the glory of God while rendering the glory of God, otherwise so completely awesome, tolerable.[3] In the case of Moses, the symbol

1. A. Jirku, 'Die Gesichtsmaske des Mose', *ZDPV* 67 (1944–45), p. 43.
2. Childs, *Exodus*, p. 610.
3. Childs, *Exodus*, p. 619. See also Sasson, 'Bovine Symbolism', pp. 386-87. Sasson concludes: 'In this... one single depiction of a horned Moses, symbolizing the old pagan faith being brought face to face with the God of the new creed, YHWH asserts his dominance. It is he who gives the orders. Moses does no more than present them to the people'. The issue here is not, as Sasson suggests, the translation of the *crux interpretum* as 'shiny' or 'horned'. The issue lies in evaluation of the term in what Sasson calls a metaphorical sense suggesting vanity, pride, force, dignity, and power.

derives from his close association with God. Thus, it appears first when Moses returns from the mountain, a characteristic which Moses himself is not aware of. And the description is similar to one that depicts God's own glory (so Hab. 3.4). But it is not sufficient to interpret the phenomenon simply as derived glory, as the glory of God reflected in his face. Rather, the symbol points specifically to the authority Moses holds before God and, incidentally, before the people. In Hab. 3.4, the shining symbol refers clearly to the glory shining from the hands of God. And the veil covers his power. Moreover, the noun in Hab. 3.4, to which the denominative verb in Exodus 34 is related, refers commonly to personal virtue, personal authority, and not to authority that simply reflects the glory of another party.[1]

In sum, the challenge to Moses' authority led to rejection of the people, a broken covenant. And it was only through Moses that the people are invited into a renewed covenant. The shining face finally countermands the challenge and affirms the authority of Moses before the people, indeed, his stature and favor before God. 'Aaron and all the Israelites saw Moses, and behold the skin of his face shone. And they were afraid to come near him...The Israelites saw the face of Moses, that the skin of the face of Moses shone. So he returned the veil on face until he should go in...'

Intercession and the Authority of the Leader

The tradition in Exodus 32–34 demonstrates the character and force of revolution. The people want a new leader. So their action crowns a new leader (a new god) and at the same time expels the old one. The action is decisive, the response of Moses and Yahweh equally decisive. An ambiguity in the call for obedience, however, comes sharply into focus when the relationship between Moses and Yahweh is examined.

---

1. Sasson, 'Bovine Symbolism', p. 386, discusses problems in the Habakkuk parallel. But to recognize difficulties in the text is not to dismiss easily the text as relevant evidence. Again, the issue is the metaphorical value of 'horns' or 'rays of light'. In either case the text refers in some manner to the force, dignity, and power of God. Compare the transfiguration of Jesus whose face shines like the sun (Mt. 17.1-7 and par.). In some sense the shining face of Jesus is also a reflection of God's glory. But it is more; it shows an explicit intention to affirm Jesus' authority, coming after the question put to Peter, 'Who do you say that I am?' (Mt. 16.15) and closing with the affirmation, 'This is my beloved son...listen to him' (Mt. 17.5).

Moses behaves toward God in a manner that is not always obviously distinct from the revolutionary action of the people. This point is clear, not only in the accusatory question at the center of the intercession, not only in the repeated moves to negotiate the concessions he sought through his intercession, but also in the threats involving his own life, in his bold identification with his own people whom he himself recognized as rebels. Yet, the tradition carries no condemnation of Moses for such audacious behavior. On the contrary, Moses' revolutionary innovations before God, his refusals to take the directive as it stood, are understood consistently as obedience and faithful loyalty.

Thus, an initial problem not only for interpreting the tradition but also for developing an ethical perspective of more general scope is to probe the difference between the two sides. The ambiguity in Exodus 32–34 suggests that the line between obedience and revolution can never be rigidly drawn. To do so reduces obedience to mechanical legalism. To the contrary, each new generation faces the necessity for determining where the line might be, and what loyalty to the right—or left—side of the line should look like.[1]

But even more, Exodus 32–34 suggests not only that God attempts to persuade his rebellious people, but that Moses attempts to persuade God. And, moreover, he succeeds. He is not simply an instrument in the hands of an omnipotent God. Rather, he contributes along with God to the emerging present. This facet of the tradition is bound up in some manner with the pattern of divine promises in the tradition. Moses appeals for God to alter an announced intention on the basis of a prior promise. And so the intercession might be understood as the result of efforts on the part of any generation to depict the intentions of God, judged in the final analysis by the character of the promises that have endured throughout the generations. But that does not do justice to the central role of Moses as a leader of major magnitude. Persuasion depends on the trust enjoyed by the participating parties of a negotiation. Moses trusts God on the basis of the traditional promises. But God also trusts Moses. Thus, Moses stands in a significant position that opens the door for him to persuade God. Does the tradition not suggest very forcefully that God reveals himself as a king who wields the power to coerce or persuade, but also as a king

---

1. The same point would apply to questions about the authority of scripture. To draw the line rigidly would reduce canonical status in the community to oppressive biblicism.

who offers freedom to his subjects even to the point of being himself coerced or persuaded? Is it possible to understand, much less appropriate, the impact of that image in the representation of God's sovereignty as the sovereignty of a king?

The question is relevant, not only for the task of formulating concepts of God as King or the character of his persuasive lure, but also for the complementary task of formulating concepts of the subjects. What does the tradition suggest about the intercessor? L. Dunlop has caught the force of the question: 'Why should such and such a person be qualified to pray for others...?'[1]

The tradition presents Moses as a creative innovator who defends his people at the risk of the favor he holds with God. The basis of the relationship is, to be sure, a mutual *trust*. And out of the assumptions established by the trust, God apparently takes the audacious intercession as the work of a loyal devotee, a loyal servant. But the qualification moves beyond mutual trust to the personal virtue of the man, the position of stature which he holds in the eyes of God. It is significant, then, that appeal to the favor Moses holds before God replaces an appeal to God's prior promises. Thus, Moses defends his people before God with the same loyalty to the people, the same courage and vigor apparent in his defense of the people before the Amalekites. Is not that stature and authority, that qualification or worth, a part of the pattern of traditions about Moses as heroic man?

The hermeneutical force of the observation, then, is that it is not necessary to divert that which is worthy and qualified from the man simply as reflected glory. It is possible to see the man as a primary agent in that real world. To live in full acceptance of that responsibility is the task of the loyal subject of the king, whether his response to the king is immediate support or opposition.

The heroic stature of Moses contributes, moreover, to the hermeneutical task posed to any subsequent generation by the tension inherent in an innovative action. How does any loyal subject of the king develop innovative programs without being dismissed as a heretic guilty of revolution? The image of the heroic servant of God establishes a context for making such choices in the demand of the moment. To be sure, the image is subjective. Its power to create such a context depends on the commitments of the generation struggling with the

---

1. Dunlop, *Intercessions of Moses*, p. 1.

question. So Moses is obedient; the devotees of the calf cult are not. Jesus is the Christ for his disciples, a pretender for those who do not believe. Given the belief in the heroic figure, however, the power of the heroic image to create a context for making such decisions is strong. The point is not that the disciples do what Moses did, in simple imitation, but that the heroic figure instructs the faithful by the power of his stature. And decisions about revolution or obedience are made in the light of that instruction. Thus, each new generation recasts the Mosaic law. But for each generation, the new law is a law that roots in the authority of Moses. Each recasting is undertaken out of loyalty to the image, loyalty to the stature and power of the figure. Such responsibility must be a part of what it would mean to believe in Moses (Exod. 4.31; 14.31).

This perspective can be evaluated more adequately, perhaps, in the categories suggested by L. Ford. There is a sense in which the power of the heroic figure is the power of the past. And that facet in the tradition must always be there. But the power of the past can be destructive for the present. The laws of the hero can be frozen into hard and fast bonds. Indeed, the image of the hero itself can be frozen, so that rather than instructing each new generation, it reminds each generation of its shortcomings. Or, should the new set of people more or less succeed in matching the image, it may find itself robbed of any genuine vitality.

The context provided by the heroic figure, however, does not mean that the new generation lives in the past. Rather, it orients the new generation toward decisions to be established in the present.

> The locus of productive activity thereby shifts from the past causes to the present effect, which is active in virtue of its own power. The past causes determine the content of the present actuality, but only as this content is appropriated and unified by the present activity...Our freedom lies in the power of the present to select and to organize that which we inherit from the past.[1]

The power of the present, which is already operative in the description of reality at the basis of the heroic tradition, feeds from the heroic tradition as a new present emerges.

But even more. The audacious quality of the hero's innovation, particularly as it assumes the form of intercession for the hero's

---

1. So Ford, 'Divine Power', p. 12.

people, suggests that the hero participates in the power of the future. Ford observes: 'Through Jesus' faithful response to the Father, his human activity became the vehicle for divine activity, for Jesus' own power of the present allowed the divine power of the future to be fully effective'.[1] In something of the same manner, Moses' faithful intercession for his people, as a part of his own power of the present, allows the divine power of the future to take its own shape. And the process, both from the promises of the past and from Moses' own stature and authority, becomes fully effective in the present. It is, moreover, to such participation in the power of the future that Moses' disciples or Jesus' disciples are called. That call arises from the context created by the heroic tradition.

Mosaic authority may be understood, then, out of his participation in the power of God. This point may be already apparent in the narrative about the divine call. The call grounds Mosaic authority, both for Israel and for Egypt. It may be apparent in the signs. The demonstration of power in converting water to blood (not just blood-red water) or in the execution of rebels by the earth opening its mouth brings a coercive facet to his authority. The strength of that authority resides, then, in the power of God at the basis of his leadership. But the strength of Mosaic authority lies at least as much in his heroic identification with his people, in his protection and defense of them not only against hunger, thirst and attacks from various enemies, but also against threats from God. We will obey Moses because he is *our* leader.

---

1. So Ford, 'Divine Power', p. 12.

Chapter 6

LEGENDARY MOTIFS IN THE MOSES DEATH REPORTS

Death reports are characteristic features in the narratives about the giants among Israel's fathers: Adam, Noah, Abraham, Jacob, Joseph, Moses, Aaron and Joshua. All of the figures appear in variegated tales depicting each in collective memory, each with distinctive traits. Yet each shares a fate in common with his fellow giants, in common as well with every other man. And the mortality of these giants demands its share in the narrative accounts of human deeds. Nevertheless, despite the common refrain of death reports among the tales of the giants, not all the death reports in biblical narrative look alike. Some are mere notices (cf. Gen. 5.5). Some develop a longer report of death. But in the process only the essential data come to light (cf. Gen. 50.22-25). And some decorate a longer report of essential data with motifs that at first seem incredible. Thus, the Moses death reports note not only the demise of the giant, but also his incomparable character at the time of his death. The purpose of this paper is to explore those distinctive motifs[1] in order to determine what they are, how they function, and what insight they offer into the Moses traditions generally.[2]

The working hypothesis of the paper is that the characteristic motifs

---

1. By motif, I mean 'a characteristic of a work's design; a word or pattern of thought that recurs in a similar situation, or to evoke a similar mood within a work or in various works of a genre'. Cf. *Dictionary of World Literature* (ed. J.T. Shipley; Totowa, NJ: Littlefield, Adams, 1972), p. 274. If one is to understand the design of various death reports, the function of motifs peculiar to some is crucial.

2. On the Moses traditions, cf. E. Osswald, *Das Bild des Mose in der Kritischen alttestamentlichen Wissenschaft seit Julius Wellhausen* (Theologische Arbeiten, 18; Berlin: Evangelische Verlagsanstalt, n.d.); R. Smend, *Das Mosebild von Heinrich Ewald bis Martin Noth* (BGBE, 3; Tübingen: Mohr, 1959); F. Schnutenhaus, 'Die Entstehung der Mosetraditionen' (Unpublished dissertation, Heidelberg, 1958); H. Schmid, *Mose, Überlieferung und Geschichte* (BZAW, 110; Berlin: Töpelmann, 1968).

in the Moses death reports are heroic. By heroic I mean motifs whose primary intention is to describe outstanding virtues and feats, either moral or physical, not in God, but in a man.[1] Of course the virtue may derive from God. The virtue may be faithful obedience to God's word.[2] But the virtue belongs to the man. The feat may root in divine strength. But it characterizes the statuture of the man.[3] In order to expand perception of this facet in the Moses traditions, I propose to isolate a series of heroic motifs in the Moses death reports, specifically Num. 27.12-23 and Deut. 34.1-12.[4]

I

The first motif in the series highlights Moses' strength at the end of his life. 'Moses was a hundred and twenty years old when he died; his eye was not dim, and his natural force had not fled' (Deut 34.7).

Three members in the statement carry the weight of the motif. The first one specifies the age at the time of death. While Moses' age is not as extensive as the age of figures in the primeval history, not even as extensive as Abraham and Jacob, it must be seen as a complete and full period. The summary statement marking Abraham's death seems harmonious for Moses as well: 'These are the days of the years of Abraham's life, which he lived, a hundred and seventy-five years. Abraham breathed his last breath and died in a good age, an old man and full...' To die in a good age is in itself a sign of strength and suggests that particularly the excessive ages in the prediluvian lists can be understood as legendary fragments from traditions about the ancient heroes.

An age of one hundred and twenty years is in itself, however, not excessive for biblical tradition, even if it does move beyond the range

---

1. On heroic tradition, see J. de Vries, *Heroic Song and Heroic Legend* (trans. B.J. Timmer; London: Oxford, 1963).
2. G.W. Coats, 'Abraham's Sacrifice of Faith', *Int* 27 (1973), pp. 389-400.
3. Coats, 'Moses versus Amalek: Aetiology and Legend in Exod. XVII 8-16', in *Congress Volume Edinburgh* (VTSup, 28; Leiden: Brill, 1975), pp. 29-41. See ch. 3 above.
4. On the relationship between these two reports, cf. M. Noth, *Überlieferungsgeschichtliche Studien* (Tübingen: Max Niemeyer Verlag, 2nd edn, 1957), pp. 190-216. The argument must consider other texts related to a report of Moses' death, such as Deut. 32.48-52, as well as Deut. 31.1-23. But the primary discussion will not focus on these texts.

of average contemporary experience. Emphasis on Moses' strength comes from the following two members. These, too, offer some problem for interpretation. The last one involves a noun with no clear biblical parallels: $w^e l\bar{o}$'-$n\bar{a}s$ $l\bar{e}h\bar{o}h$. Perhaps a related adjective, lah, provides some insight, suggesting the fresh, moist character of vital trees and fruit. At one hundred and twenty years Moses would have been as supple as a youth. But the member is formulated in the negative and does not tie down the nature of the strength imputed to Moses.[1] The other member is more helpful. Also formulated in a negative, the sentence depends on the verb $k\bar{a}h\hat{a}$; lo'- $k\bar{a}h^a t\hat{a}$ '$\hat{e}n\hat{o}$. The verb is paralleled in a negative formulation by Isa. 42.4, a text emphasizing the servant's legendary strength to persevere until justice reigns in the earth. Moreover, formulations without a negative show the verb as a means for denoting the opposite of strength. Zech. 11.17 sets the verb in a curse, with the arm of the victim without strength, the eye without sight ($z^e r\bar{o}$'$\hat{o}$ $y\bar{a}b\hat{o}\check{s}$ $t\hat{i}b\bar{a}\check{s}$ w^e'$\hat{e}n$ $y\bar{e}m\hat{i}n\hat{o}$ $k\bar{a}h\bar{o}h$ $tikheh$). And in Gen. 27.1 (perhaps of more importance) the verb describes Isaac's sight at the end of his life, an old man virtually blind and ready for death. With a negative formulation, Deut. 34.7 insists that Moses is not that way.

Furthermore, this formulation stands out by contrast from a parallel text, not a death report, but a Moses speech in Deut. 31.2: 'I am a hundred and twenty years old this day; I am no longer able to go out and come in'. The Moses who speaks in Deuteronomy 31 is an old man, feeble, unable to lead his people, ready to die. In the heroic motif, however Moses is strong, able to do what he always had done. At one hundred and twenty years he is a young man. Indeed, he appears virtually immortal.[2] And death comes, not because of natural decay, or at least not very much of it, but because the appointed time for the end of a man's life has arrived.[3] Thus Moses' strength places

1. But cf. W.F. Albright, 'The "Natural Force" of Moses in the Light of Ugaritic', *BASOR* 94 (1944), pp. 32-35.
2. E. Auerbach, *Moses* (trans. R.A. Barclay and I.O. Lehman; Detroit: Wayne State University Press, 1975), pp. 170-71. 'Moses died, not because the enormous vitality of this giant was exhausted; he appeared to be almost immortal. He died a special death: the deity summoned the loved one to it. God ordered him to die, and die he did in full vigor. The narrator has in great simplicity molded this into a powerful image'.
3. Cf. the heroes of the Nibelungenlied and Beowulf. Siegfried appeared to be immortal because he had been immersed in a dragon's blood. One tiny exception to

him in a unique category. The characterization appears overdrawn, unreal. Moses is almost superhuman, a figure whose attributes stretch the imagination beyond average human experience. That characterization typifies heroic legend.[1]

The second motif in the series singles out Moses' spirit as a spirit of authority never to be equalled in the leadership of any other single man. In Deut. 34.9 the legendary character of this motif is not obvious. The spirit motif is tied closely to Joshua as Moses' successor. And the spirit is a spirit of wisdom now filling Joshua (not the spirit of Moses). Yet the spirit fills Joshua because ($kî$) Moses laid his hands on him, a symbolic act for transferring the spirit from one head to another. In Num. 27.18-21 the same motif appears. Joshua is filled with the spirit. But the act of ordination in this case functions as a means for transferring *some* of Moses' authority, $mēhôd^ekā$ (cf. Pss. 21.6; 45.4) to Joshua. The partitive *min* seems to me to be significant, for Joshua cannot carry all of Moses' authority, Moses' vigor and strength. Nonetheless, the explicit consequence of the transferral is that the congregation will now obey Joshua as they had obeyed Moses (cf. Num. 27.20; Deut. 34.9). The same motif appears in the addition to the quail story in Num. 11.16-17, 24-30, the account of the spirit falling on seventy elders. To be sure the motif as it now stands has been converted into an etiology for ecstatic prophecy. But the primary intention of the motif lay in the transfer of authority from Moses, the head of the people, to lieutenants who would assist Moses in administration. (It is somewhat surprising that the spirit motif is absent from Exodus 18. Cf. also Deut. 3.28; 31.7, 14, 23.) Thus it is significant that the partitive *min* appears again: 'I shall take *some* of the spirit

---

complete immersion left a small but vulnerable spot. And there treacherous friends attacked, killing the hero in his prime. Beowulf defended his people against a dragon, although advanced to extremely old age. To be sure, he had lost some of his youthful vigor. Yet he withstood the dragon's attack. And though mortally wounded, he succeeded in slaying the attacker and saving his people.

1. Beowulf's struggle with the dragon occurs under the watchful eye of his aide, Wiglaf, who comes to Beowulf's aid in his time of crisis. And the struggle proves fatal. Yet the struggle is an individual feat, a display of legendary strength in the hero's old age. Cf. the work on legendary reports of battles of J. de Vries, *Heroic Song and Heroic Legend*, pp. 189-90, 203. For a working definition of legend, cf. R.M. Hals, 'Legend: A Case Study in OT Form-Critical Terminology', *CBQ* 34 (1972), pp. 166-76.

(min-$hārûaḥ$) which is on you and put it on them' (Num. 11.17).[1] Not even seventy men can carry all of Moses' spirit. Again, the superhuman ability characterizes heroic legend.

The third motif in the series describes the relationship Moses enjoys face to face with God. That kind of intimacy had not been known previously and would not be known again (Deut. 34.10). Num 12.6-8 parallels this motif closely, although the point of communication shifts from face to mouth. Moreover, that relationship stands in contrast to the prophets who must depend on visions or dreams. The point of comparison, however, is not to denigrate the prophetic office but to elevate Moses. This point can be established clearly by the parallel motif in Exod. 33.11 with a notation that such intimacy is the intimacy of friendship. The image of Moses descending from that intimacy with a shining face too awe-inspiring for average people to behold (34.29-35) doubtlessly reflects the dynamics of such a hero. But perhaps of even greater importance, in Num 12.7, in the notation that this man, whom God addresses personally, God has trusted with his entire house (cf. Gen. 39.3-4, 22).

Deut. 34.11-12 moves the content of this motif from the relationship Moses enjoys with God to the mighty acts Moses did in the sight of all Israel, not God, but Moses. To be sure, the signs and wonders Moses did to the Pharaoh, his servants, and his land, had been commissioned by God. In the plague cycle, the Pharaoh witnesses the signs and wonders in order to know that Yahweh is Lord. In the Sea tradition, for Israel to witness the great work of their salvation was to witness a great work Yahweh did against the Egyptians. And on the basis of that

---

1. A parallel can be seen in 2 Kgs 2.9. Elisha requests, in all probability, not a double portion of Elijah's spirit, but one-half or two thirds. And the issue is not so much a question of inheritance, a double portion as the right of the first born, but a reasonable portion of the master's spirit ($b^e rûh^a kā$). R.A. Carlson, 'Elisée—le successeur d'Elie', *VT* 20 (1970), p. 403. As a consequence of the emphasis on Elijah's spirit, the story seems to me to be an Elijah story, not an Elisha story, or even a story primarily about God. Against G. von Rad, *Old Testament Theology* (trans. D.M.B. Stalker, 2 vols.; New York: Harper, 1960), II, pp. 25-26. Num. 20.22-29 has another parallel, the death report for Aaron with Eleazar designated as successor. Yet here the legendary characteristics of such texts seems totally missing. There is no reference to Aaron's spirit. To the contrary. Aaron is simply stripped of his clothes. And Eleazar is invested with them (cf. the mantle of Elijah, 2 Kgs 2.13). There is no concern to give Eleazar only part of his successor's authority. There is nothing here but transfer of office.

witness Israel believed in Yahweh. But she also believed *in his servant Moses*. And the heroic formulation of that tradition in Deut. 34.11-12 makes those faith-provoking deeds the deeds of Moses. Again, Moses' special character, above all others, sets the pace for heroic legend.

II

Yet despite all this legendary aggrandizement, the Moses death reports carry another motif, apparently contrary to their presentation of the hero as a superhuman of very little fault. That motif shows Moses as the sinner who cannot enter the promised land. In Deut. 34.4 the motif is brief, simply a note that Moses will see the land but will not cross over into it. In Num. 27.13-14, however, the prohibition against Moses' entry into the land is grounded in his rebellion at Meribah (cf. Num. 20.2-13). And that element appears again, strongly, in Deut. 32.48-52. Moses suffers death at the edge of the promised land as punishment for his rebellion (cf. esp. Deut. 32.51-52). Thus, the question: How is this negative element in the Moses death reports to be evaluated vis-à-vis the positive, heroic motifs so replete in the same reports?

It seems to be clear that the reference to Moses' death as punishment for his rebellion at Meribah of Kadesh is a late rationalization of the tradition, an effort (on the part of Dtr or P) to resolve the theological hiatus caused by the memory of a strong and capable leader who did not make it into the land. Thus the explicit references to Moses' sin at Meribah appear only in late texts, all in some way dependent on Dtr or P.[1] A comparison between the priestly version of the Meribah story and its earlier counterpart establishes an intentional change in the formulation of the story. That act which constitutes obedience to God's command in the older form of the story becomes explicitly an act of disobedience for P. And for the disobedience, although in a relatively minor and technical move in executing God's instructions, Moses falls before reaching the land.[2]

Noth observes:

---

1. N. Noth, *A History of Pentateuchal Traditions* (trans. B.W. Anderson; Englewood Cliffs: Prentice Hall, 1972), p. 170 n. 479.
2. For details, cf. Coats, *Rebellion in the Wilderness: The Murmuring Motif in the Wilderness Traditions of the Old Testament* (Nashville: Abingdon Press, 1968), pp. 53-82. Also Auerbach, *Moses*, p. 170.

> Of course the Deuteronomistic historian hardly came to the idea on his own that Moses...died as a result of divine wrath before the crossing of the Jordan and the entrance into the promised land (Deut. 3.26, 27b). In this respect he was certainly bound to the received tradition, only we are no longer in a position to ascertain how the wrath of God against Moses was explained in this tradition.[1]

Noth hypothesizes, however, that the older traditions knew a motivation for Moses' punishment rooted in a vicarious substitution for punishment intended for the people. In Deut. 3.26 this element can be seen: 'The Lord was angry with me on your account' (cf. also Deut. 1.37; 4.21; Ps. 106.32).[2] If the hypothesis is correct, then Moses' character takes on a decidedly different hue. As a vicarious sufferer he bears his burden in a way that increases his stature rather than diminishing it. Indeed, the vicarious element would gain its most intense expression if the sufferer should bear the guilt of his people even though he himself bears no personal guilt at all (cf. Isa. 53.4-9). It is thus perhaps significant that behind the rather artificial designation of Moses' sin lies a tradition that did not report any sin on Moses' part.

Yet Deut. 34.1-12 notes neither punishment for a sin at Meribah nor a vicarious suffering in the place of the people. There is no explicit indication in this text that Moses' death should be taken as punishment. Rather, there is only a display of the land before Moses' eye and an announcement: 'I have let you see it with your eyes, but you shall not go over there' (Deut. 34.4). Must we not therefore reckon with a stage in the death tradition that offers no explanation at all for Moses' death? Would that kind of tradition not fit exactly with the heroic motifs so common elsewhere in the death reports? Rather than dying a normal death, the result of natural decay, Moses disappears into the mountain to die, alone, full of the vigor of life. And his death is tragic.[3] He does not die young, as does Samson. But he dies before he reaches his goal. As a consequence his death is as untimely as the typical death of a young hero like Siegfried in the

---

1. Noth, *Pentateuchal Traditions*, p. 170.
2. On the vicarious death of Moses, cf. G. von Rad, *Deuteronomy, A Commentary* (trans. D. Barton; London: SCM Press, 1966), pp. 209-10. Also Coats, *Rebellion*, pp. 79-81.
3. H. Barzel, 'Moses: Tragedy and Sublimity', in K.R.R. Gros Louis, J.S. Ackerman and T.S. Warshaw (eds.), *Literary Interpretations of Biblical Narratives*, (Nashville: Abingdon Press, 1974), pp. 120-40.

Nibelungenlied. Moreover, there is in Deuteronomy 34 no element of punishment, any more than the death of Siegfried stands as punishment. Moses dies. And that is that.

Yet, despite the tragic element in Moses' death, there is also a comforting vision of this hero facing the fate of every man. God's oracle to Jacob promises that the point of death 'Joseph's hand shall close your eyes' (Gen. 46.4). For Moses no man was present to close his eyes. Yet God was present. 'So Moses the servant of the Lord died there in the land of Moab, according to the word of the Lord. And he [the Lord] buried him in the valley in the land of Moab opposite Bethpeor. But no man knows the place of his burial to this day'. The legend of Elijah's death moves in the same direction, although with markedly more intense drama. He dies in a way that no man sees, not even his successor. Rather, he disappears from sight, full of life, free to face an unknown fate, his work as yet incomplete.[1] Death, I assume, is never timely. It threatens a terrifying loneliness (cf. Mt. 27.45-50). It cuts short work as yet unfinished. But in the heroic death of Moses or Elijah death carries a confirmation of a life's work, an affirmation of God's presence.[2]

III

One conclusion appears firm: legendary motifs casting Moses as an incomparable figure from the past constitute the building material for the Moses death reports. These motifs obviously do not call on subsequent generations to 'go and do likewise'. To the contrary they enmphasize the impossibility for fitting any other man into the mold cast by Moses. Yet, the image of Moses casts a model of leadership and strength for subsequent generations. And it is that model that functions as

1. De Vries, *Heroic Song*, p. 216: 'Heroes often die young, like Achilles, Siegfried and Cuchulainn. In many cases their death is miraculous. Romulus is taken up into heaven... and Kag Chosrev vanishes into the desert'. Cf. also 2 Kgs 13.14-21. Cf. also Lord Raglan (F.R. Somerset), 'The Hero of Tradition', in A. Dundes (ed.), *The Study of Folklore* (Englewood Cliffs: Prentice Hall, 1965), pp. 142-57.

2. Noth, *Pentateuchal Traditions*, pp. 170-75. He assumes that the earlier form of tradition knew something of the way Moses died and some precise information about the location of his grave. Cf. also von Rad, *Deuteronomy*, p. 210. But the pursuit of that original tradition seems to be misdirected. The absence of such precise information is characteristic for legendary material. And an effort to tie it down, as perhaps P did, appears to me prosaic.

edification. Leaders in the line of Mosaic succession can live and work successfully if only a portion of Moses' spirit, an approximation of the full model falls on their shoulders. This construction of a death report stands in sharp contrast to the Aaron death report in Num. 20.22-29.

A second conclusion seems to me to be justified: the motif casting Moses' death at a premature moment suggests a close relationship between the legendary elements of leadership and heroic legend, not necessarily the same generic literature.[1] If this conclusion should stand, it would raise the possibility of unity with other Mosaic traditions such as the birth story (Exod. 2.1-10), the marriage story (Exod. 2.11-22),[2] and a battle story (Exod. 17.8-16).

Two caveats to this conclusion must be considered. (a) Is such legendary aggrandizement authentic? How close are these legendary motifs to authentic tradition? At stake in the questions is the means for authentication of any tradition, particularly any legendary tradition. A means for such procedure is to establish the relationship between the legendary tradition and its historical rootage.[3] But, it seems to me,

---

1. On heroic literature in general, cf. H.M. Chadwick and N.K. Chadwick, *The Growth of Literature* (Cambridge: Cambridge University Press, 1932), I, pp. 1-376; III, pp. 679-772. J. Campbell, *The Hero with a Thousand Faces* (The Bollingen Series, 17; New York: Pantheon Books, 1949), pp. 356-64. For a contrasting position, see B.W. Anderson, *Understanding the Old Testament* (Englewood Cliffs: Prentice-Hall; 3rd edn, 1975), p. 48. 'The Exodus story is not a heroic epic told to celebrate the accomplishment of Moses as the liberator of his people. The narrator's major purpose is to glorify the God of Israel, the "divine warrior" whose strong hand and outstretched arm won the victory over his adversaries, Pharaoh and his host'. That purpose is apparent in the Song of the Sea. It is not, however, the only purpose in the Exodus story'.

2. B.S. Childs, *Exodus: A Critical, Theological Commentary* (Philadelphia: Westminster Press, 1974), p. 31. Childs observes: 'The Writer is extremely restrained in his description of this intervention. He is obviously not interested in portraying Moses as a folk hero. (Contrast this reservation with the description of Samson or Jonathan in action.)'. Yet, it seems to me questionable to deny heroic quality because of restraint in description. In terse style the narrative depicts Moses' intervention on behalf of the young women, a typical concern in heroic patterns. And the intervention parallels Moses' earlier intervention on behalf of his own people, the event that caused his flight from Egypt. Moreover, the intervention highlights his *strength*, since he sets himself against heavy odds, more than one unchivalrous shepherd.

3. D.M. Beegle, *Moses, the Servant of Yahweh* (Grand Rapids: Eerdmans, 1972), p. 30. Cf. also pp. 96-122. Beegle is concerned to establish the authenticity of Mosaic tradition by reconstructing 'Moses as he was and not what various periods of

such procedure of authentication is not consistent with legendary tendency. Insofar as the tradition itself is concerned, legend gains authenticity by virtue of its ability to influence the shape of mores and morals in subsequent generations, not by virtue of its preservation of data useful for reconstructing past generations.[1] (b) Does such legendary aggrandizement not apotheosize the hero? There is a natural aversion to such a position since for biblical tradition such exalted status must be reserved for God alone.[2] As a consequence one may observe that Moses' grave remains unknown to subsequent generations precisely in order to prevent formation of a cult around his shrine.[3] Yet, there is no evidence for such a cult. There is certainly no evidence that Moses was elevated to the position of a god or even a demigod. There is not worship directed to Moses. Thus, it seems to me that the legendary tendency in the death reports does not carry with it the baggage of deifying Moses.

Yet, one must be careful here. Moses appears as more than the average human. He stands as the perfect example of leadership. And if my thesis is correct that he dies (for the people) without the taint of rebellion from Meribah, his perfection would shine even more brightly, so brightly that we might even request a veil to cover his face. The line between heroic leader and god becomes remarkably thin. And should that tendency continue to its logical conclusion, theologians would be forced to consider some thesis about Moses' two natures. Is he not after all both human and divine, marked by a special relationship with God unparalleled by any previous servant. The fact, remains, however, that biblical tradition never moves the legend of Moses that far. It is easy to shift from legend to myth. But it is not necessary. And so the emphasis of the legendary motifs in the death reports remains on the human nature of Moses, an incomparable nature, but nonetheless human.

A third conclusion seems to me to be in order, the opposite pole of caveat (b) G. von Rad once wrote:

---

tradition attributed to him'. Cf. p. 82. A similar concern to evaluate Moses tradition in terms of historical authenticity can be seen in the work of Auerbach.

1. See de Vries, *Heroic Song*, pp. 194-209. Further exploration of this point seems to me to be a crucial hermeneutical task for research on biblical narratives.
2. Cf. M. Greenberg, 'Moses', in *EncJud* (New York: Macmillan, 1971), XII, pp. 378-88.
3. Beegle, *Moses, the Servant of Yahweh*, p. 347; Greenberg, 'Moses', p. 387.

> Not a single one of all these stories in which Moses is the central figure
> was really written about Moses. Great as was the veneration of the writers
> for this man to whom God has been pleased to reveal himself, in all these
> stories it is *not* Moses himself, Moses the man, but God who is the
> central figure.[1]

There can be no doubt that von Rad pinpoints a prime characteristic of the Moses traditions with this assertion. Commonly Moses recedes into the background as God himself takes center stage (cf. Exod. 7.17). Regularly the 'little historical credos' identify God's mighty acts without reference to the acts of Moses. Indeed, if M. Noth's thesis about Moses has any validity at all, then Moses was not originally so omnipresent in the exodus, wilderness and Sinai traditions.[2] He would have been originally a minor character on a stage filled with diverse plots, advanced to top billing for human characters only after the plots were in some degree unified.

Yet, for all of its value, this extreme formulation of Moses' role in the Moses traditions misses the impact of the legendary motifs. It seems to me that a conclusion about the Moses traditions that denies the central role of Moses in all the stories does not do justice to the legendary elements in the tradition. To be sure, God was present with Moses at his death. But the central figure, the one to whom the legendary virtues belong, is the man Moses, the Servant of the Lord. This problem takes on new weight by virtue of the challenge to exegetical work on the Pentateuch laid down by W. Brueggemann. Brueggemann attacks a one-sided exegesis, characteristically centered on the exodus, that stresses '*the helplessness of man and the grace of God*'.

> This [one-sided exegesis] is easily and consistently translated into social
> irresponsibility because man is helpless and into the centrality of Church
> authority because it dispenses the grace needed by helpless man and
> granted by a gracious God.[3]

---

1. Von Rad, *Moses* (World Christian Books, 32; London: Lutterworth, 1960), pp. 8-9 (italics mine). Von Rad (*Theology* 2, p. 24) makes a similar comment about Elijah: 'The fact is that the subject of the Elijah stories is basically not the prophet himself, but Jahweh'. Cf. also Beegle, *Moses*, pp. 347-48.
2. Noth, *Pentateuchal Traditions*, pp. 156-75.
3. W. Brueggemann, 'The Triumphalist Tendency in Exegetical History', *JAAR* 38 (1970), pp. 367-80. Cf. also his book, *In Man we Trust: The Neglected Side of Biblical Faith* (Richmond: John Knox, 1972), pp. 13-28.

Brueggemann's observation seems to me to be confirmed by von Rad's opening remarks on the Moses traditions or Noth's reduction of Moses to a minor character in one originally independent theme. The traditions, traditions that report Israel's salvation from Egyptian bondage, could not emphasize a man so much, given the context of the contemporary theological vision of man. But the fault lies not so much in the theology of the Pentateuch, with its legendary motifs tied to giants like Moses, or Abraham, or Joseph, or Balaam. The fault lies in the exegesis. My point is that the same tendency Brueggemann attacks as part of the cause for ignoring the image of man in the royal model or in wisdom also accounts for ignoring legendary traditions presenting Moses as the central figure of a heroic series. Moses is the man whom God trusted, the man with responsibility for his people. To be sure, God stands behind him. But he stands behind the royal model as well. And through that grace the man (Moses or David) plunges ahead into a tragic, heroic, brilliant future.[1] Brueggemann might well object that in the Pentateuch God intervenes when his fallible servant makes mistakes. The creature is not really to be trusted. In contrast the royal model stands alone, free to rise or fall by his own decision. But in legendary tradition, also, God does not intervene directly.[2] Thus, biblical theology needs, it seems to me, a more extensive examination of heroic, legendary material in the OT. For in these legends may lie a vision of man valuable for an age devoid of confidence in man and a hedge on the power of men who violate the legendary image by presenting themselves as gods.[3]

---

1. Cf. my comments about the same points in 'Moses Versus Amalek', pp. 39-41.
2. Cf. my discussion of Joseph as a wise administrator who interprets dreams by his own skill, not as a puppet dancing on a string in 'The Joseph Story and Ancient Wisdom: A Reappraisal', *CBQ* (1973), pp. 285-97.
3. This essay was presented as a lecture to the Sixth World Congress of Jewish Studies in Jerusalem in August, 1973.

Chapter 7

HUMILITY AND HONOR: A MOSES LEGEND IN NUMBERS 12

Interpretation of Pentateuchal narratives commonly begins with assumptions about disunity. If, for example, a word or sentence in a pericope appears on the surface to be disruptive or unnecessarily repetitive, the interpreter may simply excise the problem without considering the possibility that the word or phrase may have had a role to play in the rhetoric native to the narrator's own world of narration technique. If the excision should be completed too quickly, the contribution intended by the problem may be completely lost. That loss would, moreover, distort the interpreter's perception of the narrative's function and meaning simply by virtue of the fact. Rhetorical patterns function not only as elements of beauty in ancient art but also as keys for seeing clearly what the narrator wants to say. It is therefore of critical importance in any effort to recover meaning from any example of narrative art to recognize whatever sense of rhetorical unity may be at the heart of the piece.

For past interpreters, Numbers 12 constitutes a prime example of literary and traditio-historical disunity in Old Testament narrative. The tradition embodied by the narrative reveals at least three stages of growth. The oldest would have been an account of reproach against Moses for his Cushite marriage.[1] The culpable rebel in this stage appears to be Miriam alone. Thus v. 1 begins with a third feminine singular imperfect verb and apparently assumes that Miriam alone was the subject. In accord with a singular subject, the conclusion of the chapter describes the punishment of God for the rebellion as leprosy exacted against Miriam alone (v. 10). Aaron appears in the tradition as a part of a second stage. Here he and Miriam together reproach Moses for his audacious behavior as leader of the people and claim for

1. M. Noth, *Numbers, A Commentary* (OTL; Philadelphia: Westminster Press, 1968), p. 93.

themselves in the process the right of leadership, expressed as a mediation of God's word to the people (v. 2). The disunity between these two stages emerges most sharply in the ambiguous role of Aaron. He apparently joins Miriam in rebellion against Moses. But he stands at a distance simply as an observer when punishment for the rebellion comes from God. The third stage in the tradition's history loads the narration with various accounts of Moses' position before God and his people.[1] In the received text this stage functions as a response to the rebellion. Yet, the response loses contact at key points with both the tradition about a Cushite wife and the one about rebellion over rights of leadership. In what manner is v. 3, for example, with its depiction of Moses as the meekest of all people, a fitting response to the challenge against Moses as leader? Not only does Moses' retirement as meek fail to present a response suited to such an aggressive challenge as the one represented by v. 2, so it would appear, but it also presents an image of Moses incompatible with other pictures of his leadership (contrast Num. 16).

The disunity of this chapter represents not only a problem in the history of the tradition, however. It also reflects a literary disunity. Thus, M. Noth observes: 'The modest reserve on the part of Moses is particularly stressed in v. 3. In any case v. 3 is a later addition which disrupts the close connection between v. 2b and v. 4'.[2] The older literary critics tended to define this disruption as a late redaction of the story without attributing the insertion to a particular source. Baentsch observes simply that 'in any case the verse does not belong to the old narrative'.[3] It is possible, however, to see critics who are bolder in their literary constructions. In his comment on v. 3, de Vaulx avers that 'the redactor, *the Elohist*, who has narrowly tied down the two accounts compares the claims of the $n^eb\hat{\imath}'\hat{\imath}m$ of the northern kingdom of the ninth century with the ancient relics of family opposition against Moses'.[4] Yet, Noth refuses to analyze the literary disunity of

---

1. Noth, *Numbers*, p. 93: 'From a literary point of view, the present chapter... presupposes these insertions [about leadership] in ch. 11'.

2. Noth, *A Commentary*, p. 95.

3. B. Baentsch, *Exodus-Leviticus-Numeri* (HKAT 1.2; Göttingen: Vandenhoeck & Ruprecht, 1903), p. 512.

4. J. de Vaulx, *Les Nombres* (Sources Bibliques; Paris: Gabalda, 1972), p. 159, italics mine: 'L'rédacteur, élohiste, qui a étroitement lié les deux récits compare les prétentions des "nebi'im" du royaume du nord au ixe siècle aux vieux souvenirs des

the chapter in terms of a combination of sources:

> The reproach with regard to the Cushite marriage actually comes originally from Miriam, who is the one who is punished for it, whereas the dispute concerning the special place accorded to Moses in matters concerning the receiving of revelation is reported as stemming from 'Aaron and Miriam'...The two subjects of the chapter...are now so closely joined together that it is impossible to pursue a division into separate literary sources...It must therefore be accepted that in the complex of this chapter, a complex which, from the literary point of view, can no longer be disentangled, two different strands have been combined.[1]

If this chapter appears so completely disjointed, both in tradition history and in the literary structure of the received text, then one must ask whether there is any sense of unity at all within its limits. In what fashion can the chapter be classified as a unit? In answer to this question I propose a hypothesis. I do not deny the complexity of the tradition's history outlined in some detail by Noth. I do not even contest the apparent disunity at points in the literary construct. I propose, however, that a pattern of unity does emerge in the received text and that it overshadows the disjointed facets still preserved from the tradition's past. That pattern can be identified by paying attention to questions of structure and genre in the received text. Thus the hypothesis: The narrative as it has been preserved (by J) is no longer a tale designed primarily to narrate the events of rebellion against Moses by Miriam or by both Miriam and Aaron. To the contrary, that old, now hypothetically reconstructed tale was transformed in the course of its history into a legend.[2] As a legend the narrative now focuses on the virtues of Moses. Although the rebellion tradition lies in the immediate background for the narrative, it is not now the primary subject for narration. Rather, the subject is now the unusual status of Moses among all the people of the world. That hypothesis would mean that while v. 3 may be disruptive vis-à-vis the old narrative tradition about a rebellion, it is now the center of the unit. And it provides the necessary key for defining the unity of the pericope.

oppositions familiales contre Moïse'.
    1. Noth, *Numbers*, pp. 92-93.
    2. By legend I mean a narrative specifically structured to emphasize the virtues of the principal figure. See R. Hals, 'Legend: A Case Study in OT Form-Critical Terminology', *CBQ* 34 (1972), pp. 166-76.

I

The virtues of Moses constitute a vital part of the OT tradition about Israel's famous leader. In Exod. 17.8-16, for example, the story of Israel's struggle against the Amalekites, v. 12 depicts Moses as a leader with steady hands: $way^eh\hat{\imath}\ y\bar{a}d\bar{a}yw\ '^em\hat{u}n\hat{a}$. His steady hands endure all the way to the conclusion for the day's work: $'ad$-$b\bar{o}'\ ha\check{s}\check{s}\bar{a}me\check{s}$. This picture decribes Moses' peculiar quality in leading his people in the face of wilderness crises. Moses sticks to his job despite physical difficulties. And his ability to stand by his responsibilities shows his integrity as a leader of the people. Thus, the form of the story sets this unit among the OT legends about the leaders of Israel.[1]

This picture of Moses' virtues enlarges when Num. 12.1-15 comes into consideration. The immediate point of contact appears not simply in a common interest in the virtues of Moses, but more particularly in repetition of the virtue announced in Exodus 17. Num. 12.7b observes: 'He is entrusted with all my house': b^ekol-$b\hat{e}t\hat{\imath}\ ne^em\bar{a}n\ h\hat{u}'$. The apparent image of this verse, though based on a different grammatical form, draws on the same root word and meaning ($'mn$) from Exod. 17.12. Moses shows himself as a responsible steward in God's house, and his responsibility undergirds the picture of Moses as a person with integrity. The image would be like the one depicting Joseph in Gen. 39.1-6. Joseph, the steward over all the house of Potiphar, shows himself responsible in the administration of his responsibilities, even when his master's wife makes such responsibility very difficult.[2] The Joseph parallel does not use the key word. It is not difficult, however, to find parallels with $ne'^em\bar{a}n$ as a designation of virtue. In 1 Sam. 22.14, the term describes David in a manner that reveals integrity. It is a virtue that should set him above Saul's rampage (compare also 1 Sam. 2.35; 3.20; Isa. 7.9). To be $ne'^em\bar{a}n$ is to be honest in fulfillment of duty (cf. Gen. 42.20).

But how, we might ask, does the unit in Num. 12.1-15 function to give expression to this virtue? And what precisely is the virtue of

---

1. G.W. Coats, 'Moses Versus Amalek: Aetiology and Legend in Exod. 17.8-16', *Congress Volume Edinburgh* (VTSup, 28; Leiden: Brill, 1975), pp. 29-41. See ch. 3 above.

2. Coats, *From Canaan to Egypt: Structure and Theology in the Joseph Story* (CBQMS, 4; Washington: Catholic Biblical Association, 1973).

faithfulness in the house of God? In order to clarify the virtues of Moses as they appear in this unit, we must define the crucial role of v. 3.

What is the significance of the attribute '*ānāw* in v. 3? 'The man Moses was very *meek*, more than every other person on the face of the earth'. The key term '*ānāw* refers to a leading virtue of Moses who exemplifies the virtue better than any other person in the land.[1] It is not, however, clear that the words, 'meek' or 'humble', do justice as tools for translating the term.[2] If meek means 'deficient in spirit and courage' or 'submissive', then it does not describe the Moses of this pericope. The virtue of v. 7 has nothing to do with humility. There is no way to depict Moses as deficient in spirit when he intercedes for Miriam before God (v. 13). What kind of virtue, then, belongs to Moses more than to all other persons who are on the face of the earth? And how does that virtue relate to the description of Moses as responsible in v. 7?

My intention here is not to present a full etymology for the term '*ānāw* but rather to build on work already established. The basic thesis is that the word derives from a root, '*nw*, connoting responsibility or integrity. The following observations seem to me relevant to that end: (i) Written without a yod, the form of the word now preserved in the MT ('*ānāw*) is without parallel. This masculine singular noun would suggest derivation from a root '*nw*, with some intimate relationship to the feminine noun *^anāwâ* (cf. Isa. 29.19; 32.7; Amos 8.4; etc.).[3] (ii) A traditional analysis of '*ānāw* derives the word from the verb '*ānâ*, 'to be bowed down, afflicted'. Support for this derivation lies at hand, not

---

1. Noth, *Numbers*, p. 96. See also J. Schildenberger, 'Moses als Idealgestalt eines Armen Jahwes', in *A la recontre de dieu: mémorial Albert Gelin* (Le Puy: Xavier Mappus, 1961), p. 72.
2. The problem appears also in German translations. The terms 'demütig' or 'sanftmütig' seem inadequate to me. Cf. the comments of Schildenberger, 'Moses', pp. 71-72. G.B. Gray (*A Critical and Exegetical Commentary on Numbers* [ICC; Edinburgh: T. & T. Clark, 1903], p. 123) recognizes the conflict between such a translation and the context: 'The word is generally rendered "meek", and interpreted to mean "patient", "given to bear wrongs without resistance", but this is a sense which it bears nowhere else in OT'.
3. The Qere in Num. 12.3 reads, however, '*ānāyw*, suggesting a form of the adjective (cf. '*ānî*, Isa. 49.13). The Qere is nonetheless a problem, since it preserves the waw of the MT. The yod has traditionally been interpreted as a *mater lectionis* designed to insure pronunciation of the final syllable (Gray, *Numbers*, p. 124).

only from the Arabic root *'nw*, but also from the parallel alignment of the plural *ᵃnāwîm* with 'poor', *dallîm* (cf. Amos 2.7; etc.). J. Schildenberger opens this connotation a step farther: 'The attitude or virtue of *ᵃnāwâ* is revealed precisely in the fact that Moses does not defend himself but rather that Yahweh takes over responsibility for Moses' justification'.[1] (iii) Except in a very limited context, however, *'ānāw* does not mean 'oppressed', nor even 'reticent'. L. Delekat suggests rather that the word comes from the verb *'ānâ*, 'to answer'.[2] Moreover, the verb connotes 'answer' in a very particular way. It suggests the kind of relationship that obtains between a master and his servant. The servant devotes himself in obedience to his master. He complies with the master's designs for his affairs. Ps. 149.4 offers an appropriate parallel: 'For the Lord takes pleasure in his people; he adorns the humble (*ᵃnāwîm*) with victory. Let the faithful exult in glory'. The *ᵃnāwîm* parallel the *ḥᵃsîdîm*. They are not oppressed. They are committed in loyalty to the Lord.[3] The same parallel appears in Sir. 1.27: 'For the fear of the Lord is wisdom and instruction, and he delights in fidelity and "meekness" '.

If *'ānāw* derives from such a stem, *'nw*, with denotation of obedient response, the connotations of the word in Numbers 12 should follow in unforced sequence. Delekat observes, for example, that the verb *'ānâ*, comes from before such public honor. Indeed, public display of honor may spell the destruction of an honored person. But if *'ānâ* can suggest *willfährig* or *hörig* with certain tones of complacency, loss in

---

1. Schildenberger, 'Moses', p. 72. Translation mine.
2. L. Delekat, 'Zum hebräischen Wörterbuch', *VT* 14 (1964), pp. 35-49. Delekat observes: 'Nach Ges.-Buhl, Brown-Driver-Briggs und Köhler heisst überall "demütig". Das ist offensichtlich falsch'. His thesis is that *'ānāw* and *'ānî* are synonyms and mean 'elend' or 'willfährig', 'hörig', 'ergehen'. See also R. Martin-Achard, "*nh II* elend sein', in E. Jenni and C.Westermann (eds.), *Theologisches Handwörterbuch zum Alten Testament* (München: Kaiser, 1976), II, pp. 341-50.
3. A. Gelin, *The Poor of Yahweh* (Collegeville: Liturgical Press, 1964). See also A. Rahlfs, *'ānî und 'ānāw in den Psalmen* (Leipzig: A. Dries, 1891). Rahlfs recognized an important distinction between the two. For the Psalms *'ānî* means 'in Knechtsstellung befindlich' while *'ānāw* would mean 'sich in Knechtsstellung versetzend' (p. 73). Specifically, *'ānî* appears as a synonym for *'ebyôn*, but not *'ānāw* (p. 54). This distinction supports the point defended here. *'ānāw* describes one whose personal integrity facilitates his work as a servant, not simply a poor or retiring person.

immediacy in responsibility.¹ This kind of passive quality does not do justice to the pericope. The context highlights rather obedience within the context of personal responsibility. Moses' characteristic quality as *'ānāw* is not a strictly inner personal virtue, but comes to expression in his role as servant with responsibility for the Lord's house: *b^{e}kol-bêtî ne'^{e}mān hû'*. Thus, if one considers the context of the crucial term *'ānāw*, a conclusion lies at hand: to be 'meek' is to be responsible for the whole household of the master.

The range of connotation in the word emerges even more clearly when one compares the virtue with 'honor', *kābôd*. *kābôd* is the honor imposed on a person by his supporters. It implies recognition, public celebration of deeds or character. Prov. 15.33 and 18.12 suggest that *'ānāw* comes before such public honor. Indeed, public display of honor may spell the destruction of an honored person. But if *'ānāw* precedes the public display of honor, if the fear of the Lord prepares a person for honor in the same way that *'^{a}nāw* does, then honor may be embraced as good. *'ānāw* is therefore the personal honor, the integrity of character that makes public honor well bestowed. Num. 12.3 might thus read: 'The man Moses was the most honorable of all persons who are on the face of the earth'. This connotation for the masculine noun *'ānāw* can be confirmed by reference to all other parallel feminine nouns. In every case the noun appears to be more clearly defined if it is taken as a term for honor or integrity. Moreover, in two cases the word *'ānāwâ* creates an impossible combination if the meaning is related to meek or humble. But integrity or honor serves both well. Thus, 2 Sam. 22.36 describes an attribute of God: 'You have given me the shield of your salvation, and your "honor" made me great' (cf. also Ps. 18.36). And in contrast to the RSV emendation, Ps. 45.5 requires such a translation: 'In your majesty ride forth victoriously for the cause of truth (*'al-d^{e}bar-'^{e}met*) and the honor of right (*w^e'anwâ-ṣedeq*)'.

II

What can be said, then, concerning genre and structure in this pericope? In its final form the unit appears as a legend. A legend builds its narrative in order to emphasize a virtue in the central hero.² Typically

---

1. Delekat, 'Zum hebräischen Wörterbuch', p. 42.
2. Hals, 'Legend', pp. 166-76. See also A. Jolles, *Einfache Formen* (Tübingen:

the story line recedes behind the various points that advance the virtue, while the virtue itself becomes a central datum in the narrative, either by repetition or by structural elevation. In Numbers 12, both v. 3 and v. 7 depict the same virtue of responsibility in the administration of God's household. Both refer to the quality of Moses' leadership as a man of honor who fulfills the responsibility God gives him. Behind the emphasis on the virtue lies a tale of opposition to Moses. Indeed, the tale itself shows some evidence of growth, for an early account of the opposition because of Moses' marriage to a Cushite woman becomes a story of opposition to Moses' role as leader of the people and mediator of the divine Word. Miriam and Aaron struggle against Moses' exclusive right to represent the Word of God to the people, and the struggle leads to an appropriate punishment of the rebels in a manner that at the same time affirms the authority of Moses. This tale thus becomes a legend, a vehicle for presenting Moses' virtue.

But what is the relationship between the tradition as tale and the legendary emphasis on Moses' honor? In its final form the pericope appears as a legend. But are the legendary elements simple addition to the text that disrupt the story?[1] It seems to me that the genre distinctions between tale and legend cannot serve as evidence that the legendary elements in vv. 3 and 7 are simply disruptive. Legends typically appear as transformations of original tales, but nonetheless as significant stages in the history of the tradition. As a significant stage, the legend demands serious effort in interpretation. But of more importance, the transformation effected by the legend does not spell simple disunity in the pericope. It spells rather a new attempt to advance interpretation of the tradition. The question of unity in the pericope is thus the more pressing.

The working hypothesis for defining the unity of the pericope is that the responsibility as connoted by *'ānāw* is clearly demonstrated in the event of intercession as described in vv. 9-14. The structure of the pericope supports the viability of the hypothesis. Firstly, the point of tension in the story appears in vv. 1-3. A report of the conflict,

Niemeyer, 1969), pp. 23-62.

1. Baentsch (*Exodus-Leviticus-Numeri*), p. 512. observes: 'Der milde und demütige Moses gehört doch wohl erst der späteren Zeit an, die ihm mit den Tugenden schmückte, die ihr als die höchsten galten...Jedenfalls gehört der Vers nicht zum alten Bericht'. The issue affects not only the tradition history, but also the definition of structure. Is the verse simply disruptive? Or does it have a substantial role in the whole? Cf. the discussion in Schildenberger, 'Moses', pp. 71-72.

vv. 1-2, contrasts with the legendary note in v. 3. Miriam and Aaron may challenge the position Moses holds. But the storyteller assures his audience that Moses will respond with honor. The second element in the pericope, vv. 4-8, heightens the tension by introducing Yahweh as judge. Significantly, the narrative account of the hearing (vv. 4-5) merges with an oracle, vv. 6-8. And in the oracle is the legendary expansion. Moses administers the house of the Lord. He is $ne^{'e}mān$. The final element of structure in vv. 9-15 resolves the tension. The rebellion ends in dire punishment against the rebel. Moses' authority receives a just confirmation (vv. 9-10). It is important to note, however, that the resolution of the conflict does not bring the pericope to its close. Rather, announcement of the punishment motivates immediate appeal from Aaron to Moses not to punish the rebels for the rebellion. The appeal comprises both a confession of guilt (v. 11b) and a petition (vv. 11a, 12) and leads to Moses' intercession (cf. Exod. 32.21-24, 30-32). The intercession itself appears under the narrative verbal form, 'Moses cried out to the Lord' ($wayyiṣ'aq\ mōšeh\ 'el\ yhwh$), and features the stereotypes of supplication: 'O God! Heal her!' ($'ēl\ nā'\ r^ep\bar{a}'\ n\bar{a}'\ l\bar{a}h$). Yet, despite its formal polite structure, it shares in the radical opposition characteristic of the intercession in Exod. 32.31-32. Moses petitions Yahweh to change the course of his action. And the intercession achieves a compromise: in fact, the healing process which forms the content of Moses' petition. Moreover, the intercession with its result must be understood directly in relationship to the virtue of Moses at the center of the legend. The virtue focuses on Moses' integrity of leadership before God. That virtue is described in v. 8 as the unique position of Moses which enables him to speak 'mouth to mouth' with God. It is precisely the mouth to mouth relationship that facilitates Moses' position as intercessor. And his audacity to address God with such an appeal is the act that exemplifies the virtue. It would appear to me, therefore, that intercession cannot be taken simply as a sign for prophetic office. Here it appears as a contrast to the prophets.

In its final form, then, the pericope in Num. 12.1-15 appears as a well unified legend. Each element of structure in the unit exhibits a transformation from a focus on opposition to Moses' leadership to a depiction of Moses' virtue as a leader. And the final element shows the unit as a picture of an honorable man, a man whose virtue is exemplified by his intercession for his opponent.

The following outline illustrates the pattern of unity:

I Exposition 1-3
  A. Challenge 1-2
    1. Cushite wife 1
    2. Mosaic leadership 2
  B. *Virtue* 3
II Complications 4-8
  A. Summons 4
  B. Theophany 5
  C. *Affirmation of Mosaic Virtue 6-8*
    1. Relationship between God and prophet 6
    2. Relationship between God and Moses 7-8a
    3. Accusation, 8b
III Resolution 9-14
  A. Punishment 9-10
  B. Appeal for intercession 11-12
  C. Intercession, *fulfillment of virtue* 13
  D. Response 14
IV Conclusion 15

III

What kind of imagery dominates this pericope? The office of intercessor is commonly tied to the prophets.[1] Indeed, some intimate contact between the prophetic office and the Mosaic tradition can be seen. Yet, in just this pericope the virtue of Moses is denied to the prophetic office. The prophet receives the Word of God in a vision or a dream. But Moses enjoys a more personal relationship—the intimacy of direct communication and the responsibility of administration in the house of God. Thus, it is clear that reference to a prophetic office will not adequately account for this unit in the Moses traditions. The same point applies to the definition of the Mosaic tradition in terms of a royal office.[2] It is possible to see the king as a representative of this virtue, as J.R. Porter has shown. Yet, there is no concern in the Mosaic tradition at large, certainly not in this pericope, to define the imagery as royal. There is no limitation of this virtue to the royal office. It would be more likely that the Moses traditions *and* traditions derived

---

1. B.S. Childs, *Exodus: A Critical, Theological Commentary* (Philadelphia: Westminster Press, 1974), pp. 351-60. Noth, *Numbers*, p. 93.
2. J.R. Porter, *Moses and Monarchy: A Study in the Biblical Tradition of Moses* (Oxford: Basil Blackwell, 1963).

from prophetic or royal offices depend on a common third source, a pattern for depicting particular leadership figures that is not limited to one institution. That pattern, so it seems to me, derives from folklore and can best be described as heroic. The legend that depicts Moses as more honorable than any person on the face of the earth should be understood as a part of the heroic Moses tradition so common in the Pentateuch.

IV

This perspective on Numbers 12 has explicit theological consequences that need a hearing. (i) The legendary quality of leadership exemplified by Moses does not call for a deficiency of spirit and courage, a meek, retiring, unassertive leadership. It calls rather for strong, effective, responsible leadership. (ii) That leadership is not a strong, silent type. Rather, it involves articulation of needs among the led. (iii) Loyalty within the scope of such leadership belongs to God. But loyalty to God means loyalty in responsibility to the hero's people. Moses does not show his obedience to God by a meek acceptance of Miriam's punishment as the obvious will of God. To the contrary, his obedience emerges only when he stands face to face with God and defends his own.

Chapter 8

METANOIA IN ANCIENT ISRAEL:
CLUES FOR UNITY AND CHANGE

God called Israel, according to tradition, to follow a way from Egypt to Canaan. That way led Israel over mountains and through valleys littered with bitter springs, deserted deserts, enemies that threatened death, serpents that brought death with burning, agonizing bites. God marked his leadership with a pillar of cloud by day and a pillar of fire by night. The ark of the covenant moved at the head of the people. And its cherubim symbolized the moving presence of God, always with his people, always calling them to the right fork on the way to the Promised Land.

Even more significant, according to the tradition, than fire and cloud, ark and cherubim, was the compelling presence of Moses. His stature, his imperatives, his vision set the way to Canaan for the Israelites apart from the way to death in a deserted desert. In the traditions about Israel's beginnings in the wilderness, Moses dominates the relationship between Israel and God. Moreover, that domination takes a particular form. This Moses was not a weak and mild-mannered man, a simple reporter of the news about God's decisions for Israel in the wilderness. He was a leader capable of making hard decisions about the right way for his people. By his own initiative, he met and resolved crisis after crisis confronting his people on the way. Through Moses, God extended his own leadership for this people.

By God's commission, Moses found a source for water when the people were thirsty. He found meat and bread when they were hungry. He defended them against an Egyptian enemy at the sea, a serpentine enemy in the desert, and even a divine enemy at the mountain. He delivered a law to them that defined the moral fabric of their society. He delivered a covenant to them that defined their relationship with God. Indeed, before the eyes of the people, his very appearance changed to reflect the authority of the God who sent him. His identity with his people, his care for his people, the signs of authority bordering on miracles, marked Moses as a heroic man in the midst of the community and as a representative of God who saved the people from oppressive slavery in Egypt.

The stories Israel told about this heroic man began with an ironic and even miraculous birth. Out of jealousy, the Pharaoh of Egypt sought his life with royal decrees that killed a generation of Israelite boys. Ironically, the Pharaoh's own daughter preserved this hero from his royal fate. But tragically, the life-long struggle of this heroic man, tied as he was to his own people in their journey to a promised land, ended before the goal could be fulfilled. Moses died before the people could enter the land. How can a people redeemed by God but led by a heroic man continue when the man died too soon? But even more, the tradition remembers that this man, the one who faced so many crises on behalf of his people, died before the goal of his work was completed *on behalf of his people.* 'The Lord was angry with me *on your account,* and he swore that I should not cross the Jordan and that I should not enter the good land which the Lord your God gives you for an inheritance (Deut. 4.21).

This heroic man set a model for subsequent generations. Obedient to God, he nevertheless effected the delivery of his people through the way to Canaan. In his constancy, in the integrity of his leadership he defined what human character might be. The future leaders of Israel could struggle to be New Moses. Indeed, each Israelite could shape life as New Moses, the goal of created order.

But change plays its tune even in the best of traditions. The Moses image must have influenced leaders through the period of the judges. Samuel and later Elijah or Elisha, perhaps Jeroboam or Omri, Ezra or even Judas Maccabaeus represented New Moses for their people. But King David caught a different vision of leadership in Israel. At first a leader in the tradition of Samuel and Saul, David changed the face of Israelite tradition completely by moving the center of his operations from Hebron to Jerusalem. In Jerusalem he found a system of kingship already in operation. And with the system came new images of leadership. The king would be the Son of God, his reign eternal, as firm as the earth itself, as vital as the creation established by God who himself dwelt in Zion and secured its walls from all enemies. As king and priest in the order of Melchizedek, David would rule his kingdom in righteousness and justice. God's covenant, established directly with David, would be mediated through David to all of God's people.

The changes effected by the new kingship in Jerusalem reached all institutions in Israel's life. But not all of David's subjects accepted the changes with grace and poise. Indeed, one major problem facing change in any institution, religious or secular, is resistance from the representatives of the old order. Rebellions against David happened more than once. And rebellions were smashed by the agent of change with harsh force. One in particular deserves attention. II Samuel 20 tells of a revolt against David led by Sheba, a Benjaminite. Under the war cry, 'We have no portion in David and we have no inheritance in the son of Jesse. Every man to his tents, O Israel!' Sheba drew 'all the men of Israel' away from David, leaving David support only from 'the men of Judah'. By superior strength, David put down that resistance to change. And David's historian labeled the process the work of 'a worthless fellow whose name was Sheba'.

Yet, the resistance did not die with Sheba. When David's successor, Solomon, died, the men of Israel revolted again, this time under the leadership of Jeroboam. And Jeroboam, perhaps modeling his leadership for the rebels as a New Moses, called the men of Israel to arms with the same war cry: 'What portion have we in David? We have no inheritance in the Son of Jesse. To your tents, O Israel! Look now to your own house, David'. The north separated from the south. Images of Davidic leadership separated from images of Mosaic leadership.

Resistance to change by the old order is not the only problem posed by the process of change in the typical religious society. The new order can also resist contributions of value from the old system. In a new order, leaders can seek insurance for strength in the new establishment by throwing out all signs and traces of the old order. Thus, in many ancient societies, when a new king ascended the throne, he would typically slaughter all who might have designs on his position of leadership. David's theologians obviously sought to carry out such a far-reaching revision of the sacred traditions. In the southern version of the stories about Moses and Israel in the wilderness, the Israelites, the ancestors of the northern kingdom, were not faithful disciples of Moses, following his leadership and the guidance of God through the way in the wilderness with the fidelity of a bride. To the contrary, they were rebels, constantly murmuring against Moses, constantly wanting to return to Egypt and slavery, constantly wanting to depose

Moses and, with him, the God he served. At Sinai, those ancestors had the chance to enter a covenant with God. But they forfeited all rights to that covenant when they erected a golden calf and danced their worship before it. Jeroboam's golden calves in Dan and Bethel show how far those children of Moses had fallen away from the true way, the way of the God who dwells in Jerusalem. The goal of David's historians and theologians seems already to have been removal of all traces of the old in order to make way for the new. The struggle between the two parties with two distinct and conflicting traditions continued throughout the history of the divided monarchy. Indeed, at least a part of that struggle can still be seen in the Christian era in the animosity between the Jews and the Samaritans. What Samaritan would even stop to help a Jew, stripped and left for dead in a ditch? What Jew would allow a Samaritan to help, even if stripped and dying in a ditch?

If change is to be effective, it might seek its effectiveness by an alternative to resistance or rejection. If the north says to the south that hope for the future lies in a New Moses, it excludes the sacred for the south, the gains of the new age brought by David and Zion. If the south says to the north that hope for the future lies in a New David, it excludes the sacred for the north, the stability established by Moses and Sinai. But what would happen if these two warring brothers caught a vision of reconciled life without war? What would happen if someone caught a vision of a future for the people of God dominated by a leader who would be both New Moses and New David, a leader who could embody the changes of the new age with the strength and stability of the old? Ezekiel comes close to this vision with his sign act effected by two sticks. 'Son of man, take a stick...for Judah...Take another stick...for...the house of Israel...And join them together into one stick'. But where is the leader in Israel that can effect that union? Josiah, a Davidic king in Jerusalem, sought to re-establish control of the north and, in effect, to reconcile the separated brothers as the one people of God. But he died an untimely death. Ezra and Nehemiah brought political and cultic order to the New Jerusalem. But the vision faded into a radical exclusivism. It is significant that Christian tradition in the Gospel of Matthew identifies Jesus as both New David and New Moses. In his vision of reconciliation, not only for Jew and Samaritan, but for all the families of the earth, the fruit of change established first by the exodus from slavery in Egypt but carried forward by the crowning of a king in Jerusalem comes clearly to expression. And that wedding of New David and New Moses rings a clear message for all involved in change: resistance to change can cripple tradition and the institution that preserves tradition with rigidity is doomed to outmoded forms that cannot meet the crises of new days. But change for the sake of change, change that eliminates tradition, will have shallow footing. The change that proves effective, at least in the biblical tradition, is the change that combines the old and the new, the change that knows continuity with the past and yet the vitality of the new present with its vision of the future. That kind of *metanoia* produces a new creation. The old falls away, leaving an entirely new form. With it go identities from the old: New Jerusalem, New Exodus, a new heaven and a new earth, a new creature with a new heart.

Is it not ironic that the tradition of *metanoia* resident in the Bible is a tradition that speaks of a reconciliation of New Moses and New David in a second Adam, a tradition that calls its audience to repentance in the face of a broken past and commitment for a new future, lives in an institution that is itself divided between a faction that follows a dynastic monarchy centered in a New Jerusalem and a faction that speaks of a priesthood of all believers? Does one resist the change represented by the other? Does the other throw out all signs and stabilities from the old in its quest for the new? Perhaps change for the church can best be sought in a union of the old and the new, a union that is not simply the sum of the two parts, but an entirely new creation. Perhaps in the entirely new creation, the greatest value for the age-old principle of *metanoia* emerges in its most vital and effective form: a renewed Body of Christ.

Chapter 9

MOSES AS A MODEL FOR MINISTRY:
AN EXEGESIS OF EXODUS 2.11-22

1. *Definition of the Pericope*

The pericope for this exercise in exegesis appears in Exod. 2.11-22.[1] A formula that sets a temporal reference marks the beginning of the pericope. Moreover, the formula suggests that the focus for the following narrative is a new event, distinct from the subjects of the preceding narrative. It exposes the beginning of a new stage in the larger narrative: *way^{e}hî bayyāmîm hāhēm*. 'It came to pass in those days...' Repetition of a key term from the preceding unit effects some degree of unity between this pericope and its context: in v. 10, 'the boy grew up...' and in v. 11, 'Moses grew up...' But the principal function of the temporal clause is to mark a transition between Moses' life as a child who grows up and his life as a young man who has grown up. The conclusion of the pericope stands under the sign of an etiology for the name of Moses' son in v. 22. And v. 23 confirms that point with another transition formula: *way^{e}hî bayyāmîm hārabbîm hāhēm*. 'It came to pass in those many days...'

2. *Evaluation of the Hebrew Text and its Translation*

The Hebrew text of this pericope offers no pressing problems. It is important, nevertheless, to observe some variations. In v. 11, the Septuagint adds an adjective to the formula, bringing the transition in v. 11 into parallel with the formula in v. 23. And the pattern of

---

1. For a description of the methodology employed for this exercise in exegesis, see G.M. Tucker, *Form Criticism of the Old Testament* (Guides to Biblical Scholarship; Philadelphia: Fortress Press, 1971), pp. 6-17. The same methodology lies at the foundation for the commentary series, *Forms of Old Testament Literature* (Grand Rapids, MI: Eerdmans).

transition from one episode to another appears, as a consequence, even stronger. The other variations do not decisively affect form or translation of the pericope. In v. 14, for example, the Septuagint apparently eliminates the Hebrew construction, l^e'$îš$. And, in fact, the change would clarify the difficult syntax of the sentence. The changes from the Septuagint would thus appear to resolve difficult readings or harmonize similar constructions. The MT remains, therefore, the basis for the exegesis.

> [11]It came to pass in those days, when Moses had grown up, that he went out to his brothers, and he saw their burdens. He saw an Egyptian beating a Hebrew, one of his brothers. [12]He looked this way and that, and he saw that there was no one there. So he beat the Egyptian and hid him in the sand. [13]He went out on the second day, and this time two Hebrews were struggling together. He said to the one who did the wrong: 'Why are you beating your friend?' [14]He answered: 'Who made you a royal man and a judge over us? Do you intend to kill me as you killed the Egyptian?' Then Moses was afraid and said: 'Surely the thing is known' [15]When the Pharaoh heard about this thing, he sought to kill Moses. So Moses fled from the Pharaoh and stayed in the land of Midian. And he sat down by a well.
>
> [16]The priest of Midian had seven daughters. They came and drew water and filled the troughs to water their father's flock. [17]But shepherds came and drove them away. So Moses arose and saved them, and watered their flock.
>
> [18]When they came to Reuel, their father, he said: 'Why have you returned so quickly today?' [19]They said: 'An Egyptian delivered us from the hand of the shepherds. And he also drew water for us and watered the sheep. [20]He said to his daughters: 'Where is he? Why have you left the man? Call him, so that he may eat bread' [21]So Moses was content to dwell with the man, and he gave his daughter Zipporah to Moses. [21]She bore a son, and he called his name Gershom, for he said: 'I have been a stranger in a foreign land.'

3. *Structure*

The structure of the pericope comprises two principal elements: Moses defends the oppressed in Egypt, 2.11-15a and Moses defends the oppressed in Midian, 2.15b-22.[1] Element 1 has two principal parts in its composition: vv. 11-12 report an event in the life of Moses, the

---

1. For details, see my forthcoming Exodus commentary in the Eerdmans series, *FOTL*.

prince, while vv. 13-14 report a second event. The second report is again distinguished from the first by a temporal formula for transition: 'the next day' (*bayyôm haššēnî*). Both events highlight Moses' characteristic concern to defend the oppressed. In the first, Moses sees an Egyptian 'beating' a Hebrew. And he intervenes by defending the oppressed Hebrew. In the second, he sees two Hebrews 'struggling'. Again, he intervenes. And the text identifies the act as an act of defense for the wronged against the one who did the wrong. 'He said to the one who did the wrong: "Why are you beating your friend?"' Unfortunately, the oppressing Hebrew counters with a rejection of Moses' authority to intervene in the fight: 'Who made you a royal man and a judge over us?' But the tragedy of the counterattack is the revelation that the event with the Egyptian was public knowledge. In the pressure of rejection from the very people he sought to defend, under pursuit from the Pharaoh who now sought to kill him, Moses fled from Egypt, from the people he sought to defend.[1]

That pattern of defense for the oppressed is repeated in the second element. The second major element for the pericope, 2.15b-22, locates Moses in Midian. Fleeing from the wrath of the angry Pharaoh, Moses stops at a well in Midian, a traditional motif for folk tales (so, Gen. 24.11; 29.2). At the well, Moses witnesses seven women drawing water for the flocks they were tending. Others shepherds came to the well and drove the women away, taking their water. But in an act that corresponds with the intervention of the first scene, Moses 'helped' the women and even drew water for their flocks. The verb that denotes Moses' act is *wayyôši'ān*, from *yāša'* the verb that gives the tradition the names Joshua and Jesus. The result of the second intervention is an invitation from the father of the women to a meal. And the consequence of the hospitality is a long-term arrangement: "Moses was content to dwell with the man, and he gave his daughter Zipporah to Moses." Verse 22 marks the end of the unit with a report of the birth of a son for Moses and Zipporah. The hospitality provides not only shelter from the pursuit of the Pharoah who wanted to kill him, but also the intimacy of a family.[2]

The initial exploration of structure in the pericope suggests the following analytical outline:

---

1. B.S. Childs, *The Book of Exodus: A Critical, Theological Commentary* (OTL; Philadelphia: Westminster Press, 1974), pp. 30-31.
2. Childs, *The Book of Exodus*, p. 32.

I Intervention in Egypt 11-15a
   A. First scene of intervention 11-12
      1. Exposition 11a
      2. Crisis 11b
      3. Intervention 12
   B. Second scene of intervention 13-14a
      1. Exposition 13aα
      2. Crisis 13aβ
      3. Intervention 13b
      4. Rejection 14a
   C. Results 14b-15a
      1. Moses' response 14b
      2. Pharaoh's response 15a
II Intervention in Midian 15b-22
   A. Scene of intervention 15b-17
      1. Exposition 15b-16a
      2. Crisis 16b-17a
      3. Intervention 17b
   B. Scene of Hospitality 18-22
      1. Report of intervention to the father 18-19
      2. Invitation 20
      3. Results 21-22
         a. Moses with his host 21a
         b. Marriage report 21b
         c. Birth report 22

With this analysis of structure in hand, it is now possible to explore some greater detail in order to expose the significance of the structure for exegesis. It is clear that a major item of content in the unit depicts Moses as a man who intervenes on behalf of the oppressed. But in order to catch the weight of that point, the contrast between the two scenes in the first element must be examined. In the first scene, the exposition and the report of crisis emphasize a point of identification between Moses and the oppressed. It is important to note not only that Moses intervenes on behalf of the oppressed, but even more that Moses identifies the oppressed as *his people*. 'It came to pass in those days, when Moses had grown up, that he went out to *his brothers*.' That point of identity with the oppressed types Moses for this narrative as *heroic*.[1] The hero of the ancient tradition is heroic precisely in

---

1. G.W. Coats, 'The Moses Narrative as Heroic Saga', in *Saga, Legend, Tale, Novella, Fable: Narrative Forms in Old Testament Literature* (JSOTSup, 35; Sheffield: JSOT Press, 1985), pp. 33-44.

the ability of the key figure to identify with the people who profit from the intervention. And that identity comes not just from the hero's recognition of familial or tribal loyalty. It comes from the hero's identity with the people who benefit from the heroic act. Whether in Egypt with the sons of Israel or in Midian with the daughters of Reuel, Moses' people are the oppressed. And his function as hero is to 'save' them (*yāša'*).

But another problem arises at just this point in the narrative. Does the text not suggest that Moses' intervention is a furtive act, thus not an event of heroic quality? Is the event not a murder that soils Moses' reputation?[1] Is the act not an act of rage that suggests a fatal weakness, a flaw in this heroic figure? 'He looked this way and that, and he saw that there was no one there. So he beat the Egyptian and hid him in the sand'. The first point to observe here is the irony of diction in the description of the scene. The Hebrew verb in v. 11, 'he saw the Egyptian *beating* a Hebrew...', is the same one in v. 12: 'So he *beat* the Egyptian and hid him in the sand'. Whatever Moses did to the Egyptian was the same act that the Egyptian was doing to the Hebrews. Yet, the text uses the verb with a pointed and ironic play. When the Egyptian 'beats' the Hebrew, the act is oppressive. It highlights the plight of the slaves as the setting calling for God's response. But when Moses 'beats' the Egyptian, the act is redemptive. It is the beginning of God's response. That irony contributes to the heroic image of Moses. Indeed, the scene must not be classified as a picture of a cowardly act. Moses acts to protect the weak. And he does so in a manner that will not jeopardize his potential for acting for the sake of the weak again.

---

1. Childs, *The Book of Exodus*, p. 43. 'The selfless act is soon beclouded by violence and nothing of lasting effect is accomplished for Israel's plight'. Childs's discussion of the issue focuses on a critical moral question: under what circumstances can the use of violence be contained in a heroic tale that gives some kind of exposition for the larger Moses saga and the tradition about the exodus under God's leadership? Indeed, the exodus narratives embroil God in the same issue. God effects the death of the Egyptian first-born in order to redeem Israel from Egyptian bondage. Childs observes that the story does not resolve the issue. 'But it does raise a whole set of issues which are inherent in such action. By uncovering the ambiguities in the act of violence, the reader is forced to confront rather than evade those basic factors which constitute the moral decision'. One must also observe, however, that heroic tradition commonly has an element of violence. The hero vanquishes the enemy. Israel must await a new Moses in order to find an alternative to heroic violence: 'Father, forgive them!'

Moreover, the scene is duplicated in narrative function, although not in explicit content, by the heroic intervention of Moses in v. 17. In v. 17, the shepherds drive the women away from the well. In response to that act of oppression, Moses stands up to help the women. The parallel does not use the same verbs. But the point is the same. Moses intervenes to help the women, to secure the care for their sheep in the face of the shepherds who would drive the women away. Thus, the emphasis in v. 12 is not on a cowardly act,[1] Moses looking to insure that no one would see his deed, then hiding the body of the Egyptian in the sand. The emphasis is on intervention in an oppressive event on behalf of the oppressed. And that emphasis is repeated in vv. 15b-17.

Is the heroic stature of Moses who intervenes on behalf of the oppressed Hebrews compromised by the notice in v. 14? 'Then Moses was afraid and thought: "Surely the thing is known!"' One must note first that the comment plays a critical role in the narrative. It accounts for the transition between the heroic intervention in Egypt and the heroic intervention in Midian. But even in the content of the story, the report that the hero felt fear and fled does not compromise the heroic tone of the scene. Even in classical European heroic saga tradition, the hero may be faced with a frightening challenge and flee from the people who name him hero. Siegfried must leave his people for a time. But he is still the hero. The fear and, indeed, the flight are not fatal flaws in the heroic image. They mean that the hero must leave the people for a time. But he will return. Moses flees to the land of Midian. And there he remains for an extended time. Indeed, in the hospitality of the Midianite priest, he receives not only a wife and a son, but also protection from the quest of the Pharaoh. And of even more importance, it is precisely there that he confronts the awe inspiring presence of the Lord at the bush and hears the commission to return to Egypt.

Moreover, even for the extended period of time, Moses in the land of Midian does not forget his own people in Egypt. His new wife bears a son. And Moses calls the boy Gershom. 'I have been a stranger in a foreign land'. In the comfort of Midianite hospitality, Moses

---

1. Childs (*The Book of Exodus*, p. 30) observes appropriately: 'Verse 12 emphasizes the note of secrecy and stealth in the piling up of clues: he looked both ways; he observed no one; he struck him; there was no struggle as in v. 13'. But the secrecy and stealth imply no cowardly act.

cannot forget his people are oppressed in Egypt. And that point of identity renders him permanently a stranger in Midian, Midian permanently a foreign land. Moses' life makes sense only when Moses lives in relationship with his oppressed kinspeople.

This pericope shows no doublet structure, no repetition that fails to serve the effective structure of the whole. The entire frame reveals a significant unity, executed with attention to critical, artistic symmetry. In the larger unity of the Pentateuch/Hexateuch, the pericope belongs to the Yahwist (J).[1] And it sets an appropriate tone for the Yahwist's larger depiction of the heroic Moses. Indeed, one might hypothesize that behind the Yahwist's narrative about the heroic Moses lay a significant collection of heroic tales and legends depicting the great leader in various forms.[2] Some complication in the history of this tradition appears in the variation between the name of the host, Reuel, as it appears in this pericope in v. 18, and the name, apparently of the same man, in 3.1, Jethro.[3] But a resolution of this traditio-historical problem is not essential for the exegesis of the pericope. It is at least clear that the variation does not signal two different literary sources joined here by a redactor.

4. *Genre*

Some consideration of genre undergirds the analysis of structure in the unit. A tale focuses on narration of a plot in order to feature a particular event at the center of the plot.[4] The structure exposes its plot elements by introducing Moses, the hero who identifies with his own people (11a). The point of crisis comes in his observation of the Egyptian beating the Hebrew. It is heightened by his discovery that his heroic intervention, now public knowledge, threatens his life. And indeed, the storyteller adds to the tension by reporting that the Pharaoh sought to kill him. In the second scene, the crisis is repeated. Moses intervenes on behalf of the oppressed. Will he be forced to flee again? The denouement in the plot comes with the Midianite invitation. Here Moses can find refuge. Indeed, the focus event in the second scene is

---

1. M. Noth, *A History of Pentateuchal Traditions* (trans. B.W. Anderson; Englewood Cliffs: Prentice-Hall, 1972), p. 267.
2. Coats, 'The Moses Narrative', p. 34.
3. Noth, *A History*, pp. 183-84.
4. Coats, 'Tale', in *Saga, Legend, Tale, Novella, Fable: Narrative Forms in Old Testament Literature* (JSOTSup, 35; Sheffield: JSOT Press, 1985), pp. 63-70.

in some sense the resolution of the crisis created by the focus event in the first scene.

But the tale points its audience toward the future. Moses in the shelter of his Midianite father-in-law is a stranger. And the stranger status anticipates the time when he will return to his own people. Yet it must be clear that the event at the center of the tale is not the flight to Midian. That event is simply a by-product of the focal event, a feature that sets up the following scene. The centre event is also not to be found in the sojourn with the Midianite priest. Again, that event is a by-product of the focal event. The focus event for the tale is the heroic intervention on behalf of the oppressed, an event that documents Moses' identification with the oppressed. Moreover, the heroic tale would now function as an episode in a larger heroic saga. This tale shows the style of leadership characteristic for the hero of the saga.[1]

5. Setting

Who would tell this tale? Where would such a tradition as this live? The Moses saga generally and the individual tales within the structure of the saga must have circulated among Israel's storytellers.[2] The storyteller would entertain audiences by performing a tale, a legend, or perhaps even the entire saga at whatever occasion. But one should note that such stories were used not simply for entertainment, but also for building structures, for preserving community identity, moral fabric, encouragement, goals and hope for the future. The community that celebrated its tradition about a heroic leader could conspire to preserve that identity as its heritage for each succeeding generation. And that process could occur in various community events: cult, court, palace, family.

The setting takes on more precise lines when its position in the literary structure of the Yahwist comes into focus. A majority of OT scholars who write about the Yahwist place the work in the time of the united monarchy, probably in the court of Solomon or even as early as David.[3] Two problems confront this conclusion. First, some

---

1. Coats, 'The Moses Narrative', p. 37.
2. G.W. Coats, 'Vocational Identity in Ancient Entertainment Circles', *LTQ* 13 (1978), pp. 39-47.
3. W.H. Schmidt, *Old Testament Introduction* (trans. M.J. O'Connell; New

more recent exploration of the Yahwist places the work in an exilic or postexilic period.[1] Does the heroic Moses fit the late period, after the kingship had been vanquished?[2] Secondly, a conflict between the traditions about Moses and the traditions about David seems to set these two complex bodies of narrative in opposition.[3] If the story has been preserved from oral settings by the Yahwist, and if the Yahwist was in some sense David's theologian, why would that person or persons preserve a tradition that depicts Moses as hero? Would a heroic Moses create less conflict for the society and indeed inspire that society to some hope for the future if the society had already lost its Davidic line of leadership? The answer to that question depends on a definition of intention for the tradition.

6. *Intention*

The tale describes the heroic Moses in order to depict his leadership as an event that unites leader and led in a very intimate bond. The leader does not simply tolerate the people who live under his care. This shepherd of the sheep identifies with his people so that their suffering becomes his suffering, their cry for redemption his cry. For the structure of the larger saga, this identification serves as a transition from the youth in Egypt, the hero of the people who is not yet ready to act publicly on behalf of all the people but whose act anticipates that great intervention, to the shepherd in Midian, the hero of the priest's daughters who awaits the call of the God of the oppressed. But this hero does not simply identify with the suffering and ache with their pain. This hero embraces the task for doing something about their plight. This hero acts to defend the oppressed, indeed, to liberate the oppressed from their oppression.

The intent of this tale moves beyond its depiction of the ministry of

York: Crossword, 1984), p. 76.

1. H.H. Schmid, *Der sogennante Jahwist: Beobachtungen und Fragen zur Pentateuchforschung* (Zurich: Theologischer Verlag, 1976), pp. 167-83. J. van Seters, *Abraham in History and Tradition* (New Haven: Yale University Press, 1985), pp. 149-53.

2. R. Knierim, 'The Composition of the Pentateuch', in K.H. Richards (ed.) *Society of Biblical Literature 1985 Seminar Papers* (Atlanta: Scholars Press, 1985), pp. 393-415.

3. G.W. Coats, 'Metanoia in Ancient Israel: Clues for Unity and Change', *Midstream* 23 (1984), see ch. 8 below; 'II Samuel 12:1–7a', *Int* 40 (1986).

Moses, however. It represents the ministry of Moses as a model for all subsequent leaders in Israel. The tale captures its audience not only by describing Moses as a hero who identified with his people, but also by suggesting that David and all heirs who stand in his line should be heroes like Moses. Indeed, the adequacy of any particular Davidic heir as leader of the Lord's people might be judged on the basis of that person's success or failure in matching the Mosaic model.[1] A David who ignores the plight of the people and gives power to his own greed and passion stands under the judgment of the Mosaic model for Israelite leadership. The force of that intention does not suggest that royal leadership in Israel had already passed from the scene when the model saga addressed its audience. That kind of model affected stages of prophetic theology after the fall of the monarchy. Perhaps Moses was the model for the suffering servant of the Second Isaiah. Perhaps the Gospel tradition employs Moses as a model for depicting the beautiful relationship between Jesus and his disciples. But it also provides a check for the times when a Davidic heir magnifies himself beyond the heroic at the expense of his people. Such a procedure can be seen in the Deuteronomistic history, particularly in the presentation of Joshua, but also in the picture of Josiah. It is legitimate to suggest that the heroic Moses models a vision for the coming messiah for a people who have lost their kings. But it would also be an effective tool in the hands of a theologian who addresses a Davidic monarch still on the throne. Indeed, the heroic model might make its greatest impact by showing people and king what leadership ought to be. The king is not above the people, set apart from the suffering of the people. To the contrary, the king lives with the people. Their suffering is his suffering. And the power of the story calls a king to meet that model even if the process means royal suffering. The Davidic heir, the son of God, must also be the suffering servant.

Thus, the primary intention of the tale proclaims not only that Moses as hero identified with his people, but also that all new Mosaic leaders, including the scion of David, should identify with their people. A new David must also be a new Moses. And only in the combination can the full image of the messiah emerge.[2]

In the larger structure of the Moses saga, this tale functions as a

---

1. Is this process not the pattern for the Deuteronomistic history? The point is particularly clear in the Dtr section on Josiah.
2. Coats, 'Metanoia'.

transition: from Egypt to Midian. And in that transition, the stage is set for the tradition about the event at the burning bush. But for the larger saga, the tale is not simply a transition. It sets the tone for the entire scope of the Moses tradition: Moses is the hero who gives his life, his work for the sake of his oppressed people.

7. *The Pericope in the Context of the Canon*

It is important to note that this tale, and indeed, the entire scope of the Moses saga, addresses not only the community of faith with its leaders from the past, but also the community of the faithful with its leaders in each succeeding generation. This image of the heroic leader helps the first century evangelists understand who Jesus was. Jesus, the new Moses as well as the new David, was hero for his people because he identified with them in their suffering, their sin, their death. The leader in the church of the twentieth century can understand ministerial leadership modeled on the pattern of the heroic Moses. The minister of the church does not stand over the parish as if by heroic status he or she were above the congregation. The minister does not stand above the moral codes of the faith. The minister does not look down a self-righteous nose at the congregation of sinners beneath the high pulpit. Rather, the minister models ministry according to the pattern of the heroic Moses. As shepherd, the minister identifies with the sheep, knows their needs (so, Ezek. 34). The Mosaic model provides a heuristic tool for interpreting modern ministry.[1]

---

1. The process is reflected in the midrashic pattern of interpretation described by J.A. Sanders, *Canon and Community: A Guide to Canonical Criticism* (Guides to Biblical Scholarship; Philadelphia: Fortress Press, 1984).

Chapter 10

THE FAILURE OF THE HERO:
MOSES AS A MODEL FOR MINISTRY

Modern culture requires that heroes who set their mark for members of the society to imitate must be successful. The corporation executive who maintains a position in the modern world of business can continue in that position only if the position basks in the rich light of success. The modern coach, whether responsible for the work of junior high squads or the leader of a National Football League team, remains a modern coach only if the won-lost record breaks in the coach's favor. The minister of a modern congregation marks the character of ministry by the number of additions to the congregation's membership. In the world of success, the failure can find no room at the inn. The person who fails finds no continuation from the board of executives who tolerates only signs of success. The person who fails finds no disciples who imitate the failure's particular pattern of work.

Yet, failure is a realistic factor of modern life. Businesses in today's world will occasionally close because of bankruptcy. Ministers in today's churches will occasionally face a move because of poor support. Marriages will occasionally end in divorce. Students will occasionally drop out of school. Some students even flunk out of school. Nations struggle to find excuses for policies gone awry. Even presidents struggle to cover procedures that have obviously failed.

In the literature of the ancient world, the hero carries the banner for success in leading the people who respond to heroic leadership. The hero successfully defends the people against enemies who would reduce the people to slavery, against hunger or thirst that would drive the people to the edge of death, and against confusion that would capture the people in aimless wandering through endless wilderness. If the hero were unable to lead the people to the end of the wilderness, if the hero failed to defend the people against the dangers of life in the wilderness, then the hero would hardly be heroic.

Yet, failure is a realistic factor in the life of leaders for the modern world. In the face of failure, a typical procedure for a leader is to direct blame for the failure to some other person or even to claim no knowledge or responsibility for the event of failure at all. Some other official must have been responsible for the failure. 'The woman whom you gave to be with me, she gave me the fruit of the tree, and I ate'. Will a leader accept responsibility for a military failure like the Bay of Pigs? Or will a leader deny any responsibility for the sale of arms to one faction seeking to overthrow another faction when once that sale becomes public knowledge?

Moses appears in the OT narrative as a hero who commits his life to the task of leading the Israelites out of the oppressive bondage in Egypt.[1] The narrative captures the dynamic task assumed by Moses as a task so overwhelming that from the beginning Moses must struggle with its gigantic portions. 'Who am I that I should go to Pharaoh, and bring the sons of Israel out of Egypt?' God responds to this self-abasement from Moses by promising Moses that the divine presence would accompany him in the process of executing the commission.[2] Moses apparently feels the enormous proportions of the task as a seal for failure, given the understanding of himself that controls the response. The promise for presence in executing that kind of ministry must certainly be a promise for success. And indeed, the presentation of plans for this ministry to the people brings an initial mark of success. 'And the people believed: and when they heard that the Lord had visited the people of Israel and that he had seen their affliction, they bowed their heads and worshipped'.

Exodus 5 is, however, an account of heroic failure. Opening with a single transition word, $w^e ahar$, a word that ties the chapter to the preceding narrative, this brief tale reports the execution of the divine commission that sent Moses and Aaron to the Pharaoh. 'Afterwards Moses and Aaron went to Pharaoh and said, "Thus says the Lord, the God of Israel, 'Let my people go, that they may hold a feast to me in the wilderness.'"' According to the pattern of success, particularly success in presenting God's word for people to obey, the Pharaoh

---

1. G.W. Coats, *Moses: Heroic Man and Man of God* (JSOTSup, 19; Sheffield: JSOT Press, 1987). A principal goal for the monograph is to show that the Moses narrative should be understood as heroic saga.

2. Coats, 'Self-Abasement and Insult Formulas', *JBL* 89 (1970), pp. 14-26.

should have acquiesced immediately to God's demand. Or at least the Pharaoh should have opened negotiations in order to work out a compromise. But the Pharaoh responds to the demand in a way that creates immediate tension for the plot of the story. 'Who is the Lord, that I should heed his voice and let Israel go? I do not know the Lord, and moreover, I will not let Israel go'. Moses and Aaron continue the negotiations by offering a compromise. 'The God of the Hebrews has met with us: let us go, we pray, a three days' journey into the wilderness, and sacrifice to the Lord our God, lest he fall upon us with pestilence or with the sword'. The compromise offer fails, however. Indeed, the Pharaoh not only refuses the request of Moses and Aaron that the people be allowed to go into the wilderness for a short period in order to sacrifice to their God, but he also increases their burdens of work. In vv. 7-9, the text notes the Pharaoh's commands for the task masters and foremen,

> You shall no longer give the people straw to make bricks, as heretofore: let them go and gather straw for themselves. But the number of bricks which they made heretofore you shall lay upon them, you shall by no means lessen it...Let heavier work be laid upon the men that they may labor at it and pay no regard to lying words.

The Pharaoh strongly rejects the efforts of Moses and Aaron to achieve release of the people by negotiations. Indeed, the text paints a picture of the Pharaoh as a man of power who believes that Moses and Aaron are lying to him. He knows that if he permits the Israelites to go a three-day journey into the wilderness to sacrifice to their God they will not come back. They will continue their march away from Egypt. And, in fact, he is right in his impression. The appeal to the Pharaoh for permission to go into the wilderness a journey of only three days is clearly an excuse to get out of Egypt. Indeed, even if they do in fact hold a feast to the Lord at some point in the journey, it is clear for the storyteller that they would have no intention for coming back. They would continue their journey. The Pharaoh is thus right in his suspicions that the appeal to God's demand for a festival in the wilderness is an excuse to escape the power of the Pharaoh. The plot depends on deception.

But even worse, the Pharaoh responds to the negotiation with an insult to the Lord. In v. 2, 'Who is the Lord, that I should heed his voice and let Israel go?¹ I do not know the Lord, and moreover, I will not let Israel go'. The question implies that the Lord, the subject of the question, does not demand enough authority to meet the goal of the negotiations to let Israel go. Thus, with an insult to God, the Pharaoh rejects the petition of Moses and Aaron.

Verses 10-14 demonstrate the intensification of the Egyptian oppression against the Israelite people. In v. 14, 'the foremen of the people of Israel [who were Israelites themselves] who Pharaoh's taskmasters had set over them, were beaten...' The effort to carry out the commission of God for securing the release of the people thus ended in failure. Indeed, it ended with increased oppression against the Israelites. In this case, failure facilitates even greater tension.

The plot of the tale continues its progression by intensifying the crisis even beyond the mark of heavier oppression. Verses 15-19 depict the efforts of the Israelite foremen to secure some softening of the labor. 'Why do you deal thus with your servants? No straw is given to your servants, yet they say to us, "Make bricks"! And behold, your servants are beaten: but the fault is in your own people'. But the Egyptians reject the appeal with a stubborn repetition of the demand to meet the quota of bricks, 'You shall by no means lessen your daily number of bricks'. The negotiations end not only in failure to achieve the goal of freedom from oppression, but also an increase in the oppression.

The failure scene comes to a pitched focus in v. 20. The storyteller describes the anticipated confrontation between the Israelite foremen and Moses/Aaron. Their immediate attack is an appeal for judgment against Moses and Aaron. 'The Lord look upon you and judge...' The effort by Moses and Aaron to resolve the oppression of the people ends in a lawsuit by the people against Moses and Aaron.² No more forceful sign of failure could appear. The very people the heroes intend to lead to freedom turn on them and reject them with a lawsuit.

Moses and Aaron have now made an initial effort to win the release of the people. And that effort ends in failure. But the irony in the failure is that the lawsuit depicts the efforts of Moses and Aaron to save the people from their bondage as an attempt to kill them. 'Because you have made us offensive in the sight of Pharaoh and his

1. So, Coats, 'Self-Abasement and Insult Formulas'.
2. H.J. Boecker, *Redeformen des Rechtslebens im Alten Testament* (WMANT, 14; Neukirchen–Vluyn: Neukirchener Verlag, 1964), pp. 25-34.

servants, and have put a sword in their hand to kill us'. The people see the move to save them from oppression as a move to kill them. The image of failure in the scene is not simply a rejection of the hero. It is a rejection of the hero's principal work, the heart of Moses' identity as the hero of the people.

The irony in this tragic rejection develops another level of tension. With the rejection by the people heavy on the shoulders of Moses and Aaron, with the failure of the negotiations to win the freedom of the people still sharp in the pericope, Moses turns the rejection on God. In v. 22, 'Then Moses turned again to the Lord and said, "O Lord, why hast thou done evil to this people? Why didst thou ever send me?"' Again, the question is in the form of an accusation. Formally, it calls for some kind of response from the addressee. Moreover, Moses states the case for the accusation, 'since I came to speak to Pharaoh to speak in thy name, he has done evil to this people, and thou hast not delivered thy people at all'. The hero recognizes his own failure in delivering the people. The foremen of the people make the point clear. But now Moses makes a similar accusation against God. In Moses' eyes, God has also failed. Thus, the issue for the pericope arises from the pressure of failure. Moses, the hero, failed to win the freedom of his people by negotiations with the Pharaoh. And that failure Moses places under God's responsibility. When Moses fails, for Moses that means that God, the God who commissioned Moses for the task, also fails. Now what will God do? And as a part of that issue, what will Moses do?

The pericope in Exodus 5 is not structurally a part of the cycle of scenes in the long narrative about Moses' repeated negotiations with the Pharaoh in tireless efforts to win the release of the people. In fact, the tale in Exodus 5 contains the narrative tradition in its most primitive form, a form that provides the traditio-historical roots for the larger negotiations narrative. In Exodus 7–12, an expanded narrative elaborates the kernel of tradition in Exodus 5. Indeed, the end of the negotiations as a narrative motif, Exod. 10.29 puts the issue of tension in the narrative at the very point left hanging in Exodus 5. The complicated process of negotiations between Moses and the Pharaoh ends in failure for Moses. And that failure implies failure for God. In the face of that failure, what will Moses do next? In face of failure, what will God do next?

The cycle of scenes about Moses' repeated negotiations with the

Pharaoh develops in a specialized form. The storyteller constructs the cycle as a palistrophe, a pattern that sets the first scene as a structural parallel with the tenth scene, but not with any other scene. In the same way, the second scene parallels the ninth scene. The third scene follows the pattern with the eighth scene. The fourth scene parallels the seventh, and the fifth parallels the sixth. In the palistrophe, the Passover has no place. It is not a part of the tight structure in the story and thus not an original account of the climax for the narrative. Rather, the narrative in the palistrophe comes to an end in Exod. 10.28-29. 'Then the Pharaoh said to him, "Get away from me. Take heed to yourself. Never see my face again. For in the day you see my face, you shall die." Moses said, "As you say! I will not see your face again".' With that exchange, the negotiations between Moses and the Pharaoh end.[1] But the Pharaoh has not agreed to release the people. At this point, the negotiations process stands clearly as a failure. And the failure characterizes not only Moses but also God.

At least one exegetical problem arises just at this point. The storyteller notes, just before reporting that the Pharaoh dismissed Moses with a death sentence as the penalty for continuing the negotiations, that the Lord hardened Pharaoh's heart, and he would not let them go. With that comment, the storyteller announces that the repeated failure in the negotiations process was the result of God's design for the event. With this element in hand, the exegete can conclude that Moses and God did not fail after all. It was all a part of God's design. When one asks about the tradition history of the negotiations narrative, the problem with the pattern sharpens. In some sense, the motif is a narrative technique designed to enable the storyteller to move from one scene in the sequence to the next. And, indeed, the movement sets up the Passover scene. If the initial audience between Moses/Aaron and the Pharaoh had ended in success, the narrator would have lost the story—there would be no reason for the Passover scene. The hardened heart motif allows the narrative to move from one stage to the next, with the Passover at the end. But the process also depicts the narrator's view of Moses' reaction, indeed, God's reaction to the spectre of failure. When the failure occurs, the hero goes back to the drawing board and creates a new plan. And then he tries again. Indeed, the hero receives a new plan from the hand of

---

1. D.J. McCarthy, 'Moses' Dealings with Pharaoh', *CBQ* 27 (1965), pp. 336-47.

God. When God's plan for saving the people fails, then God tries a new plan. The hero demonstrates the tenacity of God to pursue the plan of salvation despite repeated failures in the plan.

The point can be pursued a step farther for this tradition. Exodus 5 shows the traditio-historical basis for the narrative as a tradition about failure. The negotiations cycle ends in Exodus 10 with failure. Where does a resolution for this narrative tension appear? In every respect, the Passover event marks the climax of the tension in the narrative as it now stands. God resolves the issues of failure in the process by creating something new. In a dramatic strike against all of the Egyptians from the poorest to the Pharaoh himself, God kills the first-born of every Egyptian family. But by proper preparation of the ritual, the Israelites protect their first-born from the plague that puts Egyptians in their place. It is a scene of rank violence. But the violent attack forces the Egyptians to submit to the demands of the Israelite hero. They free the Israelites from their dehumanizing slavery. Indeed, they drive them away. Finally, in one fatal blow, the Israelite and the God he serves win success in delivering the people from their slavery. The issue of the violent means remains a problem at tangent with the design of this paper. The principal point here is that failure did not thwart the work of the hero.

The traditio-historical complexity in the cycle adds to this picture of response to failure. A part of the tradition brings the cycle of negotiations between Moses and the Pharaoh to a conclusion without success in convincing the Pharaoh to release the slaves. The roots of that tradition shape the narrative in Exodus 5. The narrative moves beyond the failure in order to depict Moses' return to the people, prepared to develop a new and quite different plan. In Exod. 12.35, the narrative notes that 'The people of Israel had also done as Moses told them, for they had asked of the Egyptians jewelry of silver and of gold, and clothing...' The point of this motif emerges with a different description of the exodus event itself, a description unrelated to the Passover, 'the Lord had given the people favor in the sight of the Egyptians, so that they let them have what they asked. Thus they despoiled the Egyptians'. The same motif appears in Exod. 3.21-22 and 11.2-3 (cf. also Ps. 105.37). This depiction of the exodus assumes that all of the efforts of the heroes and even the efforts of God end in failure. In the face of the failure, this tradition shows Moses preparing a new plan. He will lead the people out of Egypt in a secret escape, without the permission of the Pharaoh.[1] To escape in the middle of the night would require preparation for movement at a moment's notice, 'your loins girded, your sandals on your feet, and your staff in your hand; and you shall eat it in haste' (Exod 12.10). Indeed, the picture of the people with dough for the bread on their backs, before it had time to rise in response to leaven, sets the pattern for a Feast of Unleavened Bread (12.34). That this event might have been originally distinct from the Passover seems clear.[2] Yet, in both cases, the narrative describes procedures of the hero in the face of failure. When the first plan fails, then the hero tries again. Whether the try appears as the Passover event or as the event celebrated during an originally distinct Festival of Unleavened Bread, still the tradition depicts the hero as the servant of God who does not give up in the face of failure. Rather, when one who does not succeed with an initial plan responds to the failure in the manner of the hero Moses, that one develops a new plan and tries again.[3]

This pattern of failure and renewed effort to gain success by approaching the issue from a new direction marks the entire history of God's efforts to save the people. In the wilderness, Moses fails again. The people murmur against Moses and God. They rebel against Moses' leadership and threaten to execute him. At the mountain, God establishes a covenant with the people through the hand of Moses. But the people fall from the covenant in a rank act of apostasy with the Golden Calf. Joshua leads the people across the Jordan into the land of the promise. The ark of the covenant symbolizes God's presence in this Holy Land at the event of a covenant renewal at Shechem (so, Jos. 24.12). But the people fall from that covenant again and again. The

1. Coats, 'Despoiling the Egyptians', *VT* 18 (1968), pp. 450-57.
2. R. de Vaux, *Ancient Israel: Its Life and Institutions* (trans. J. McHugh; New York: McGraw-Hill: 1961), pp. 484-89.
3. As a model for ministry, the Moses figure functions for the modern church in much the same way that it functioned for the Deuteronomistic historian in a critique of the kingship. Modern ministers might profit by developing Mosaic characteristics as marks of their ministry. One mark would be the pattern of response to failure. In the face of failure, the temptation is strong to give up. But the challenge of the model calls the minister confronted by failure back to the drawing board. The admonition is clear: 'Get up! Dust yourself off, and start all over again'. But the model goes a step farther. In the discouraging and often very lonely setting that emerges in the wake of failure, how can the minister find enough courage to try again? 'Fear not! I am with you'.

tragedy at Baal Peor is only a prime example of repeated failures. Moses, Joshua, the judges of the tribal confederation, Samuel, all experience leadership for the people of God under a constant threat of failure. And each searches for new ways to meet the challenge of leadership.

A radical new plan to meet the failure in salvation history emerges with the rise of the kingship. David would be God's special envoy. From the perspective of tradition in Jerusalem, David would be the Son of God, the heir of Melchizedek. And with David and his dynasty in Jerusalem, God would rule the world with justice and righteousness. Yet, even here the ideal world of peace as the place for God's salvation for all people under the authority of a Davidic king, such as the messiah described in Isa. 11.1-9, seems to fail. David corrupts the rule of God in Jerusalem with Bathsheba and a rank failure to show compassion in his dealings with her husband, Uriah.[1] Solomon demonstrates wisdom in administration of the kingdom. But at his death, his son Rehoboam shows no wisdom. And his failure leads to the division of God's people between the north and the south. The Deuteronomistic historian looks for a king in the line of David that would correct the failure in the ranks of the Davidic dynasty. Indeed the model for that successful king would be a Davidic heir who would match the model of leadership for Israel provided by Moses.[2] Josiah almost completes the job. His move to unite the north and the south under the aegis of a Deuteronomic reform opened the door for a pattern in his own leadership that stands out for its Mosaic qualities, its new law and new covenant. But Josiah failed through no fault of his own. On top of a lonely mountain, he met an untimely death, and the dream of success, so close to realization, ended in failure effected by an Egyptian King. The New Moses, the Davidic King Josiah died in the midst of apparent success. How could God avoid another tragic failure? In the face of so many failures, it is remarkable that God has continued in a constant pursuit for salvation of the world's human creatures.

Another new Moses, another Davidic messiah, brought hope for God's salvation for all the world. Under the reign of Jesus of Nazareth, God's kingdom of peace comes in a new form to the world.

1. Coats, 'II Samuel 12: 1-7a', pp. 170-75.
2. G.E. Gerbrandt, *Kingship According to the Deuteronomistic Historian* (SBLDS, 87; Atlanta: Scholars Press, 1986).

Yet, even here apparent failure dominates the scene. Where is this new kingdom, a kingdom that will mark God's rule of peace for the world? 'My kingship is not of this world'. Is that not a false promise? What other world is there for experiencing the success in God's redemption, in God's rule of peace? But the marks of a kingdom uncontrolled by a political king do emerge. Political kings sell arms to two sides in a war, just to see how much destruction money can buy. The king in the Kingdom of God does other things. 'The blind receive their sight and the lame walk, lepers are cleansed and the deaf hear, and the dead are raised up, and the poor have good news preached to them'. Each year, the Christmas celebration marks the hope for God's success in delivering the people of the world from their petty wars. But the apparent success meets the same tragic failure that met Josiah. On a lonely hill, the New David, the New Moses met the callous lack of compassion that belongs to a world of hostile people. They killed him, just as the Egyptians killed Josiah, just as the people threatened to do with Moses. Thus, God's plan ended again in failure. The hope offered by Christmas ends in the despair of Dark Friday. What will God do now in the face of still another failure?

'Now, after the Sabbath, toward the dawn of the first day of the week, Mary Magdalene and the other Mary went to see the sepulchre.'

Chapter 11

THE GOLDEN CALF IN PSALM 22

The narrative in Exodus 32 describes the tragic event in Israel's wilderness experience marked by construction of the Golden Calf. According to the tale in these verses, Moses had left the people, apparently in the care of Aaron, in order to climb the mountain for an audience with God. The problem posed by the narrative, the plot at the foundation of the tale, emerges with clarity in the first verses of the unit. Now anxious because Moses tarried so long on the mountain, the people address Aaron with instructions designed to resolve the source of their anxiety. 'Up! Make us gods who shall go before us. As for this Moses, the man who brought us up out of the land of Egypt, we do not know what has become of him'. In the face of their anxiety, the people call for Aaron to construct gods who could continue the leadership for the people in their journey through the wilderness.[1]

The present form of the text interprets this speech as rank heresy. Not only do the people request construction of an object that would serve as leader of the exodus and wilderness journey, an object defined as gods and thus an idol that violates the second commandment, but they also identify the object as 'gods' and thus violate the first commandment. Indeed, the noun is plural, constructed with a plural verb. The first commandment prohibits service of other gods, a

---

1. J.W. Davenport, *A Study of the Golden Calf Tradition in Exodus* 32 (PhD dissertation, Princeton Theological Seminary, 1973), pp. 93-97. Davenport suggests that the collocation in Exod. 32.1, *zeh mōšeh*, is a divine epithet. So, p. 63. Since Aaron took the initiative in creating the calf, it might follow that the calf belongs to Aaron. So, Moses Aberbach and Leivy Smolar. 'Aaron, Jeroboam, and the Golden Calves', *JBL* 86 (1967), p. 135. But contrast M. Noth, *A History of Pentateuchal Traditions* (trans. B.W. Anderson; Englewood Cliffs: Prentice-Hall, 1972), p. 244. Noth argues that the calves functioned as a symbol of leadership for Jeroboam 1. But in the Pentateuch, the calf reflects the leadership of Moses. So, J.M. Sasson, 'Bovine Symbolism in the Exodus Narrartive', *VT* 18 (1968), pp. 384-87.

noun also clearly defined as plural by the plural adjective that follows it. From the point of view of the storyteller, the event highlights the tragic apostasy of the people that violates the critical first two items in the Mosaic decalogue.

Yet, it is important to note that the call for construction of gods to effect the leadership of the people in the wilderness journey is not a call for replacement of the Lord as the God of the event. To be sure, the people ask for gods. But the gods defined by the people would replace Moses, not the Lord. 'Up! Make us gods who shall go before us. As for this Moses, the man who brought us up out of the land of Egypt, we do not know what has become of him' (Exod. 32.1). The tradition carried by the narrative rests on an assumption that the 'gods' to be constructed stand in very close association with Moses. Is it possible that behind the present polemic in the narrative lies a tradition that accepted a positive role for the golden calf in Israel's cult? Is it possible that positive tradition recognized a close association between the golden calf requested here and Moses? Was the object at one time, perhaps before its interpretation as an object of apostasy that would replace the absent Moses, a symbol of Moses' leadership? Perhaps the allusion to Moses in this verse, *zeh mōšeh hā'îš*, hides a reference to the God of Moses: 'This one of the man Moses who brought us up out of the land of Egypt...'

Moses responds to God's announcement that the people have become apostate with the golden calf by interceding for the people and in fact securing their pardon, at least for the moment.[1] God's intention was to destroy the apostates and begin anew with Moses. But Moses announces his unity with the worshippers of the golden calf and wins a stay of execution. Then Moses and Joshua descend the mountain in order to confront the people involved with the new object that serves as leader for the people in the wilderness journey. In the descent, Joshua responds to the noise from the camp with an apparent foreboding announcement. 'There is a noise of war in the camp'. The noise, in Hebrew, *qôl*, of the people is identified as the 'voice' of war, the *qôl milḥāmâ*. But the play on the voice as the term for the noise coming from the foot of the mountain only highlights Moses' response

---

1. On the intercession element in the tradition, see G.W. Coats, 'The King's Loyal Opposition: Obedience and Authority in Exodus 32–34', in G.W. Coats and B.O. Long (eds.), *Canon and Authority: Essays in Old Testament Religion and Theology* (Philadelphia: Fortress Press, 1977), pp. 91-109. See ch. 5 above.

to the event. 'It is not the voice (*qôl*) of shouting for victory. It is not the voice (*qôl*) of shouting for defeat. It is the voice (*qôl*) of shouting that I hear'.

This strange exchange, a picturesque definition of the noise from the camp that leaves the final stage unqualified in its effort to color the sound from the camp, fits into the picture of rank apostasy in the celebration with the golden calf. The following verses observe that when Moses arrived at the camp, his own anger burned, and in that rage he broke the tablets of the covenant, thus breaking the covenant itself.[1] The people of Moses, so newly members of a covenant relationship with God, now lose their covenantal status.

Yet, the problem posed by Moses' response to the voice from the camp remains. Moses hears a voice. It is not the voice of victory. It is not the voice of defeat. It is simply the voice. An effective parallel for this construction appears in the Elijah saga (1 Kgs 19.8-12). Following the great victory over the prophets of Baal, Elijah climbs the mountain at Horeb and stands alone, ready for God to act. In this text, Elijah witnesses a strong wind, an earthquake, and a fire, all natural symbols associated with the presence of God. But for the Elijah text, God's presence does not appear for Elijah in any of the normal forms that demonstrate the presence of God, just as in the Moses story, the voice of victory and the voice of defeat both fail to define the character of the theophany. The alternative for Elijah, the source that effects God's presence for Elijah, is the voice. The voice is defined explicitly as a still, small voice: *qôl d^emāmâ daqqâ*. But the point is that the critical event involves simply the voice. The connection between the voice that dramatizes God's presence to Elijah and the voice that dramatizes God's presence to Moses, both at Horeb/Sinai, suggests that Elijah must be seen in line with Moses, a new Moses. But it also suggests that the event described by the shouting voice in the Moses tale can have a positive tone. And in that positive tone, would the voice not fit the implied positive tradition represented by the calf that must have functioned originally as a Moses symbol?

Another element emerges from this tradition that calls for some caution at this point, however. The 'voice' in the refrain from the Moses story precedes an apparent infinitive construct from the verb

---

1. On the function of the act as a symbol for breaking the covenant, see B.S. Childs, *The Book of Exodus: A Critical, Theological Commentary* (OTL; Philadelphia: Westminster Press, 1974), p. 569.

'*ānâ*, 'to answer'. The third element in the refrain doubles the *nun* in the infinitive construct. With the break in pattern sharply obvious, would some other explanation of the word be appropriate? Davenport suggests, for example, that the voice may be understood not simply as an answering voice, but as the voice of Anat.[1] If that hypothesis should prove to be sound, the character of the tradition as polemic would reveal even sharper polemic traits.

The hypothesis that the calf was originally a positive symbol gains strength, on the other hand, in the light of Aaron's response to Moses' inquiry about the nature of the celebration. In v. 21, Moses confronts Aaron: 'What did this people do to you that you have brought a great sin upon them?' Clearly the polemic functions here since Moses labels the act with the golden calf as a great sin. And in light of the accusation, Aaron responds with a statement that appears to be lame and foolish in its fabrication. 'Let not the anger of my lord burn hot. You know the people, that they are set on evil. For they said to me: "Make us gods who shall go before us."' But Aaron's explanation continues: 'As for this Moses, the man who brought us up out of the land of Egypt, we do not know what has become of him'. And I said to them: "Let any who have gold take it off". So they gave it to me, and I threw it into the fire, and this calf came out'.

Yet, in the light of the hypothesis that a positive tradition once lay at the basis of this now negative story, can we not hypothesize that the lame explanation hides a serious cultic aetiology that accounted for the origin of the calf?[2] The calf came out of the fire as an act of God who must have been enthroned on the back of the animal. From the Canaanite world, the picture of the deity standing atop the bull in a position for war would document the accuracy of the image.

Many commentaries observe the connection between the golden calf in Exodus 32 and the golden calves of Jeroboam I, established at the northern sanctuaries at Dan and Bethel.[3] 1 Kgs 12.25-33 sets the event at Dan and Bethel at the center of the polemic against the event in the

---

1. So, Davenport, *Golden Calf Tradition*, p. 158. See also F.I. Andersen, 'A Lexicographical Note on Exodus xxxii 18', *VT* 16 (1966), pp. 108-12. R. Edelmann, 'To *'annôt* Exodus xxxii 18', *VT* 16 (1966), p. 355. R.N. Whybray, *'annôt* in Exodus xxxii 18', *VT* 17 (1967), p. 122.

2. So, Davenport, *Golden Calf Tradition*, pp. 190-91. See also pp. 26-31.

3. So, Noth, *Exodus, A Commentary* (trans. J.S. Bowden; OTL; Philadelphia: Westminster Press, 1962), p. 246. See also Aberbach and Smolar.

Deuteronomistic History. In the scholarly discussion, the suggestion that the negative cast for the tale in Exodus 32 reflects a polemic against the bull cult of Jeroboam is not new.[1] Indeed, the suggestion that the original form of the tradition in Exodus 32 was positive is not new.[2] One can hypothesize that originally the calves in Dan and Bethel, the calf in Exodus 32, functioned as symbols for the throne of God who sat invisible above them, just as the cherubim functioned for the Lord in the Jerusalem temple. But the weakness in the hypothesis lies in the fact that positive evidence to support the hypothesis plays little role in the discussion.

The principal goal for this paper, then, is to develop an argument as support for the position that interprets the calves as positive symbols. The first texts for consideration under that rubric are Num. 23.22 and 24.8. 'God brings them out from Egypt. He has the horns of a wild ox'. The initial question for exploring these texts focuses on the 'horns of the wild ox'. What does it mean for God to be described as a deity that has the horns of a wild ox? The RSV confuses the picture of this text by translating the line in a plural. 'They have as it were the horns of the wild ox' (so, LXX). But the Hebrew line is simple. 'The horns of a wild ox are his'. But what precisely does that mean?

1. Regardless of the interpretation of the horns of the wild ox, it is clear that the text sets the provocative image of God with the horns of a wild ox in the context of the exodus. Apparently, the affirmation that God has the horns of a wild ox has something to do with the execution of the exodus event.

2. The noun, 'wild ox', in Hebrew, $r^e\,'\bar{e}m$, is rare in the Old Testament. But it apparently has the connotations of a bovine animal. One might then ask where in the tradition a bovine animal has anything to do with the exodus. I suggest that the noun denotes the creature that served as the symbol of Moses in the exodus.[3] Yet, one must observe, the noun for the creature in the Exodus 32 text is not $r^e\,'\bar{e}m$. It is '$\bar{e}gel$. I suggest that the designation of the creature in Exodus 32 as 'golden calf', as '$\bar{e}gel$, reflects the polemic against the symbol, a term that carries negative connotations of symbols and idols from the

---

1. Davenport, *Golden Calf Tradition*, p. 121.
2. Davenport, *Golden Calf Tradition*, pp. 50-83.
3. Davenport, *Golden Calf Tradition*, p. 133 n. 181. He notes simply that this collocation may be 'another expression of Yahweh as a bull who delivers his people from their enemies...'

Canaanite enemies.[1] The identification of the same creature in Num. 23.22 as r^e'$ēm$ reflects the positive side of the tradition. The r^e'$ēm$ was the creature, the symbol of Moses, that effected the exodus. And that event is memorialized by the allusion to the exodus effected by the r^e'$ēm$ in the Balaam oracles. The term also appears in Deut. 33.17. In that text, it functions more generally but appears to be connected with the northern tribes (cf. also Ps. 92.11). The polemic against the golden calf was strong. It dominates most of the received text, that canonical form of the OT now at the center of theological discussion. Yet, something of the original positive nature of that tradition shines through the poetry of the Balaam oracles, untouched by the polemic. Is it not typical for such polemic to change intentionally the traditions of the opposing community from positive to negative forms? And if some sign of the positive form of the tradition is preserved in the received text, that canonical text that reflects a heavy domination by the negative polemic, must the interests of canonical theology not explore the nature of that positive evidence?

Additional evidence for the positive form of the golden calf tradition and, indeed, additional evidence for a hermeneutic of change in the tradition as a tool for the polemic against the golden calf appears in another occurence of the noun r^e'$ēm$ in Ps. 22.22 (English 22.21). Psalm 22 is a lament psalm that follows the typical structure for the lament in precise order. The invocation for the psalm in v. 2 introduces the lament question. 'My God! My God! Why have you forsaken me?' Verses 4-5 mark a typical shift in the structure of the lament. The worshipper reminds God of the relationship established by the fathers with the God who could be trusted. In v. 6: 'They cried out to you and were saved. They trusted in you and were not disappointed'.

Again in typical fashion for the lament, v. 7 shifts to a self-description for the psalmist, a description that catches miserable suffering. 'I am a worm and not a man, scorned by men and despised by the people.' Variations on these elements continue through v. 11. Verse 12 then introduces a new structural element, a petition. 'Be not far from me, because trouble is near, and there is no helper.' Then vv. 13-20a return to a description of the plight of that motivates the lament. Verses 20b-22a repeat the petition. 'But you, O Lord, be not far off! You, my help, hasten to my aid. Deliver my life from the

---

1. But see Davenport, *Golden Calf Tradition*, pp. 68-70.

sword, my only one from the power of the dog. Save me from the mouth of the lion.' Verse 23 carries the typical affirmation of faith that concludes the lament'.[1] The shift from lament to affirmation is marked formally by a shift from direct address to God to the direct address to the congregation. 'I will tell your name to my brethren in the midst of the congregation. I will praise you. You who fear the Lord, praise him.'

The issue in defining the structure of the poem lies in the formal position for v. 22b.[2] The LXX sets this verse as a part of the petition. That interpretation requires identification of the word, ^{a}*nîtaî*, at the end of v. 22 as a noun. But it is clearly a verb. The RSV follows the LXX by translating: 'Save me from the mouth of the lion, my afflicted soul from the horns of the wild oxen'. If, however, the MT should be preserved as the proper reading of the text and the key word maintained as a verb, the translation would read: 'Save me from the mouth of the lion. You have answered me from the horns of the wild ox (r^e*'ēm*).' The shift from petition to affirmation would thus occur between v. 22a and v. 22b. Moreover, the word 'wild ox' is the same word that appear in the Balaam oracle as the term for the golden calf, r^e*'ēm*. The hypothesis is that the golden calf functions as the throne of God. This text would then describe God enthroned on the horns of the Golden Calf. When the lament addresses its petition to the God enthroned on the Golden Calf, then God speaks from the horns of the golden calf, the symbol of the throne, indeed, the symbol of the place of power for the one enthroned there. And that speech answers the petition of the psalmist. The horns of the Golden Calf symbolize the seat of God who answers petitions with power, just as the wings of the

---

1. J. Begrich, 'Das priesterliche Heilsorakel', *BZAW* 66 (1936), pp. 63-88. He suggests that the shift in the structure of the *Klagelied* from the words describing the plight of the psalmist to the words of praise reflects the intervention of a 'priestly oracle of salvation'.

2. A. Weiser, *The Psalms, A Commentary* (trans. H. Hartwell; OTL; Philadelphia: Westminster Press, 1962), p. 224. H.J. Kraus, *Psalmen 1* (BKAT, 15; Neukirchen–Vluyn: Neukirchener Verlag, 1961), p. 182. Kraus takes the key verse in the positive element of the psalm as an affirmation: 'Du hast mich erhört!' M. Dahood, *Psalms 1* (AB 16; New York: Doubleday, 1965), p. 142. He takes the key word as an element that balances the imperative at the beginning of the verse and thus as a part of the petition. The word would be parsed as precative perfect from *'ānāh*, 'to conquer, triumph'. It would be translated thus: 'Over the horns of the wild oxen make me triumph'.

cherubim in the Jerusalem temple symbolize the seat of Yahweh's power.[1] Indeed, the importance of the act as an answer to the petition of the worshipper picks up the verb *'anôt* from Exod. 32.18. The verb would then maintain an original positive connotation rather than a negative allusion to *'Anat*.

It is important to note just here that the Balaam texts and the Psalm text complement each other in defining the nature of the affirmation about the bull as a symbol of God's presence and power. The God enthroned on the bull, the one who was involved in the exodus, acts to save the oppressed from Egyptian oppression. The God who speaks from the horns of the bull in Psalm 22 responds to the petition of the lamentation. And that petition reflects oppression from a 'company of evildoers' that bring the psalmist to the point of death. The God of Moses is a God who responds to the plight of the oppressed.

The polemic that changes the golden calf to an idol, the cult at Dan and Bethel to apostate centers, must have some connection with the polemic against Jeroboam I. Would it not be possible to see the lines of that polemic reflected at other points in Israel's life? Perhaps the struggle between the Davidic kingship and the various kings in the north, symbolized in their decision to separate from Jerusalem and its Davidic king by Jeroboam I, accounts for the interpretation that changes the r^e'*ēm* to *'ēgel*, made especially for the 'golden calf' in Dan and Bethel. The competition between the two communities of faith sharpens precisely over the golden calf. And the southern bias of the Yahwist leaves the golden calf as an idol, the symbol of northern apostasy, northern rejection of Jerusalem and its symbols of power.

The question then arises: under what circumstances can the division represented by that polemic ever be healed? The question is sharpened: under what circumstances can the division between the Davidic traditions in Jerusalem and the Moses tradition in Dan and Bethel (Samaria) ever be healed? But there is more. The obvious polemic between the north and the south may account for the tradition of the Golden Calf that connects its function with idolatry. The southern

1. L.R. Bailey, 'The Golden Calf', *HUCA* 42 (1971), pp. 97-115. He argues specifically that no evidence for interpreting the golden calf as pedestal for the enthroned deity appears. So, pp. 98-100. Yet, the description of God responding to the petition of worshippers from the horns of the calf opens evidence for just such an interpretation. The horns of the calf would function as the pedestal, if not the throne for the deity who answers petition.

point of view in the Yahwist might be a good example of that. Yet, Hosea, the northern prophet, indicts the bulls of Gilgal, the calf of Samaria, with sharp rejection of the bull cult. Perhaps the polemic reflected in the received text was already present in the northern cultic traditions before they migrated to the south and fell into the hands of the Judean storytellers. Perhaps the polemic focused the issue of character in the northern cult as a struggle between the people who held the golden calves to be the effective symbol of God's presence in the exodus and the wilderness and the people who held the ark of the covenant to be that effective symbol. Is it not too simple to define the issue singularly as the product of the struggle between the Moses people and the David people? The issue might be clarified at still another level by an exploration of the Joshua/ark traditions in the mix of the early narratives. It is sufficient at this point, however, to note that, especially for the book of Joshua, but also in the earlier traditions of the Pentateuch, the ark functions as a symbol of Joshua's leadership in the conquest.[1] In the temple, the ark rests under the wings of the cherubim. The Joshua symbol has a position in the temple, even though it is dwarfed by the cherubim. But the Golden Calves do not appear there. They have been explicitly rejected. Indeed, Hezekiah removes the other Mosaic symbol by destroying the Nehushtan (2 Kgs 18.4). The polemic between the north and the south, effected by rejecting the symbols of leadership central for each side, comes to explicit focus in the rejection of the calf as an effective form of leadership.

But still the question remains. With such polemic, with overt rejection of central symbols, how could reconciliation between the opposing parties occur? The issue posed by the Golden Calf is not simply the polemic that reduces the calf to an idol. The issue beyond the effective symbols is the prospect of reconciliation. Does any symbol in this mix of competing traditions serve the role of reconciliation? Another Moses symbol serves precisely that role: 'It is too light a thing that you should be my servant to raise up the tribes of Jacob and to restore the preserved of Israel. I will give you as a light to the nations that my salvation may reach to the ends of the earth' (Isa. 49.6).

A principal issue in any dialogue between Christians and Jews must

---

1. G.W. Coats, 'The Ark of the Covenant in Joshua: A Probe into the History of a Tradition', *HAR* (1985), pp. 137-57.

be, so it seems to me, what we do with each other's symbols. In a world where the star of David can become a yellow arm band, in a world where the cross can be converted into a Christian sign of Jewish rejection, symbols can still serve to divide us. Does the Moses tradition not suggest that in the final analysis, those serious battles should be set aside for a common symbol? Moses, the servant of the Lord, becomes Israel, the servant. And from that symbol, Christians inherit a common cause to fulfill a role as servant of the Word of God, so that the light of divine salvation may reach to the ends of the world.

But the servant also has responsibility to Torah. 'He will not fail or be discouraged until he has established justice ($mišpāṭ$) in the earth and the coastlands wait for his law ($l^e tôrātô$). It is easy for some Christians to claim status as a New Testament church and to mean by that a rejection of the OT, specifically the Torah. Yet, the focus on salvation in the Second Isaiah includes the function of the servant to bring Torah. Salvation without justice made plain by God's Torah does not come from God. Another text in the tradition of Moses catches the point:

> I hate, I despise your feasts. I take no delight in your solemn assemblies. Even though you offer me your burnt offerings and cereal offering, I will not accept them. The peace offerings of your fatted beasts I will not look upon. Take away from me the noise of your songs. To the melody of your harps I will not listen. But let justice roll down like waters and righteousness like an ever-flowing stream (Amos 5.21-24).

Whatever we do with each other's symbols, our final push toward a common life as servants of the Lord must involve dedication to the task of establishing justice and righteousness as a light to all the nations of the world.

Chapter 12

HEALING AND THE MOSES TRADITIONS

According to the Yahwist, God created humans for intimacy, for special relationships that would flower in the garden established by God for their support.[1] But the humans broke that intimacy by disobeying God's instructions. And as a consequence, they lost their place in God's garden. The instrument for the tragic event that broke the intimacy in the garden was the serpent. 'The serpent was more subtle (*'ārûm*) than all the creatures of the field which the Lord God had made'. This introduction to the scene (Gen. 3.1) shows that the serpent is not a personification of Satan, a primordial being co-eternal with God. The serpent is one of the creatures from the field, subtle to be sure, but simply a creature. Indeed, the text establishes the creaturely status of the serpent with a subtle word play. The serpent is *'ārûm*. The humans are *'ᵃrûmmîm*. That subtle serpent poses the question that effects the broken intimacy between the man and the woman, and then between the humans and God. 'Did God say, "You shall not eat from any tree of the Garden?"'

In defence of God's instructions, the woman explains to the serpent that only one tree has been forbidden. But the serpent objects: God's instructions hide the truth about the tree. So the woman eats and gives the fruit to the man. And he eats. With that event of rebellion, intimacy disappears. God responds to this act of rebellion by expelling the humans from the garden. The following folk etiologies explain the woman's pain in childbirth, the man's work to earn food for life, and the serpent's form that requires crawling as the consequence of the rebellion. But no reference to the serpent as essentially evil appears.

---

1. For a definition of the term intimacy in the context of the Yahwist's presentation of the primeval saga and the stories about the fathers, see G.W. Coats, *Genesis, with an Introduction to Narrative Literature* (FOTL, 1; Grand Rapids: Eerdmans, 1983), pp. 13-34.

Thus, the principal question about the tradition sharpens: in what manner does later tradition alter the shape of the fate for the man and the woman? And what role does the serpent play in that process? The man must always work to obtain food for his family. The woman must always bear pain in childbirth. The serpent must always crawl in the dust without legs. But can the lost intimacy be restored? And if so, what role does the serpent play in the process?

For the Yahwist, an important step in the journey occurs under the leadership of Moses. The people of Abraham's family had become strangers in a foreign land. And in that foreign land, they had fallen into slavery. Under incredible oppression, even a pogrom matched in cruelty only by the heralds of Herod, the descendants of Abraham cry to God for relief from their slavery. God heard that cry and responded. 'I have seen the affliction of my people who are in Egypt and have heard their cry because of their taskmasters; I know their sufferings, and I have come down to deliver them out of the hand of the Egyptians...' (Exod. 3.7-8). And in the same act, he sent Moses to effect their redemption from slavery: 'Come, I will send you to Pharaoh that you may bring forth my people, the sons of Israel, out of Egypt'. Armed with a validation of his commission expressed in the very name of God, a validation that promised the immediate presence of God to Moses and to the people, Moses addressed his own people, confronted Pharaoh, and then led the people from their oppression into the wilderness.[1]

In the wilderness, the people bind themselves to God in a new act of intimacy. A covenant at Sinai gives the people the means for living in intimacy with God, with nature, and with themselves. But the problems posed by overt acts that break the intimacy also arise. At the sea, the people rebel against Moses and against God. At the mountain, their golden calf brings the covenant to ruin. And only Moses' intercession saves the rebels. Away from the mountain, into the wilderness again, the people continue their rebellion. So the question posed by the narrative is sharp: what will God do now?

Various motifs in the Moses traditions constitute the basis for an answer to this question. The Moses figure functions as a model for the suffering servant of Second Isaiah.[2] And, of course, the suffering

---

1. B.S. Childs, *The Book of Exodus: A Critical, Theological Commentary* (OTL; Philadelphia: Westminster Press, 1974), pp. 178-214.
2. A. Bentzen, *Messias, Moses redivivus, Menschensohn: Skizzen zum Thema*

servant establishes an essential model for the NT's presentation of Jesus. Moses, the intercessor, prefigures the picture of Jesus who intercedes with a petition specifically for the unity of the disciples, a unity established by a messiah who could be both new David and new Moses.[1]

One motif out of the Moses tradition that affects the shape of the suffering servant appears under the rubric of healing. In the Moses tradition, healing events can involve a serpent image. And within the Moses traditions, the sorry saga of broken humanity continues. What will God do now about restoring intimacy for the human community? God destroyed that community once in a flood of cosmic proportions. God scattered them over the face of the earth with no means for communication. But then God moved to bless these human creatures. Abraham could have been the open door for all of the world (so Gen. 12.1-3). But how can God use a broken family to bring blessing to all of the world's people? God gave the people a covenant through Moses. But they rejected it. And as a result, the rebels could not enter the land of promise. But there is another motif, namely, the conviction that God will heal the people. God will heal them at the depth of their lives, their relationships, not lightly as if superficial surgery would solve the problem (so Jer. 6.14; 8.11). Ironically, that healing process in the Moses traditions relates to the serpent.

In the wilderness traditions, the narratives appear regularly under the stamp of the murmuring tradition, although an older, more positive form of the tradition may report Israel's faithful obedience during a bridal period in the wilderness.[2] Exod. 15.22-26, a tale, reports a particular crisis in the sequence. From the event at the sea, the people moved under Moses' leadership three days without water. Then they came to Marah, a place where water was available. But they could not drink that water because it was bitter. Rebellion follows. Moses intercedes before God, and God shows him the way to solve the problem. Implicit in the crisis is a threat of death from thirst for the people in a hostile wilderness (so Exod. 16.3). The resolution thus meets not only the threat of rebellion against Moses' leadership but also the threat of imminent death. Verses 25b-26 probably represent a Deuteronomistic

Weissagung und Erfüllung (ATANT, 17; Zurich: Zwingli Verlag, 1948), pp. 16-17.

1. Coats, 'Metanoia in Ancient Israel: Clues for Unity and Change', *Midstream* 23 (1984), pp. 185-88. See ch. 8 above.
2. Coats, *Rebellion in the Wilderness: The Murmuring Motif in the Wilderness Traditions of the Old Testament* (Nashville: Abingdon Press, 1968), pp. 16-17.

expansion of the tale.¹ The expansion suggests that intimate relationship with God could be restored by keeping the law. But the content of the restored intimacy is characterized explicitly in terms of healing. The diseases God put on the Egyptians will not affect the Israelites. In this pericope, the promise establishes God's response to the rebellion. Instead of death from the diseases of the Egyptians, life would come from God for those obedient to the covenantal law. That promise motivates the epithet for God: 'I am Yahweh your healer'. Healing belongs to God. Moses functions here as the mediator, the instrument for God's healing act.² But specifically, healing is an alternative to the diseases that attacked the Egyptians. Those diseases were fatal, just as God's response generally to the rebellion in the wilderness was fatal (so Num. 14.35). Deut. 28.60 reflects the same tradition in opposite dress. A threat warns Israel that failure in keeping the law will bring the diseases of Egypt. Those diseases mean death for Israel (so vv. 61, 63). Ironic for the description, the disease that brings the death now represents an intimacy for the Israelites. 'They [the diseases] shall cleave to you' (v. 60). The word is the same verb as the one that describes the intimate relationship between a husband and a wife (so Gen. 2.24). But the event that proffers God's healing comes to the Israelites through the hand of Moses, the man of God. Whether the act of throwing the tree into the water or proclaiming the new law, the instrument of God's healing comes from Moses. Moses pulls his people from the threat of death back to life.

Two texts in the Moses traditions relate the healing event more directly to the action of Moses himself. In Num. 12.1-16, a legend, Miriam and Aaron challenge Moses' unique authority for leading the people. Verse 3 identifies Moses as a man of integrity, the validated leader of the people.³ Then the remaining section of the legend shows what Moses' integrity as a leader looks like. God responds to the challenge by striking Miriam with leprosy. Moses intercedes for her, despite the fact that her challenge threatens his position before the people. The content of this intercession is of critical importance for the

---

1. M. Noth, *Exodus: A Commentary* (OTL; Philadelphia: Westminster Press, 1962), p. 129. But see also Childs, *Exodus*, pp. 266-68.
2. Childs, *Exodus*, p. 270.
3. Coats, 'Humility and Honor: A Moses Legend in Numbers 12', in D.A.J. Clines, D.M. Gunn and A.J. Hauser (eds.), *Art and Meaning: Rhetoric in Biblical Literature* (JSOTSup, 19; Sheffield: JSOT Press, 1982), pp. 99-107.

Healing and the Moses Traditions

139

study of the healing motif. Aaron petitions Moses for the intercession on behalf of Miriam, vv. 11-12. And in the petition, he identifies Miriam's plight as death: 'Let her not be as one dead...' Moses responds to Aaron's petition with intercession addressed to the Lord: 'Heal her, O God, I beseech thee'. The Lord responds by giving Moses the proper ritual for restoring Miriam to the community. When the ritual was properly executed, then the healing occured.

The same conclusions noted for the first pericope apply here as well: (1) The healing event belongs to God. (2) Moses effects God's healing by intercession and, in this case, properly carrying out the ritual. (3) The healing restores the one at death's door, isolated from the community by some kind of strife, to intimacy within the community. Miriam's return to the community marks the resumption of Israel's wilderness march under the leadership of Moses and, through Moses, under the leadership of God. Return to the community, the result of healing effected by Moses, constitutes restored intimacy for its members. One step toward paradise regained results in continuation of the wilderness march.

The second text that relates the Moses traditions directly to the healing event, and thus to a reconciled community for God's people, appears in Num. 21.4-9. This tale describes an attack on the Israelites in the wilderness by fiery serpents. In this case, the wilderness crisis is not the cause for rebellion among the people but rather its result. The fiery serpents, as the instrument of God's wrath, attack the rebels who have rejected Moses because of problems with food, water and the worthless manna (v. 6). And the consequence of their bite was death (so v. 6). In response to the crisis, Moses intercedes for his rebellious people. And God accedes to his petition. The instructions to Moses call for construction of a bronze serpent ($n^eha\check{s}\ n^eh\bar{o}\check{s}et$) erected on a pole ($n\bar{e}s$). There is some connection between this Nehushtan and the rod of God in Moses' hand that turns into a serpent ($n\bar{a}h\bar{a}\check{s}$) before the Israelites and the Egyptians. Moreover, there appears to be an ironic relationship between the bronze serpent ($n\bar{a}h\bar{a}\check{s}$) and the serpent who challenges Eve in the garden ($n\bar{a}h\bar{a}\check{s}$). In addition, the bronze serpent becomes a symbol of Moses' position as leader of the people (cf. 2 Kgs 18.4). But the important point here is that the symbol functions as an instrument for healing. People bitten by the serpent and thus doomed to die had but to look at the symbol and, *ex opere operato*, death would be converted into life. The key verb for healing does not appear in this pericope. But the process is the one described elsewhere as healing. Death is converted into life (so v. 9). The irony in the scene must not be missed. The serpent is an instrument of death. But, by the miracle of ritual, the bronze serpent becomes an instrument of life.

Moreover, the new life effected by the healing event with Moses' bronze serpent, the resolution of the rebellion against Moses and God, would enable the Israelite community to be restored. The event of healing brings new life not only to the body, a process of the natural world, but also to the community, a process of the social world. This healing process restores relationships of intimacy between the rebels and Moses, between the leader and the led. As a gift of God, the healing event restores relationships between the rebels and God. The healed community does not enjoy the intimacy of the garden, the peace of Isaiah's paradise, at least not yet. But it anticipates that kind of life. Healing effected by the bronze serpent ironically as the opposite of the serpent's gift to humanity in the garden prefigures the messianic kingdom where no hurt can be found in all of God's holy mountain. 'As Moses lifted up the serpent in the wilderness, so must the son of man be lifted up, that whoever believes in him may have eternal life' (Jn 3.14). As a foretaste of that kingdom, the bronze serpent stands as a symbol of reconciliation between Moses and David, the north and the south, the suffering servant and the messiah. For the Yahwist, the Moses who heals points toward restored intimacy for all of God's people. Does the presence of the bronze serpent in the Jerusalem temple at least until the time of Hezekiah not point to some sign of that reconciliation (so 2 Kgs 18.4).

There is another dimension in the serpent tradition with its role of healing the broken intimacy within the people of God. Through the serpent Moses calls his people not only from broken intimacy to a new sense of community, but also from death to life. Elijah, a new Moses in the wilderness, intercedes for the son of a widow. And the child lived. But the new life stands not only for restored nature in the body of the child. 'Elijah took the child...and delivered him to his mother' (1 Kgs 17.23). With the restoration of life for the dead child, there is restoration of intimacy within the family, within the community.[1] Elisha responds to the cry of the Shunammite woman whose son died in her arms. And again, the ritual of healing effected by this disciple of

---

1. B.O. Long, *1 Kings, with an Introduction to Historical Literature* (FOTL, 9; Grand Rapids: Eerdmans, 1984), p. 185.

Elijah, this new Moses, brings healing, life, even resurrection for the dead.[1]

The suffering servant poem from the Second Isaiah depicts the death of the new Moses (Isa. 53.8).[2] But the death of this particular servant did not occur for his own rebellion. He carried the rebellions of his people. And the result was death, like Moses cut off from the promised land, like Moses 'stricken for the transgressions of my people'. But the critical point is that the salvation offered the people of God by this new Moses is explicitly healing. 'With his stripes we are healed'. The death of the servant brings healing, restoration to the people.

I suggest, therefore, that a critical root in the OT for understanding the proclamation of reconciliation is the picture of Moses, the healer who brings restored intimacy to the community by healing their diseases, their wounds, their strife, and their rebellion. Indeed, I suggest that resurrection motifs in OT traditions must be understood in relationship to the healing paradigm, rooted essentially in the Moses traditions. The point can be defended generally from the verb itself. In Deut. 32.39, the verb relates to its negative pole, 'to wound'. But the pair, 'I wound and I heal', stands synonymously parallel to a resurrection statement: 'I kill and I make alive'. Ps. 30.3-4 makes the same point: 'O Lord my God! I cried to you for help, and you healed me. O Lord, you have brought up my life from Sheol, restored me to life from among those gone down to the pit'. In Jer. 33.6, the promise 'I will heal them' stands in contrast to the threat in v. 5, 'to fill them with dead bodies of men whom I shall smite in my anger and my wrath'. In Jn 3.14, following a Son of man saying that connects resurrection and ascension to an explicit tradition about the pre-existence of the Son of man, the Moses tradition appears. 'As Moses lifted up the serpent in the wilderness, so must the son of man be lifted up, that whoever believes in him may have eternal life'. Son of man theology is obviously present. But what does the Moses theology contribute to the saying? The function of the symbol, by virtue of its history within

---

1. For details, see O.H. Steck, *Überlieferung und Zeitgeschichte in den Elia-Erzählungen* (WMANT, 26; Neukirchen–Vluyn: Neukirchener Verlag, 1968), pp. 11-12.
2. Bentzen, *Messias*, p. 51. For an interpretation of the poem in terms of death, see C. Westermann, *Isaiah 40–66: A Commentary* (OTL; Philadelphia: Westminster Press, 1969), pp. 265-69.

the Moses tradition, is clear. The son of man, lifted up like Moses' serpent in the wilderness, is an instrument of healing. The dominant point is that like the Israelites in the wilderness, the people who see, the disciples of Christ, will also be healed. The broken intimacy shared by all with the people of the garden can be converted into reconciliation, restored intimacy, and peace with God, with fellow humans, and with the world. The glorification of Jesus, the resurrection that heals the broken body, heals the broken body of the disciples as well. Looking at the bronze serpent brings healing to the Israelites in the face of death from the bite of the wilderness serpents. Believing in the crucified, glorified new Moses brings healing to the body of Christ. Indeed, that healing carries a promise for eternal life.

Yet, where does this healing happen? For Israel, rebellion in the wilderness continued to the border of the land. Apostasy at Baal-peor marked the land not simply as the symbol of God's presence with the people but as the place of their worst apostasy (Jos. 22.17). For the Yahwist, intimacy is related to the figure of David (so Num. 24.7-9, 17). And for the Chronicler, that notion of intimacy is confirmed. For Deuteronomy, the place for intimacy must be associated with Moses (Deut. 26.5-11; Jos. 24.1-28). But the contrast between appeal to David and appeal to Moses highlights a fundamental point of strife in the community of God's people. Is the dream for restored intimacy anything more for the OT than the dream of the Yahwist?

Josiah tried to realize that dream. Something of a new David, Josiah launched a reform built around proclamation of a new Mosaic law. Indeed, an apparent goal for the reform must have been the unity of the people under the new law of Moses. But Josiah died at Meggido, and the attempt at reform proved to be little more than an appetizer (2 Kgs 22–23). The gospel interprets Jesus as the new David and new Moses together.[1] Just as Josiah worked for unity among the people of God, so Jesus prays for the unity of the people of God (Jn 17). Indeed, Jesus died on a lonely hill, just as Josiah did. Does not the event require still further projection toward the future? This projection focuses precisely in the resurrection, an event of healing for the body of Christ. Precisely in the resurrection, reconciliation occurs. Intimacy is restored for humanity, the world with humanity, and humanity with God. The resurrection brings healing to the whole body of Christ.

---

1. So Coats, 'Metanoia'. See also R.E. Brown, *The Gospel according to John* (AB, 29; New York: Doubleday, 2nd edn, 1983), pp. 210-15.

But still humanity is divided. The resurrection is not the fulfillment of healing for the whole body of Christ, the restoration of intimacy for the community. It only prefigures that healing. As prolepsis, it promises incredible good news. Broken humanity can be healed. But where does humanity share the fruit of that good news? In the Eucharistic sacrament, the unity of the healed body of Christ stands most sharply in the light of God's word. The sacrament effects the healed body of Christ, the place of restored intimacy for God's people, the new Garden of Eden. And its symbol is as ironic as the Mosaic bronze serpent. The serpent was a creature of death, representing broken intimacy for those who look at it in obedience to its command for disobedience. It symbolized punishment for rebellion against Moses and against God. Yet, it becomes the symbol of life, representing restored intimacy for those who look at it in obedience to the word of God through Moses. The symbols of the sacrament are symbols of violence, rejection, broken intimacy, death. Broken bread stands for a broken body. The wine stands for spilled blood. But in the sacrament, these symbols become the symbols of peace, harmony, restored intimacy, healing, new life in resurrection. In the sacrament, the healing of the body of Christ occurs in advance of the final new creation.

The serpent facilitates an act that destroys human intimacy. The bronze serpent facilitates a healing process that restores intimacy. Ritual can effect new community. Yet, the risk of performing the ritual without the appropriate intimacy raises questions about the healing process. In effecting the healing by ritual, exploitation may occur. When confronted with exploitation, someone must raise a prophetic voice of protest. Jeremiah objects to the prophets of his day: 'They have healed the wound of my people lightly, saying "peace, peace," when there is no peace' (6.14; 8.11). The same point can be found throughout the prophetic traditions (so Ezek. 13.10, 16; Mic. 3.5).

Interestingly, there is some connection between the healing process at home in the Moses tradition and the healing process linked to the so-called false prophets.[1] The following points show a common tradition:

First, the verb associated with the action of the so-called false prophets is the same as the one that appears in the two key units of the

---

1. G. Quelle, *Wahre und falsche Propheten* (BFCT, 46; Gütersloh: Bertelsmann, 1952). See also J. Lindblom, *Prophecy in Ancient Israel* (Philadelphia: Muhlenberg Press, 1962), pp. 210-15.

Moses traditions: *rāpā*.' The object of that verb is 'wound'. A wound is a prelude to death, a condition that stands in sharp contrast to healing, a condition that calls for the healing process (so Jer. 15.18; 30.12; Mic. 1.9; Nah. 3.19). In the case of the prophets attacked by Jeremiah, the threats in 6.14 and 8.11, 'the wound of the people', become death for those who fall under the Lord's punishment. And ritual cannot resolve the tragedy. The people who would be healed by the ritual of the prophets of peace remain separated from the Lord. Intimacy that would create genuine peace is broken precisely by the failure to execute the ritual properly. Ritual without the intimacy of integrity cannot produce intimacy.

Secondly, the fruit of the healing process expected by the prophet who pronounces the ritual is 'peace'. The character of *šālôm* is defined by the model of messianic justice and righteousness (so Isa. 11.6-9), although in that text the word *šālôm* does not appear. An oracle in Isa. 9.1-6 makes the same point. Messianic rule will be marked by righteousness and justice, by *ṣ^{e}dāqâ* and *mišpāṭ*. But the fruit of that model is peace, *šālôm*. And the peace is perpetual, without end. There can be no peace without righteousness and justice. From the perspective of this exploration, there can be no healing, no intimacy, without righteousness and justice. The intimacy produced by the healing process, symbolized by the bronze serpent within the Mosaic tradition, involves a relationship that does not support exploitation. Intimacy is defined by righteousness and justice, signs of the new life effected by healing. There can be no healing without righteousness and justice. Any relationship short of that character approaches slavery.

Thirdly, the condition that calls for healing, that stands in contrast to peace, intimacy with God, nature and fellow human beings, is not simply a physical disease, although obviously physical disease provokes a call for healing (2 Kgs 20.5; cf. also Lev. 13.37; 14.3, 48). The condition is primarily moral. In the wilderness, the people rebel against Moses and against God. That violation brings on the attack by fiery serpents. Healing with the bronze serpent brings not only recovery from physical agony that can lead to death but also recovery from the moral violation represented by the murmuring of the people. Indeed, healing of the moral violation, the rebellion represented by the murmuring, is a prerequisite for the healing of the physical violation (cf. Mt. 9.1-8). Thus, typical prophetic rhetoric involving the healing process calls for repentance (Hos. 6.1; 14.5; Jer. 3.22; Isa. 6.19; 19.22). Restoration of intimacy, return to peace that effects relationships between a person and God, nature, and fellow persons, is not an event that, even by ritual, can be established automatically. To the contrary, such restoration calls for obedience, the sense of integrity lost in the garden of Eden.

One must, however, ask about the negative image of the prophets of peace, who heal the wounds of the people lightly. Is it possible that the prophets of peace, with their ritual for healing, depend on the Mosaic tradition, a tradition that in the proper context might have been seen as a positive force in the Israelite religious life? Not all of the classical prophets condemn the prophets who heal, who call for peace, who effect new intimacy by their ministry.

In Hos. 14.1-8 (Eng.), an example of a prophetic oracle that functions as a proclamation of the healing, a reconciling word of God appears. The oracle has two formal elements. The first, vv. 1-3, contains an address from the Lord through the prophet to the people. The first part of the address, vv. 1-2a, admonishes the audience to repent. The opening verb, 'return', calls explicitly for the act of repentance fundamental for the healing process (cf. also Isa. 6.10; 19.22; Jer. 3.22; Hos. 14.4; 2 Chron. 7.14).[1] Moreover, the admonition is supported by an explicit description of the event that has broken the intimacy between the people and their God. Verses 2b-3 then define the confession expected from the people. The confession features a general term for violation of relationships, 'iniquity', *'āwōn*. Verse 3 names three concrete examples of the violation: dependency on Assyria, dependency on the power of horses, and definition of still some other object as 'our God'. Verse 3bβ provides a contrast to these acts of dependence on objects other than the Lord. Mercy for the orphan, for the one who has lost a natural source of intimacy, comes from God. This confession reflects acts that have broken the covenant of intimacy, leaving the people without a source of hope for renewal.

The second element in the oracle, vv. 4-8, is the proclamation of healing.[2] God announces God's intention to heal. The object of the healing is explicitly the negative acts of the people that have broken the intimacy of the covenantal relationship. Verse 4b views the act of

---

1. H.W. Wolff, *Dodekapropheten I*; *Hosea* (BKAT, 14/1; Neukirchen–Vluyn: Neukirchener Verlag, 1961), pp. 302-303.
2. For details see Wolff, *Dodekapropheten I*, pp. 302-309.

healing as parallel to an act of love that abolishes God's anger and thus God's power to maintain broken intimacy with the people (like the power to place cherubim at the entrance to the garden). Verse 8 then describes the fruit of healing, a restored relationship between people and God. 'They shall return and dwell beneath his shadow. They shall grow grain. They shall blossom as the vine. Their fragrance shall be like the wine of Lebanon'. That picture is an effective description of restored intimacy. Indeed, this verse captures the quality of šālôm, even though the word itself does not appear.

The healing described by Hosea occurs as if in response to the confession. Just as a priestly oracle of salvation responds to a lament, so a prophetic oracle of healing responds to a confession of covenant violation and establishes the event of healing, an event whose content restores the intimacy of the covenant relationship. I suggest, then, that this ritual is the event for Israel that accompanies the symbol of the bronze serpent, the event that effects the healing of broken intimacy. It is important to note that this healing oracle occurs in a prophet of the Northern Kingdom, a prophet who alludes to the role of Moses as the prophet who brought Israel out of Egypt (Hos. 12.13). In this regard, Hosea makes more effective use of the Moses traditions than he does of the David complex.[1]

In Isa. 57.14-21, there is no confession of broken intimacy, no admonition to repent introduced by the verb 'return', šûb. It may be that the admonition in v. 14 functions in the same way as an admonition to repent (cf. Jer. 42.10; Mal. 1.4). An admonition to build, to prepare the way, to remove obstructions, effects the same kind of ritual that enables intimacy to be restored. Indeed, the description of the worshipper, who partipates in the process of preparing the way, as a person of contrite and humble spirit, a point repeated in v. 15b, belongs to the ritual of repentance. Verse 16 promises God's response to the ritual depicted by vv. 14-15. That response is marked as an event of life (v. 16b). Such an event of life stands in contrast to the anger of God, the lawsuit that threatens the people with death. Verse 17 repeats the pattern, but from a new perspective. God describes God's response to the iniquity of the people. The initial response was one of punishment. 'I smote him. I hid my face and was angry' (17a). But the people did not change. The punishment did not

---

1. For details, see Westermann, *Isaiah 40–66*, pp. 21-27.

alter the character of the people. 'He went on backsliding in the way of his own heart' (v. 17b).

This oracle poses a severe question. Because of Israel's iniquity, God punished; God removed the divine presence from Israel. There could be no intimacy in that kind of life. But Israel did not repent. Thus, the tradition faces a severe question. What will God do this time? God is not blind. 'I have seen his ways'. But God acts in an unexpected way. 'I will heal him. I will lead him and requite him with comfort, creating for his mourners the fruit of the lips' (v. 18). What follows comprises the content of the healing tradition. '"Peace, peace, to the far and to the near," says the Lord. "And I will heal him".' The fruit of the ritual, the result of the oracle given the backsliding people, is *šālôm*, restored intimacy. In the context of the ritual, but by the word of God, the guilty receive peace, the intimacy lost in the garden. And that gift is explicitly the result of healing.

But the intimacy, the state of being healed, must be marked by integrity. The wicked still toss in the sea of broken intimacy. 'The wicked are like the tossing sea, for it cannot rest' (v. 20). Rest comes from restoration of the intimacy lost in the garden. ' "There is no peace," says my God, "for the wicked"' (v. 21). The notion of *šabbāt* is particularly at home in the Sabbath tradition. Perhaps the Sabbath is the most effective ritual for creating intimacy with God. The Sabbath brings healing for a wounded people, restored intimacy for those who strive with God, neighbors and nature.

Another insight into the moral dimension of healing appears in Third Isaiah. In keeping with the orientation of Isaiah 40–55, with its emphasis on a new exodus, a new wilderness journey and a new Moses, Third Isaiah also employs exodus/Moses traditions. The point is particularly prominent in Third Isaiah's focus on the Sabbath. Isa. 58.1-14 (cf. Num. 15.32-36) employs three structural elements to relate healing, the rest of the Sabbath, with restored intimacy.

First, Isa. 58.1-5 indicts the rebellious people for violating the Sabbath. 'They seek me daily and delight to know my ways...They ask of me righteous judgments' (v. 2). Specifically, these people of the broken covenant perform the ritual: fasting, humbling themselves. According to the tradition, the ritual should be effective. But the indictment is explicit. 'In the day of your fast, you seek your own pleasure and oppress all your workers. You fast only to quarrel and to fight and to hit with wicked fist' (vv. 3-4a). The ritual, unaccompanied by integrity and intimacy, fails. 'Fasting like yours this day will not make your voice to be heard on high' (v. 4b).

Secondly, in contrast, 58.6-7 describes the ritual that effects intimacy. 'Is not this the fast that I choose: to loose the bonds of wickedness, to undo the thongs of the yoke, to let the oppressed go free and to break every yoke? Is it not to share your bread with the hungry and to bring the homeless poor into your house; when you see the naked, to cover him, and not to hide yourself from your own flesh?' The content of the ritual that serves as the antidote for broken intimacy combines the operation of the ritual with integrity and commitment to a proper relationship.

Thirdly, the result of the combination (vv. 8-9a) is again explicit: 'Then shall your light break forth like the dawn, and your healing shall spring up speedily. Your righteousness shall go before you. The glory of the Lord shall be your rear guard'. But the capstone of the restored intimacy is the final assertion. 'Then you shall call, and the Lord will answer. You shall cry, and he will say, "Here I am".' Restored intimacy effected by the healing of God, centered in a ritual on the Sabbath but open to all of God's people wherever they call for an answer, offers the presence of the Lord, the opposite of the experience of the man and the woman expelled from the garden and kept at a distance from the Lord by the terrible cherubim.

Is this image or restored intimacy in the Sabbath ritual not already anticipated by the perceptive redactor who combined the tale of a paradise lost with a priestly account of creation that focuses on the Sabbath as the occasion to celebrate God's creation? But of even more importance is the power of the Sabbath to effect healing and restored intimacy. The tale in Mt. 12.9-14 (and par.) points in just this direction. 'Is it lawful to heal on the Sabbath?' The justification for the event, an event held by Jesus' opposition as a violation of the Sabbath ritual, lies precisely in the integrity of intimate relationships. If a friend has a sheep that falls into a pit on the Sabbath, each person in the audience would stop to help that friend lift the sheep out of the pit. Relationships within the community constitute the crucial norm. Indeed, this norm enables healing to occur. Moreover, the healing in Jesus' ministry occurs precisely as a response to the ritual that restores intimacy. As a result, the proclamation of forgiveness for sin effects healing (so Mt. 9.1-8 and par.). The same point appears in Paul's admonition to the Corinthians about the holy supper (1 Cor. 11.17-26). Violations of the integrity of the community undercut the operation of intimacy in the ritual. In fact, such violations can leave the community under severe threat. 'That is why many of you are weak and ill, and some have fallen asleep'. But the ritual with intimacy brings strength and health, indeed, life that provides for the integrity of the individual within the community. Healing, the ritual of the fast, combined with the integrity of intimacy, restores the reality of intimacy for the human community. In that reality, members of the community once again have access to the tree of life. In the intimacy of God's presence, resurrection gives new life to all who see the serpent-servant lifted up, to all who experience the healing that comes from that event and respond with integrity to their fellow humans. With this observation comes a final comment about the history of the healing tradition. Should the resurrection story in the early Christian tradition not be understood as a part of the OT tradition history concerning healing, specifically as it is found in the Moses traditions? The irony of the Yahwist, which sets the serpent that helped fracture human intimacy in the garden on a pole in order to facilitate restored intimacy in the wilderness, develops decisively in Jn 3.14-15: 'As Moses lifted up the serpent in the wilderness, so must the Son of man be lifted up, that whoever believes in him may have eternal life'.[1]

One must be careful at just this point, however. The description of the process might easily degenerate into a circle. Broken intimacy can be resolved by the healing touch of God, effected by the ritual. But the ritual is effective only if it occurs within the intimacy of the community, characterized by the integrity of relationships within the community. The key to the process that effects healing and restored intimacy, that opens the door of healing to the good news of the resurrection, is the moral dimension. In the healing, restoration involves not only physical and social dimensions, but also spiritual dimensions. Healing occurs with the forgiveness of sin. That element comes from God. But it also calls for commitment from the healed person. Intimacy is not a passive state. To be healed is not simply to

---

1. On the origin of the bronze serpent, see H.H. Rowley, 'Zadok and Nehushtan', *JBL* 58 (1939), pp. 113-41. My concern here is not whether the bronze serpent was originally a Mosaic symbol or how that symbol might relate to the ark. Rather, the issue is how the symbol appears in the story and how it facilitates the healing process.

receive the grace of God's healing touch. Healed intimacy is an active state, a sharing of life in mutual integrity. 'Thus you shall call, and the Lord will answer. You shall cry and he will say, "Here I am"'.

Chapter 13

STRIFE AND BROKEN INTIMACY:
GENESIS 1–3: PROLEGOMENA TO A BIBLICAL THEOLOGY

The first five books of the Old Testament, the Pentateuch, carry significant weight for the remaining sections of the Old Testament canon, indeed, for the entire Bible. These books, the Torah for the Jewish community of faith, set the pace for theology in both the Old Testament and the New Testament, not only by introducing the law, so crucial for the Jewish community in the days of Jesus' ministry, but also by introducing a critical insight into God's grace, the announcement of God's many acts designed to redeem the people from the oppression that enslaved them. The Pentateuch highlights five particular acts aimed at saving the people from their plight: (1) God's promise to the patriarchs, Abraham, Isaac and Jacob, for great posterity and for possession of a land, (2) God's response to the Egyptian oppression that enslaved the descendants of those patriarchs, (3) God's aid for those descendants when they lived in the wilderness for forty years, (4) God's gift of the law, designed to show the descendants of the patriarchs how to respond to God's acts of redemption, and (5) God's gift of the land, a place that would give identity to the descendants for all years to come.

These five themes also appear, with one exception, in brief, confessional recitations of God's mighty acts. In Deut. 26.5-9, for example, the people respond to God's gift of fruit from the ground by saying:

> A wandering Aramean was my father; and he went down into Egypt and sojourned there, few in number; and there he became a nation, great, mighty, and populous. And the Egyptians treated us harshly and afflicted us, and laid upon us hard bondage. Then we cried to the Lord, the God of our fathers, and the Lord heard our voice and saw our affliction, our toil, and our oppression. And the Lord brought us out of Egypt with a mighty hand and an outstretched arm, with great terror, with signs and wonders, and he brought us into this place and gave us this land, a land flowing with milk and honey.

There is no reference in this credo to the events at Sinai. Perhaps the Sinai traditions come from different groups of God's people than the ones who recited the credo. Perhaps the credo assumes the events at Sinai to be a part of the linkage between the exodus and the conquest, just as it assumes the entire system of wilderness stations without referring to the events that occurred there (contrast the credo in Jos. 24.2-13). But in any case, the traditions that compose the structure of the Pentateuch appear, by and large, in brief confessional articles. Perhaps the Pentateuch itself is a baroque story designed to elaborate on the articles of faith in the little, historically oriented credos. That would mean that the story in the Pentateuch is the product of faithful confession, the verbal painting that depicts the fundamental character of the people's identity.

The Pentateuchal narrative shows not only the confession of the community of the faithful from one particular generation. These traditions must have lived among the people for many generations before they were committed to writing. Then different generations preserved the verbal portrait as their distinctive document of identity for their particular time. At least two different forms of the story have been combined into an artistic whole to form the Pentateuch. The oldest form of the story dates from roughly 950 BCE, presumably under the influence of the royal Davidic court. Perhaps composed in the time of King Solomon, the source sets the confession of faith in God's mighty acts as the foundation for the kingship and the nation. The younger source, dated from roughly 550 BCE, or later, sets the story in the midst of the tragic events of the exile and shows the critical function of the ritual, formal worship, as the means for maintaining identity. Maybe a third source that would emphasize the interests of the north was composed during the eighth century. But that source, emphasizing the fear of the Lord as the character of obedience to God's law, now appears only in fragments, if at all, and cannot be reconstructed in its original form. A fourth source, represented primarily by the book of Deuteronomy from the seventh-century BCE and some editorial comments based on Deuteronomy from the sixth-century BCE, emphasizes the Mosaic law and the model it represents for the community of faith. At some point in the history of these traditions, someone put all of these sources together into one whole just as in the late second-century of the Christian era, Tatian put the four Christian Gospels together into one combined narrative called the Diatessaron.

Genesis 1–3, part of a larger unit of narrative in Genesis 1–11 commonly called the primeval saga, sets the pace for the history of God's salvation for the people of the world. It is important to note that salvation history is rooted in the creation of the world. The first act of redemption for the people of the world is the creation of the world itself, a point that already suggests that people should rejoice in the beauty of the world as a gift of God's salvation, rather than falling into the trap of exploiting the creation for whatever manipulative ends. The salvation God offers to the people of the world is in every sense a new creation. Genesis 1–3 is a combination of two distinct creation stories. The younger one, an introduction to the priestly source of the exile, shows influence from the world of culture that gave life to the Jews during the Babylonian exile. From that systematic hand of the sixth century, this account of creation describes God's creation in a systematic structure determined by a seven-day week. The focus of that seven day scheme is the institution of the Sabbath on the seventh day. The outline of the structure in the unit emphasizes this characteristic:

I	Introduction	1.1-2
II	Stages of creation	1.3-31
	A. Day one	3-5
	1. God's call for light	3-4a
	a. Command	3a
	b. Execution of the command	3b
	c. Valuation	4a
	2. God's act	4b-5a
	a. Act	4b
	b. Naming	5a
	3. Conclusion	5b
	B. Second Day	6-8
	1. God's call for firmament	6
	2. God's act	7-8a
	a. Act	7a
	b. Execution	7b
	c. Naming	8a
	3. Conclusion	8b

154   *The Moses Tradition*

    C. Third Day   9-13
        1. God's call for dry land   9-10
            a. Command   9a
            b. Execution   9b
            c. Naming   10a
            d. Valuation   10b
        2. God's call for vegetation   11-12
            a. Command   11
            (1)   Word   11a
            (2)   Execution   11b
            b. Act   12
            (1)   Report   12a
            (2)   Valuation   12b
        3. Conclusion   13

    D. Fourth day   14-19
        1. God's call for lights   14-15
            a. Command   14-15a
            b. Execution   15b
        2. God's act   16-18
            a. Act   16-18a
            b. Valuation   18b
        3. Conclusion   19

    E. Fifth day   20-23
        1. God's call for sea and air creatures   20
        2. God's act   21-22
            a. Act   21a
            b. Valuation   21b
            c. Blessing   22
        3. Conclusion   23

    F. Sixth day   24-31
        1. God's call for land creatures   24-25
            a. Command   24
            (1)   Word   24a
            (2)   Execution   24b
            b. Act   25
            (1)   Report   25a
            (2)   Valuation   25b

			2. God's call for human beings	26-31a
			a. Command	26
			b. Act	27-31a
			(1) Report	27
			(2) Blessing	28
			(3) Designation of food	29-30a
			(4) Execution	30b
			(5) Valuation	31a
		3. Conclusion		31b
III	Conclusion			2.1-4a
	A. Conclusion formula			1
	B. Seventh day			2-3
	1. Act			2
	2. Blessing			3
	C. Conclusion formula			4a

From the pattern of structure in this pericope, two items appear to be especially important: (1) The third day, described in vv. 9-13, carries two distinctive acts of creation, the creation of dry land and the creation of vegetation. But the creation of vegetation clearly functions as an extension of the creation of dry land, a natural part of establishing the land in contrast to the sea. (2) The sixth day also has two distinctive acts of creation, the creation of the land animals and the creation of the humans. In this case, the creation of the humans is not subordinated to the creation of the animals. But the two acts of creation appear together, the one a natural extension of the other. That structure does not place the human at the top of creation, the goal for all other acts of creation. To the contrary, it suggests that in two distinct acts of a single moment in creation, the human creatures and the living creatures appear. And among those creatures, the human has responsibility for the others, indeed, for the whole shape of the created world. That responsibility requires that the human secure the fertile productivity of creation, including the other species of animals. It does not grant license to the humans to exploit creation in whatever way human imagination might suggest.

But the primary point in this schematic design of creation comes in the final day. One of the signs of this special event in creation is the blessing enacted on the day. To be sure, God also blessed the sea creatures (v. 22) and the human beings (v. 28). The blessing carries a special promise for fertility. But the blessing on the seventh day is strengthened by a second verb, a verb that does not accompany any of the other blessing events. 'God blessed the seventh day, and he hallowed it...' God made the seventh day holy. The word 'holy' describes that particular character of God that separates God from all things that are not God. When the seventh day receives the character of 'holy', the hallowed day, then that day stands in a unique relationship with God. And all persons who rest on the seventh day as God rested have the blessing of that special relationship. Those who rest on the Sabbath enjoy the blessing of God on that day, a blessing that brings the faithful into a close and personal relationship with God by virtue of their observance.

This point is explicitly the content of Sabbath legislation in Exod. 31.12-17. The priestly text explicitly orders observance of the Sabbath, and the initial reason for the observance is that the Sabbath functions as a sign of the relationship between the people and God (v. 13). A sign typically functions as a symbol of a covenantal relationship (so, 31.16). But the function of this covenantal sign is made even more explicit. In v. 13, God instructs Moses to command the people to observe the Sabbath 'that you may know that I, the Lord, sanctify you'. The verb at the center of this promise, 'sanctify', is the same verb that describes the special relationship with God bestowed on the Sabbath at creation. To observe the Sabbath is to participate in the act of creation that initiates a special relationship between God and creation. The text in Exod. 31.14-17 emphasizes that special relationship by asserting the opposite: 'Everyone who profanes it shall be put to death. Whoever does any work on it, that person shall be cut off from among the people...Whoever does any work on the Sabbath day shall be put to death'. To violate the Sabbath is to break the relationship symbolized by the Sabbath between God and the people. The contrary would also apply. To observe the Sabbath is to preserve the relationship symbolized by the Sabbath between God and the people. Indeed, there is a sense of the effective ritual in the observance of the Sabbath. To observe the Sabbath is to participate in the creation event it symbolizes. It is to participate in the effective relationship with God marked by the active, decisive event, the hallowing, the sanctification of the people. It is to experience in a new way the event that effects that relationship. *Ex opere operato*, the observance of the Sabbath places the worshipper into the covenantal bond with God, the creator.

Strife and Broken Intimacy 157

The older story of creation, Gen. 2.4b–3.24, reflects a totally different culture from the Babylonian cast of the priestly account. This account, from the hand of a person or persons whom scholars call the Yahwist, since it emphasizes the name of God as Yahweh, stands at the opposite extreme from the images of the priestly account of creation. The image of the world before God began the process of creation is not one that emphasizes too much water, the $t^e hôm$ that must be placed in its proper place. Rather, here the problem facing the creator is too little water.

> In the day when the Lord God made earth and heaven, when no plant of the field was yet in the earth and no herb of the field had yet sprouted, because the Lord God had not yet caused it to rain on the earth, and no man had worked the ground, but only a mist went up from the land and watered the face of the ground...

Into that dry world, God's act of creation brings new order and fertility. The initial act of creation defines the moment with its focus on God's relationship with the man, the male. God formed the man from the dust of the ground. The word play that emphasizes an intimate relationship between the man and the ground from which God created him must not escape the attention of the audience. Man, *'ādām*, comes from the ground, *'ᵃdāmâ*. But the intimacy in this scene also emphasizes the relationship between the creature and his creator. God 'forms' the man from the ground. That is an act that normally belongs to a potter who shapes the pot with tender care, using the talented and artistic hands that show not only expertise but also a tender care that belongs to an artistic creator, a mother who forms her baby by the artistic love of deep devotion. And the intimate scene grows even more intimate. The Lord God breathed into the nostrils of the man the breath of life. And at that very moment, the man became a living person. Like a cosmic mother, the Lord God gives life to a creature shaped by the tender touch of the creator's hand.

For this new creature, the Lord God creates a Garden, with trees that could provide for every need the man could have, food for daily life, the tree of life for continuing life, and the tree of the knowledge of good and evil. And rivers provided life-giving water. Into this paradise God placed the man. But the man was not simply a guest. The man had responsibility for the garden. 'The Lord God took the man and put him in the Garden of Eden *to till it and keep it*'. It was the man's responsibility to render the Garden productive. But working together, the man and the garden could maintain creation as God had established it. And the Garden with its man would be the place for God to enjoy the leisure of rest.

But one more item of moral responsibility confronted the man. God instructed the creature: 'You may freely eat of every tree of the garden. But of the tree of the knowledge of good and evil you shall not eat, for in the day that you eat of it, you shall die'. Death here is not simply the end of life. It is the opposite of the intimacy in the Garden, the support of nature including the tree of life, the communion with God. It would be the man's moral duty not to infringe on the tree of knowledge. In the Garden, the man had access to the tree of life and could live under its fertility. But he could not use the tree of knowledge. That fruit would give him the power of life and death, the power of a king over creation. That power of kingship (see 1 Kgs 3.9) belongs only to God.

The Garden was a place of intimacy. The man enjoyed a very special relationship with God, a relationship of responsibility but also one of mutual respect and support. The Garden supplied the needs of the man, even the need for life. And in return, the man worked the Garden and kept it. But the storyteller recognizes that in neither of these poles does the man find the intimacy that completes his life: 'It is not good that the man should be alone'. To be alone in the garden is to be outside the order of intimacy created by God for the man. In order to remedy this gap in the man's creation, God announces a plan: 'I will make a helper fit for him'. The English word, 'helper', is a poor term for translating the Hebrew noun, *'ēzer*. An *'ēzer* is not a subordinate, an assistant, a servant who would do the master's bidding. To describe the next moment of creation as creation of a subordinate assistant to the man is to violate the power of the scene. An *'ēzer* is a complement, an alter ego, a counterpoint for the man (see Ps. 89.20). Without the one pole, the other pole in this human field of energy would be useless. But in the intimacy of the relationship, the man would receive the power of God to accomplish the human task—to render the earth fertile.

In order to find the 'helper fit for him', the Lord God created the animals of the field and the birds of the air. The man gave them names, a symbolic act of dominion over the creatures. But among the animals, he found no partner, no *'ēzer* who would be his opposite complement (v. 20). The next act of creation establishes the unique.

bond for the man, the 'helper' who would complement his life, the partner who would share his life with all of its responsibilities. 'So the Lord God caused a deep sleep to fall upon the man, and while he slept, took one of his ribs and closed up its place with flesh. And the rib which the Lord God had taken from the man, God built into a woman and brought her to the man'. The intimacy of this relationship is symbolized by the construction of the woman from a part of the man's body. But in addition, it is also captured by the name. The word for 'woman' is a feminine form, *'iššâ*, of the word for 'man', *'îš*. The poem in v. 23 catches this sense of intimacy, this sense of oneness in the new relationship: 'This at last is bone of my bones and flesh of my flesh. She shall be called woman (*'iššâ*) because she was taken out of man (*'îš*).' This act of naming is not the same as the man's act of naming the animals, an act that symbolizes the man's dominion over the animals. Here, the name given the woman is the man's own name, an act that symbolizes a unique and intimate sharing of a common life. Neither party is lord over the other. Rather, the two stand together, each a part of the other. And the common name, distinct only by virtue of being masculine or feminine, captures the intimate bond.

The final two verses of the chapter add two new symbols for expression of this bond of intimacy. In v. 24, the conclusion reports that the man 'leaves his father and mother and cleaves to his wife, and they become one flesh'. This description of the intimate bond catches more than a sexual union between the man and the woman. The verb 'cleaves', *dābaq*, describes the bond of intimacy between the man and the woman at every level of their lives, a bond that gives each a very particular identity. In this description of creation, neither the man nor the woman is complete without the other. There is no place here for celibacy as a sign of the holy life. The power of the word to denote intimate relationships that create community necessary for achieving identity is confirmed by by 2 Sam. 20.2; 2 Kgs 18.6; Prov. 18.24.

Secondly v. 25 observes that both the man and the woman were naked (*'ărummîm*) and they were not ashamed. The fact that the two could be together naked without shame shows the unique quality of the relaltionship. Nakedness without intimacy is for the Old Testament culture wrong (see Gen. 9.20-29; 2 Sam. 11.2-5). Nakedness within the bond of intimacy between a man and a woman is beautiful. It is in fact a symbol of the bond.

Genesis 2 captures a garden scene of beautiful intimacy, a paradise where relationships were as God intended them to be: man/woman; man-woman/God and man-woman/nature. Genesis 3 depicts paradise lost, the destruction of intimate relationships at all three levels. Verse 1 gives expression to an agonizing pun: 'The serpent (*nāḥāš*) was more subtle (*'ārûm*) than any other creature that the Lord God had made'. God created the creatures in order to find an intimate partner for the man. The symbol for that intimacy is nakedness (*ᵃrûmmîm*). The pun suggests that the serpent was the primary candidate among all the animals to be chosen as the man's companion, the one who could have been intimate with the man. But the serpent was not chosen. What happens when a rejected candidate for a position of importance meets the candidate that was in fact chosen? The temptation scene follows.

The confrontation begins with a simple question from the serpent to the woman: 'Did God say: "You shall not eat of any tree in the garden"?' And the woman responds by defending God. She explains to the serpent what God said: The two of them may eat from all of the trees in the garden except the one in the midst of the garden. The issue here is not the tree of life. That tree was apparently available to the pair. The issue is the tree of the knowledge of good and evil. The serpent challenges the truth of God's statement by asserting the opposite: 'You will not die'. Then the serpent defines the value of the tree: 'Your eyes will be opened, and you will be like God, knowing good and evil'. To know good and evil, to have the power of life and death over other members of God's creation, is to be like God. The one thing that the human creature may not do is to be like God, to try to make himself or herself a God. But the serpent points out that the human pair can do that. It is their choice.

The woman takes the fruit, eats, gives some to the man, and he eats. It was a free choice. The serpent did not force them to act in a way that would disobey God's command. And the immediate consequence is the loss of the intimacy characteristic for the garden: 'Then the eyes of both were opened. And they knew that they were naked. And they sewed fig leaves together and made themselves aprons'. They hid their nakedness. The sign of their intimacy between themselves disappears.

The signs of intimacy with God also disappear. Verse 8 reports that the Lord God who created the Garden was walking in the Garden in the cool of the day, an act that opens the door to intimate relationships with the other residents of the garden. But when the man and the woman heard God walking, they hid themselves from God. God then calls to them with a question that must be answered: 'Where are you?' The emphasis of the question does not call for information that God does not know. It calls for a confession. The man must answer. And the answer shows the evidence of a broken intimacy: 'I heard the sound of you in the garden, and I was afraid'. Why would the man and the woman be afraid in an intimate relationship? 'Because I was naked. And I hid myself'. But intimacy approves of the naked. Hiding from an intimate partner breaks the intimacy. 'Who told you that you were naked? Have you eaten of the tree of which I commanded you not to eat?' And with that challenge, the man must confess. Intimacy with God has been broken by human disobedience.

But the tragic story of broken intimacy does not end with the confession before God. The man now becomes the accuser: 'The woman whom you gave me, she gave me fruit of the tree, and I ate'. One can almost hear the man say: 'It is not my fault, Lord. It was her fault. And, after all, you gave her to me. It is really your fault'. God then challenges the woman. 'What is this that you have done?' And the challenge requires the woman's answer: 'The serpent tricked me, and I ate'.

The three poems that follow this tragic scene capture the fruit of the broken intimacy. In vv. 14-15, the serpent is condemned not only to crawl without legs but also to be in perpetual enmity with the humans. Intimacy between the creature and the human is broken. In v. 16, the woman is condemned to pain in childbirth and to a subordinate role to her husband. The position that subordinates the woman to the man is not an order of God's creation. It is the fruit of human sin. In vv. 17-19, the man is condemned to work in nature for support without the support of nature.

But the tragic scene in the account of paradise lost is not yet over. The man gives the woman a new name, an act that now symbolizes a new dominion over her. She is no longer partner, an *'ēzer* fit for the man. She is now subject to him. And new garments hide their nakedness. But vv. 22-24 add to the tragic conclusion. Verse 22 is not complete. 'The man has become like one of us, knowing good and evil.' The plural pronoun may recall the mythological tradition behind this tale of Israel, a tradition that reports the action of creation as the actions among gods and goddesses. But the important part is the announcement that the man and the woman must be expelled from the

Garden, so that they may not continue to eat from the tree of life. The expulsion means that they can no longer sustain life from the tree of life. And without that sustenance, they will die. God's word is tragically true. When they eat from the tree of knowledge, when they must leave the garden, they begin the process that leads to their death. As mortals, they now approach death day by day.

But the tragedy grows even more severe. In order to insure that the death penalty sticks, that the man and the woman can never find their way back into the Garden, back to the tree of life, God placed cherubim at the entry to the Garden. God will keep the disobedient creatures out of the Garden, away from the tree of life, away from intimate relationships with God. And on that tragic note, the older story of creation ends.

The tragic story of broken intimacy in the earliest part of the creation tradition in the Old Testament cannot stand apart from the equally tragic stories of broken intimacy in the same source, the story of the two brother, Genesis 4, the story of the flood, Genesis 6–9, and the story of the Tower, Genesis 11. In Genesis 4, Cain and Abel compete for God's attention. When God looks with favor on one but not the other, the rejected brother kills the favored brother. And God's punishment for the act of violence that breaks brotherly intimacy condemns the guilty brother to a life without intimacy: 'When you till the ground, it shall no longer yield to you its strength'. Nature will not support Cain. 'You shall be a fugitive and a wanderer on the earth'. Human community will no longer sustain Cain. And Cain responds: 'My punishment is greater than I can bear. Behold, you have driven me this day away from the ground, and from your face I shall be hidden. I shall be a fugitive and a wanderer on the earth, and whoever finds me will slay me'. In Genesis 6–9, both the older and the younger sources report God's act of destruction for a people totally broken in all relationships. The tragedy of this state is captured by the description of God in 6.6: 'The Lord was sorry that he had made man on the earth, and it grieved him to his heart'. And this story of tragic broken intimacy reaches its peak in 9.20-27. Noah, drunk from misuse of nature's fruit, lies naked. And Canaan sees that nakedness. The fruit of this corrupted intimacy is a curse on Canaan. Finally, the tower people presume to build a tower with its top in the heavens, or perhaps back in the place where God lives. In order to prevent an attack on the place where God lives, an effort that would be an attempt to make themselves God, God confuses the language. Unable to understand each other, the people scatter, broken apart from an intimacy that almost made them members of paradise again.

The question posed at the end of Genesis 1–11 is critical. For the earliest source, the issue is clear. The humans broke intimacy with themselves, with nature and with God. Now, how would they ever experience restored intimacy? Would it be possible ever to regain the paradise lost in that terrible moment of disobedience? When intimacy is broken, can it ever be restored?

In the younger source, the issue is slightly different. The ritual is critical. But can the human creature observe the ritual properly? Or will that creature desecrate the levels of relationship given by God? Will that creature desecrate the ritual and destroy the means for restoration given by God? Even when the proper form of the ritual has been defined, can it ever be executed with enough precision so that the unity of the community might be restored?

For the older source, the critical question about reconciliation opens the sagas about the patriarchs, Abraham, Isaac and Jacob. The implied answer to the question is that in the intimacy of the family, intimacy for all people might be restored. But the patriarchal sagas are stories about strife in the family, broken intimacy in family relationships that seems impossible to restore. The storyteller pits Sarah against Hagar, Abraham against Lot, Isaac against Ishmael, Jacob against Esau, and finally Joseph against the whole group of brothers. Where is reconciliation for the people of God's creation if it must come through a family broken by perpetual strife? Perhaps the answer lies in Moses who takes those people out of Egypt and brings them to a mountain in the wilderness. But the storytellers report that all along the way, the people murmured against Moses and against God. And at the mountain where God created a new intimacy for the people in a covenant bond, the people broke that intimacy immediately with a Golden Calf. How is intimacy possible for these rebellious people?

The next key in the history of God's efforts to restore the intimacy of the Garden through these people lies in the saga about Joshua and the entry into the land. Indeed, Jos. 22.1-6 suggests that intimacy returns explicitly when the people enter the land. The land is a physical sign of God's presence and thus of God's intimacy with the people. But what will happen to the Canaanites who already possess the land, and who will lead the people away from the Canaanite gods?

For the older source of the Pentateuch, the answer to this critical question about reconciliation rests with the new king, with David and his successors. The new king will create a community of unity without strife. And particularly, from the new power base in Jerusalem, that unity achieves impressive power. David, who now stands in the line of the Canaanite king Melchizedek, will unite both the north and the south around Zion. And indeed, he will unite not only the people of Moses from the wilderness with the people of his own territory, but also the Canaanite people of Jerusalem with the whole group, all who would commit loyalty to the throne in Jerusalem. And that spirit of unity would be celebrated and affirmed each year in a ritual enthronement festival. By effective proclamation, that position of power would unify all people in a royal intimacy under the aegis of the king. Psalm 78, especially vv. 67-72, gives expression to this new stage of intimacy in Israel. Moreover, the image of a creation theology undergirds the power of the king in Jerusalem. The first man in the garden is a royal man, the model for the king. God, the God who was worshipped in Jerusalem as El Elyon, is the creator of the world (so, Gen. 14.19-20). Indeed, David who sits on the throne of Melchizedek in Jerusalem, is the son of God who rules the people with the authority and intimacy of El Elyon. Is the Jerusalem of David not the restored paradise of intimacy, the new Garden of Eden? Is the festival for enthronement of the king in Jerusalem not at the same time a festival that celebrates renewal of the creation?

Yet, the tradition knows disappointment from the kingship too. The new Adam, the king on the throne in Jerusalem, breaks intimacy with his people, particularly with Uriah, and with God. The prophet Nathan indicts David with a charge that compassion, that key virtue that David should have learned from Moses, indeed, from Moses' Egyptian mother, fails in the new administration of the restored Garden of Paradise. How can a king who treats his subjects with exploitation and disdain be the Son of God who will restore intimacy to all the people of the world? The tradition of the Old Testament must now look beyond David for a new king who might finally restore intimacy for God's world.

The prophet Isaiah of Jerusalem announces the coming of a new David, an annointed one, a Messiah who would introduce the return to a garden of intimacy. In Isa. 9.2-7 and particularly in 11.1-9, the character of that Garden is painted in paradisiacal colors.

Strife and Broken Intimacy 165

> The wolf shall dwell with the lamb. The leopard shall lie down with the kid. The calf and the lion and the fatling together, and a little child shall lead them. The cow and the bear shall feed. Their young shall lie down together. The lion shall eat straw like the ox. The sucking child shall play over the hole of the asp. The weaned child shall put his hand in the adder's den. They shall not hurt or destroy in all my holy mountain, for the earth shall be full of the knowledge of the Lord as the waters cover the sea.

The intimacy in God's creation is life in a world of peace, šālôm.

The second Isaiah then announces the advent of a servant, a new Moses whose devotion to the sheep will lead the sheep to a new experience of intimacy with God. Indeed, the servant identifies himself so fully with the sheep that he offers his own life for the sake of the sheep:

> Surely he has borne our griefs and carried our sorrows. Yet we esteemed him stricken, smitten by God, and afflicted. But he was wounded for our transgressions. He was bruised for our iniquities. Upon him was the chastisement that made us whole [a new intimacy?] and with his stripes we are healed [a new life?].

Yet, just in the juxtaposition between the New David of First Isaiah and the New Moses of the Second Isaiah, the issues of the broken intimacy for the people of God come sharply into focus. The people who preserved the traditions about Moses would find themselves embroiled in a constant war with the people who preserved the tradition about David (so, 1 Kings 12). How could people at war within themselves experience restoration of a garden where intimacy and peace marked a life of harmony for all of God's people? 'It is too light a thing that you should be my servant to raise up the tribes of Jacob and to restore the preserved of Israel. I will give you as a light to the nations, that my salvation may reach to the end of the earth.' Is there any stage in the history of the tradition that marks a reconciliation between the New Moses and the New David, a stage that would usher in a New Jerusalem, a new world of peace, a new garden of Eden?

King Josiah apparently sought such a reconciliation, a reunion of the north and the south. Certainly in him, the Deuteronomistic Historian saw the combination of New David and New Moses. In him, Jeremiah identified a potential messiah. But Josiah died too soon, before the reconciliation could be completed, the victim of human aggression on the top of a lonely mountain in Megiddo. The New

Testament understands Jesus as the unique combination of the messiah and the suffering servant, the one who would usher in a new creation, a new Jerusalem. And yet, here too, tragedy strikes before the event of reconciliation that might create a new intimacy is complete. Human strife kills this man of God, this son of God, before the new Jerusalem could arrive, before reconciliation for all of the world's people could become a reality. How can reconciliation occur for people continually torn by strife and hatred?

For the disciples of Jesus, the answer lies in ritual. In the Holy Supper, reconciliation for the disciples of Jesus, indeed, for all of God's people who share in the intimacy of the occasion occurs *ex opere operato*. In the ritual, a new event of creation occurs. In the ritual, the peace of the Garden rules the community of human creatures. In the ritual, intimacy with God, with neighbor, and even with nature occurs, the effective result of God's presence.

There is, however, one more problem in the system. When reconciliation is effected *ex opere operato*, participants in the ritual may misuse the system as a magic process that simply overrides the broken intimacy of the human community. The prophet Amos reports that God rejects that kind of ritual.

> I hate, I despise your feasts. I take no delight in your solemn assemblies. Even though you offer me your burnt offerings and cereal offerings, I will not accept them. And the peace offering of your fatted beasts I will not look upon. Take away from me the noise of your songs. To the melody of your harps I will not listen.

The prophet Micah hits a similar note.

> With what shall I come before God on high? Shall I come before him with burnt offerings, with calves a year old? Will the Lord be pleased with thousands of rams, with ten thousands of rivers of oil? Shall I give my first born for my transgression, the fruit of the body for the sin of my soul?

In a similar vein, Hosea reports that God rejected the symbols of Samaria. 'I have spurned your calf, O Samaria. My anger burns against them.'

In each of these texts, the point is explicit. The ritual in itself does not create a new world. The ritual cannot establish a new intimacy *ex opere operato*. To the contrary, the ritual needs supplementing. The implication is not so much that the ritual is wrong. The ritual may symbolize a new creation, a new intimacy for all of God's people. But the ritual that effects the new world, the ritual that calls a new intimacy into existence, shows the power of a critical supplement. Verse 24 in Amos 5 makes the point: 'Let *justice* roll down like waters, and *righteousness* like an ever-flowing stream'. Verse 8 in Micah 6 makes the same point: 'He has showed you, O Man, what is good. And what does the Lord require of you but to do *justice*, to love *kindness*, and to *walk humbly* with your God'. Verse 5 in Hosea 8 captures the same thrust in a question: 'How long will it be till they are *pure*?' Each of these terms has explicit ethical content. They define the virtues of people who can live in intimacy with each other. They suggest that the order of creation cannot be restored until the people of God learn not only how to live together efficiently, but also how to live together in integrity. There is no peace, *šālôm*, without justice, *mišpāṭ*. There is no freedom from hurt in God's holy mountain without the humility (an ethical term) and righteousness (another ethical term) that marks God's relationship with the people. There is no intimacy in the ritual (with the Golden Calf) without the purity of heart (another ethical term) that marks the bond of covenant community. That sense of integrity belongs in the world from the very moment of creation. And redemption from strife and broken intimacy promises the day when such integrity will rule all of God's people.

The stories about creation do not appear now, however, as two clearly separated accounts. They have been combined as one witness to God's creative power. What is the significance of that one witness? What difference does it make that the older form of the creation tale with its tragic account of broken intimacy and paradise lost is now introduced by the younger report about God's acts in creation with its focus on the Sabbath? The impact of the juxtaposition is that God's provision for reconciliation in the face of broken intimacy lies in the Sabbath. But it is not simply a provision that restores lost intimacy *ex opere operato*. The Sabbath is not a value-neutral ritual. The Sabbath, a provision given by God as a means for restoring intimacy in a broken community, is an occasion for moral commitment. 'Remember the Sabbath day, to keep it holy. Six days you shall labor and do all your work, but the seventh day is a Sabbath to the Lord your God.' Observance of the Sabbath restores intimacy with God.

> In it you shall not do any work, you or your son, or your daughter, your manservant or your maidservant, or your cattle, or the sojourner who is within your gates, for in six days, the Lord made heaven and earth, the

sea, and all that is in them, and rested the seventh day. Therefore, the Lord
blessed the Sabbath day and hallowed it.

Observance of the Sabbath restores intimacy with all who observe the Sabbath together, the family, the servants, the cattle, the sojourner and stranger.

But there is another stage in the tradition about the Sabbath. Exodus 16 reports that nature supported the Israelites in the wilderness. By the hand of God, nature gave the Israelites the manna to meet their hunger. But even nature observed the Sabbath (vv. 22-23). When some among the Israelites violated that Sabbath rest, the community of intimacy with nature was broken (v. 20). Lev. 25.2-7 insists that even the land shall observe the Sabbath. And in that observance, the intimacy of creation confirms the support for life offered by nature. The Garden returns. Yet, even here, the community of intimacy rests on moral commitment. 'You shall not wrong one another, but you shall fear your God, for I am the Lord your God.' That moral commitment in the face of ritual execution appears in the New Testament: 'So if you are offering your gift at the altar and there remember that your brother has something against you, leave your gift there before the altar and go. First, be reconciled to your brother and then come and offer your gift'. The moral commitment in the Sabbath year sharpens the focus: 'For six years you shall sow your land and gather in its yield; but the seventh year you shall let it rest and lie fallow, that the poor of your people may eat'.

Genesis 2–3 depicts creation of a paradise for the people of God's world, a paradise marked by intimacy in relationships between people and God, people and nature, and people among themselves. But that intimacy disappears when the people break the orders of intimacy in God's creation. Those orders can be restored by effective ritual. But it is the moral commitment that renders the ritual effective.

> Is not this the fast that I choose: to loose the bonds of wickedness, to undo the thongs of the yoke, to let the oppressed go free, and to break every yoke? Is it not to share your bread with the hungry and bring the homeless poor into your house, when you see the naked, to cover him, and not to hide yourself from your own flesh? Then shall your light break forth like the dawn, and your healing shall spring up speedily. Your righteousness shall go before you. The glory of the Lord shall be your rear guard. Then you shall call, and the Lord will answer. You shall cry, and he will say, 'Here I am'.

Recommended Reading

Coats, G.W.,
Genesis: Forms of Old Testament Literature 1 (Grand Rapids: Eerdmans, 1983)
—'Strife and Reconciliation. Themes of a Biblical Theology in the Book of Genesis', *HBT* 2 (1980), pp. 15-37.

von Rad, G.,
Genesis: A Commentary (OTL; Philadelphia: Westminster Press, 1961).

Chapter 14

VIOLENCE IN THE HEROIC TRADITION:
A CHARACTERISTIC MOTIF IN BIBLICAL SAGAS

Violence characterizes much of life. Since its beginning as a nation, the United States has claimed violence as a means to establish its most outstanding heroes. The cowboy of the wild west won his position in national halls of fame by driving the Indians from their native lands. And if the Indian refused to leave that land, then the cowboy could attack and burn the Indian's village, or at least confine the Indian to restricted reservations. The American revolution itself marked the use of violence as a means for rejecting the political control of the British. American technology has created a war machine whose violence has destroyed whole cities in one touch of the bomb. That same technology, now spread to most of the nations of the world, sets the world on the edge of violent extinction. Indeed, even the effort to use that technology for peaceful ends, such as the production of electrical power, can become a nightmare of violence in a brief uncontrolled moment of time.

Unfortunately, violence does not belong exclusively to the American way of life, or even to the modern way of life. The history of humanity documents a progressive development of violence as something endemic to human society. For the ancient world, the machines of violence perfected the process for waging war in ways that for that period were as frightening and inhumane as nuclear weapons are for the modern world.

One facet of the process of relationship within human society and, indeed, with other creatures of the world is that the one most skilled in using violence can become the hero of a society, a figure to be imitated by coming generations.[1] The wild west cowboy riding down

---

1. For a definition of heroic tradition, see J. Campbell, *The Hero with a Thousand Faces* (Bolligen Series, 17; Princeton: Princeton University Press, 1949);

from some mysterious *mesa* to dispel (slaughter) some enemy who lives in a simple Indian village becomes the model for young boys who play cowboy and Indian games in peaceful hometown neighborhoods. War heroes call more readily for recognition by society than do the figures who suggest non-violence as a way to effect public policy. No one questions the heroic status of the Lone Ranger. No one objects to the honor and recognition of Dwight David Eisenhower. Yet, on that tragic day of violence when Martin Luther King fell to an assassin's bullet, some sincere American citizens objected to flying the flag at half-mast since that non-violent hero must have been subversive.

The issue of violence, however, as a mode of relationship in human society cannot submit to a simple 'right or wrong' equation. One might well adopt a non-violent life-style and yet face a challenge that would require a violent response. The issue sharpens when one considers the pattern of violence in the heroic tradition of the Bible. The hero is a hero precisely because he or she defends the people from threats posed by an outside enemy. The defense may call for a violent response to the enemy. The point can be illustrated from the heroic saga that depicts Moses as the leader of the Israelite slaves.[1] The Moses birth story sets the child in a violent world.[2] The Egyptian Pharaoh demanded, as a means for resolving the threat he perceived from the Hebrew slaves, that all sons born to the Hebrew slaves be thrown into the river. The event is memorialized by the same tragedy in the days of Herod the king. 'A voice was heard in Ramah, wailing and loud lamentation, Rachel weeping for her children. She refused to be consoled because they were no more'. The force of this violent scene for the Moses birth story sharpens with the irony of Exod. 2.1-2. Exod. 1.22 reports the speech of the Pharaoh, marking the tragic use of violence as a national policy: 'Every *son* that is born to the Hebrews you shall cast into the Nile...' Then the birth story begins. 'A man from the house of Levi went and took a wife, a daughter of Levi. The woman conceived and bore a *son*.' By the decree of the Pharaoh, the child should have been taken from his mother, obviously an act of

---

J. de Vries, *Heroic Song and Heroic Legend* (trans. B.J. Timmer; London: Oxford University Press, 1959).

1. G.W. Coats, *Moses: Heroic Man and Man of God* (JSOTSup, 57; Sheffield: JSOT Press, 1987).

2. For details about the Moses birth story, see B.S. Childs, 'The Birth of Moses', *JBL* 84 (1965), pp. 109-22.

violence, and thrown into the river—another act of violence. The Hebrew text captures this double act of violence with one Hebrew verb, *taŝlîkuhû*.

This particular baby escapes the violent slaughter of Hebrew sons by the heroic acts of the mother. Like the mother of Sargon the Great the mother of Moses preserves the child against the threat of a violent death by building an ark, securing it against the water of the river, and then floating it down the river in the hands of the fate dictated by the river or by whatever god controls the river. The apparent tragedy of that fate unfolds when the princess, the daughter of the king that had condemned this child to a violent death, discovers the child in the river and recognizes the child as a Hebrew. She could have completed the violence dictated for the child by her father at that very moment. But to the contrary, she bestows the opposite on the child: 'she had compassion for the child'. Compassion describes the event in this scene that functions as the opposite of the violence dictated by the Pharaoh.[1] She could have killed the baby but she chose to let him live; indeed, to adopt him as her own child.

Moses' life begins, according to the narrative saga, under the stamp of two opposing modes of life, each confronting the baby from the outside world as a determining factor for the baby's life—violence or compassion. And each plays its role in shaping the life of the hero. That process appears dramatically in the next pericope of the Moses saga, Exod. 2.11-15a. Verse 11 describes the violent context for the Hebrew slaves, now observed by Moses the prince. 'One day, when Moses had grown up, he went out to his people and looked on their burdens. And he saw an Egyptian beating a Hebrew, one of his people'. An essential element for the heroic status of Moses in the narrative construction comes to the surface here. The storyteller emphasizes the relationship between Moses and his people. The tradition shapes the figure of Moses as hero by emphasizing the identity between Moses and the slaves.[2] Even though an Egyptian prince, he names the people who give him identity as the Hebrews. Indeed, the storyteller calls those people 'his people'. Moreover, his people suffer in a violent captivity. He saw an Egyptian *beating* one of his people. The Hebrew verb, *makkeh*, from the root verb *nākâ*, connotes a violent act, and the Hebrews are victims of that violence. Moses responds to that act of

1. G.W. Coats, 'II Samuel 12.1-7a', *Int* 40 (1986), pp. 170-75.
2. So, Coats, *Moses*.

violence with an act of violence: 'He looked this way and that, and seeing no one, he *killed* the Egyptian and hid him in the sand'. The key verb in this verse, obviously a verb that denotes an act of violence, is the same verb that describes the Egyptian's act against the Hebrews: *wayyak*, again from the root verb *nākâ*. Moses did to the Egyptian the very thing that the Egyptian was doing to the Hebrews.[1] And now, since Moses buried the Egyptian in the sand, it is clear that that violent act is an act that brings death to the victim. Moses' life style here, a key text that marks Moses as hero for the Hebrews, belongs to the category of violence rather than compassion.

Yet, just in this contrast, the issue of violence in the heroic tradition sharpens. The hero shows compassion for his own people by violently removing any threat that endangers those people. It is thus inappropriate to suggest that, at least from the point of view of the storyteller, Moses 'murders' the Egyptian. The English term 'murder' connotes a negative use of violence. Had the attempt on Hitler's life that cost the life of the hero in the German confessing church, Dietrich Bonhöffer, been successful, then Bonhöffer would not have been labeled a murderer by the Christian community. He would have been an international hero. In the case of Bonhöffer, as in the case of Moses, the cause of compassion was served by violently removing, or at least violently attempting to remove, the enemy of the people.

The same construction appears in the following Moses pericope, Exod. 2.15b-22. Moses fled when he discovered that his violent act against the Egyptian had become public knowledge. That news comes to him when, attempting to mediate a quarrel between two of his own people, Moses feels the stinging rebuff from his own people that carries the public information about his act: 'Who made you a prince and a judge over us? Do you mean to kill me as you killed the Egyptian?'[2] Typical for the heroic tradition, this pericope then reports that the hero had to leave his people for a time.[3] Yet, the same heroic image of violence follows Moses to Midian. Resting at a well in the

---

1. M. Buber, *Moses: The Revelation and the Covenant* (TB, 27; New York: Harper & Row, 1946), pp. 36-37.
2. On the formal character of these questions as a legal accusation, see H. J. Boecker, *Redeformen des Rechtsleben im Alten Testament* (WMANT, 14; Neukirchen–Vluyn: Neukirchener Verlag, 1964), pp. 25-34.
3. On the separation between the hero and the people, see de Vries, pp. 210-26, especially p. 216.

land of Midian, Moses observes female shepherds watering their sheep. Then male shepherds drive the females and their sheep away. The scene is one of violence. The male shepherds obviously exert violent power against the females. The Hebrew verb is *waygārᵉšûm*. The verb, *gāraš*, can depict Israel's expulsion of the Canaanites from their land (so, Exod. 34.11). The LXX translates the verb with an equally strong term of violence: ἐξέβαλον. The verb is ἐκβάλλω. That verb can have a non-violent connotation. But here it translates a Hebrew verb that carries clear connotations of violent expulsion, the use of violence for a cause that handicaps the people of the hero. The text then reports that Moses helped them (*wayyōši'ān*). The act implies the use of violence on behalf of those whom the male shepherds treated violently. When the women report the event to their father, the storyteller puts another verb into their speech to describe Moses' act. The verb is *hiṣṣîlānû*, again a verb that implies an overt use of violence on behalf of the oppressed. The violent act of the hero destroys the enemy or at least reduces the enemy to a powerless position. And that act redeems the people of the hero from the enemy's oppression. Both verbs also describe God's act in delivering the people from the hands of their oppressors (cf. Hos. 13.4; Exod. 18.8). Violence thus characterizes not only the hero's action, but also, in some sense serves as an extension of that action, God's action of salvation, delivery from Egyptian oppression.

The series of stories about the negotiations process between Moses and the Pharaoh depicts the use of violence as a tool for delivering the people from Egyptian oppression.[1] The series begins with events that are innocuous, simply demonstrations of power. But each scene increases the serverity of the demonstration. The first sign appears to be a simple trick of magic. Aaron throws his rod to the floor before the Pharaoh, and it becomes a serpent. But the wisemen of Egypt do the same thing. Yet, the foreshadowing of violence in the series comes when the serpent-rod of Aaron and Moses eats the serpent-rods of the Egyptians. The second sign turns the water of the river to blood, again a simple trick of magic duplicated by the Egyptians. But the act

---

1. D.J. McCarthy, 'Moses' Dealings with Pharaoh', *CBQ* 27 (1965), pp. 336-47. See also A.M. Vater, 'A Plague on Both Our Houses: Form- and Rhetorical-Critical Observations on Exodus 7–11', in *Art and Meaning: Rhetoric in Biblical Literature* (ed. D.J.A. Clines, D.M. Gunn and A.J. Hauser; JSOTSup, 19; Sheffield: JSOT Press, 1982), pp. 62-71.

from Moses and Aaron kills the fish in the river. The third sign, frogs over the land, infests not only the land generally, but also the food supply. And when the frogs die by the hand of Moses and the Lord, the land stank with their decaying bodies. Again, the act shows an overt show of violence as a tool for securing the goals of the negotiations. The next sign, the swarm of gnats, attacks both humans and animals. The swarm of flies does the same. The violence increases with the attack on the cattle of the Egyptians, with the cattle of the Israelites free from the plague. The next sign brings boils to the skin of the Egyptians, again an act of violence in the hands of the Lord and Moses and Aaron, the servants of the Lord. And this act reduces the Egyptians' magicians to helpless victims. The hail kills humans and animals alike and destroys the crops. The swarm of locusts consumes whatever crops remained after the hail. And the final sign, darkness in the land, closes the series with an attack on the visible symbol of the Egyptian god Re, personified by the solar disc. The series, leading to some kind of climax, builds on successively more severe and violent events. And it poses the pressing question: what will the final act of violence look like?

The violence in the series functions as an instrument of pressure for the negotiations with the Pharaoh. Again, violence in the heroic tradition, both in the acts of the hero and in the acts of God, functions on behalf of the people for whom God and Moses, the servant of God, have compassion. To express compassion for the oppressed calls for violent destruction of the oppressor. The violence comes to a sharp focus in the climax of the series. The obvious conclusion to the series in the structure of the text as it now stands is the Passover scene. By proper execution of the ritual which in itself calls for a violent act, the slaughter of the Passover lamb, the people of God prepare for the final confrontation with Egypt. That preparation protects the people from God's final act of violence against their enemies: 'At midnight, the Lord smote all the first-born in the land of Egypt, from the first-born of Pharaoh who sat on his throne to the first-born of the captive who was in the dungeon, and all the first-born of the cattle...There was not a house where one was not dead'. The result of the violent attack on the Egyptians was the royal decree that sent Israel out of the land: 'Rise and go forth from among my people...' The violent act secured the redemption of Israel from slavery. Indeed, it forced the submission of the enemy to the God of Moses and Aaron: 'And bless me also'.

The tradition at the heart of this Passover narrative reflects evidence of a second way for describing the event. The sign involving the darkness over Egypt brings a closure to the negotiations with no success in the struggle to obtain release for the captives (so, 10.28-29). There is some evidence to suggest a tradition about the exodus arising from failure in the negotiations process. With the process closed and no success in convincing the Pharaoh to release the people for a three-day march into the wilderness, Moses apparently returns to the people and leads them away from Egypt in a secret escape.[1] This tradition is obviously less violent than the Passover. Yet, it carries its own form of violence. At Moses' bidding, the people borrow jewelry of silver and gold and also clothing from the Egyptians. And when they leave Egypt in secret escape, they take these goods with them. That act the storyteller now labels as an act of despoiling. The act is not overtly violent. Yet, the act of despoiling, a military event that marks a victory over an enemy, is normally the fruit of violence. In this context, the storyteller defines the event at least as covert violence, the signs of a military victory against the enemy.[2] Thus, again, violence effects God's salvation of the people from the hands of their oppressors.

Violence as a constitutive part of the heroic traditions, a part that appears in the construction of the story as a necessary response of the hero or of God to a violent enemy, appears in other parts of the Moses traditions. In Numbers 16 the Yahwist describes the rebellion against Moses by Dathan and Abiram. The priestly source adds Korah to the ranks of the rebels. The confrontation leads to a contest of power between the opposing principals. Moses prays that the issue could be resolved if God would demonstrate Moses' proper position as leader of the people by rejecting the rebels. Verses 29-30 show a public declaration by Moses that would resolve the right of leadership in the community. That declaration calls for an event of divine violence: 'If the Lord creates something new and the ground opens its mouth and swallows them up, with all that belongs to them, and they go down alive into Sheol, then you shall know that these men have despised the Lord.' The story then reports that God did just the violent thing that Moses called for. 'So they and all that belonged to them went down alive into Sheol. And the earth closed over them, and they

---

1. G.W. Coats, 'The Failure of the Hero: Moses as a Model for Ministry', *Ashbury Theological Quarterly* 41 (1986), pp. 15-22. See ch. 10 above.
2. G.W. Coats, 'Despoiling the Egyptians', *VT* (1968), pp. 450-57.

perished from the midst of the assembly.' The event provoked fear among the Israelites that the violence would spread: 'All Israel that were round about them fled at their cry, for they said: "Lest the earth swallow us up:"'. But in fact the violence did spread. 'Fire came forth from the Lord and consumed the two hundred and fifty men offering the incense.' The violence demonstrates rejection of Moses' opposition and, by that fact, an affirmation of Moses' authority as the leader of the people.

Also in the Moses traditions, a part of the tale that describes Israel's apostasy with the Golden Calf, Exod. 32.25-29 reports an order from Moses to the Levites: 'Thus says the Lord God of Israel, "Put every man his sword on his side and go to and fro from gate to gate throughout the camp and slay every man his brother and every man his companion and every man his neighbor."' The violent slaughter of the Israelites involved in the Golden Calf incident becomes a formulation of the ordination for the Levites that requires all who serve as Levites to abandon familial ties.[1] But in the story, the ordination is effected by the slaughter of brother, companion and neighbor.

When Joshua leads the people across the Jordan into the promised land, he effects the fulfillment of God's promise for the land by submitting all captured Canaanites to the $ḥērem$: 'They utterly destroyed all in the city, both men and women, young and old, oxen, sheep, and asses, with the edge of the sword'. When Elijah confronted the prophets of Baal on Mt Carmel, the demonstration of divine power on behalf of Elijah, like the demonstration of divine power against Dathan, Abiram and Korah on behalf of Moses, leads to an execution of the prophets of Baal: 'They seized them. And Elijah brought them down to the brook Kishon and killed them there'. Even Ezra, the new Moses after the exile, employs violence in order to maintain the purity of the congregation: 'You have trespassed and married foreign women, and so increased the guilt of Israel. Now make confession to the Lord, the God of your fathers, and do his will. Separate yourselves from the people of the land and from the foreign wives'. The event does not call for the slaughter of the foreign women. But the verb, $w^ehibbād^elû$, connotes a violent disruption of family structures. In Ezra 10.3, the same violence appears: 'Therefore

---

1. G.W. Coats, *Rebellion in the Wilderness: The Murmuring Motif in the Wilderness Traditions of the Old Testament* (Nashville: Abingdon Press, 1968), pp. 66-67.

let us make a covenant with our God to put away all these wives and their children'. The verb of violence here, *lᵉhôṣî'*, is the same verb that functions in a theologically critical context to denote the exodus. Finally, the Gospel of Matthew reports an event in the ministry of Jesus when Jesus responds to the desecration of the temple by the money-changers: 'Jesus entered the temple of God and *drove out* all who sold and bought in the temple. He *overturned* the tables of the money-changers and the seats of those who sold pigeons'. The scene depicts an act of overt violence. The violence is active and dramatic in the account of overturning the tables of the money-changers. But the principal verb in the scene, depicting Jesus in the violent act of driving the people who bought and sold in the temple out of the sacred precincts, is ἐξβάλλω, the same verb used by the LXX to translate the Hebrew verb for the violent act effected by the male shepherds against the daughters of Jethro. To be sure, the verb can connote a non-violent act. When Jesus sends the seventy out on a missionary journey, the text depicts the act with this same verb. But in the temple scene, as in the scene with the male shepherds against the daughters of Jethro, the verb captures a violent show of force.[1]

In each of these examples, the hero of the tradition acts in a violent manner in order to dispell the enemy of the people who is at the same time the enemy of God. Moses kills the Egyptian who is killing his people. Joshua kills the Canaanites who occupy Jericho in order to open the promised land for God's people. Elijah kills the prophets of Baal who subvert the people's loyalty to the Lord. Ezra calls for the expulsion of foreign wives who might force the Israelites into compromise in their loyalty to the Lord. Jesus drives the people who conduct commerce in the temple out of the sacred area so that the sacred temple would not be profaned. From the point of view of the hero and

1. W.F. Albright, C.S. Mann, *Matthew* (AB 26; New York: Doubleday, 1971), p. 255. In Jn 2.13, the tradition captures the violence in the act of Jesus by showing Jesus driving the money changers away with a whip. The verb for the event is again ἐξέβαλον, from the root, ἐκβάλλω. Here the violent element in the verb is unmistakeable. The tradition is followed here by the resurrection saying concerning the temple. 'Destroy the temple, and in three days I will raise it up'. The tradition is followed in Matthew by a report that the blind and the lame came to him in the temple and he healed them. That element, too, must be understood as a resurrection tradition. Cf. G.W. Coats, 'Healing and the Moses Traditions' in G.H. Tucker, D.L. Peterson and R.R. Wilson (eds.), *Canon, Theology, and Old Testament Interpretation* (Festschrift B. Childs; Philadelphia: Fortress Press), 1988, pp. 131-46. See ch. 12 above.

those who hold the hero as their leader, this use of violence on behalf of the people is appropriate. It suggests that the people must kill the enemy—or at least drive the enemy away—before the enemy can kill the people. In that setting of hostility, who could exercise the opposite of violence on an enemy? Who could show the enemy compassion?

There is, unfortunately, another dimension in the role of violence for the heroic tradition. The people whom the hero leads can reject the hero with a threat of violence against the hero. In the spy tale, Numbers 13–14, the people respond to the report of the spies with the most overt rebellion in the narrative sequence. 'Would that we had died in the land of Egypt...would it not be better for us to go back to Egypt?' The narrative frame for the discourse of rebellion calls for another speech to make the rejection of Moses' leadership complete: 'Let us choose a captain (a different captain) and go back to Egypt'. This scene of rebellion against Moses and Aaron then develops its dimensions of overt violence, a factor made explicit by the narrative frame. 'But all the congregation said to stone them with stones. Moses' lament in Exod. 17.4 catches the same threat of violence: 'So Moses cried to the Lord: "What shall I do with this people? They are almost ready to stone me"'. In a world of violence, the violence can be turned by the people oppressed by violence back onto the heroic leader.

For the Moses tradition, the threat of death by violent rejection appears in other tales as well. The rebellion of Dathan, Abiram, and, in P, Korah features a violent resolution of the rebellion in favor of Moses. The rebellious attacks highlight Moses' position of leadership: 'All the congregation is holy...why then do you exalt yourselves above the assembly of the Lord?' The accusation threatens Moses with rejection and even death. The contest between the rebels and Moses involves a death sentence for the loser, whoever that may be. The rebellion of Aaron and Miriam, Numbers 12, ends with graphic violence infecting Miriam. But the threat of their rebellion would have been a similar violent threat against Moses, had he lost the appeal. Certainly the most tragic element of violence turned back against the hero appears in the heroic tradition about Jesus. The purpose of the life and ministry of Jesus, according to the gospel tradition, was to redeem the people of the world from their bondage to the world's way of violent oppression. The signs of the new way, the new Kingdom of God, seem explicitly to be non-violent. 'The blind receive their sight and the lame walk, lepers are cleansed and the deaf hear, and the dead are raised up, and the poor have good news preached to them.' The series of healing events, including the resurrection of the dead, mark the compassion of the new Kingdom, the opposite of the rule of human violence. In fact, the hero who experiences the violence of his own people turned back against himself responds to that violence, not with a new act of violence, but with the opposite: 'Father, forgive them. For they do not know what they do'. Compassion is defined by the prayer from the cross.

The compassion of that intercession parallels the compassion reflected in the intercession of the Moses tradition. In Exodus 32, God responds to the Golden Calf apostasy with an announcement of violent destruction for the apostates: 'Let me alone, that my wrath may burn hot against them and I may consume them'. That threat of violence against the people is coupled with a promise of new status for the hero: 'Of you I will make a great nation'. Moses could have remained still, observed God's violent destruction of the people, and then become the father of a new people. Divine violence would have honored Moses with the position of a new Abraham, the father of a new people. But Moses chooses the opposite. Rather than watching the violent destruction of these rebels with the honor in hand for becoming the father of a new people, Moses intercedes for the rebels, prepared to suffer their violent end with them, or even for them, should God choose to pursue a violent dismissal of the people: 'Alas. These people have sinned a great sin. They have made for themselves gods of gold. But now, if you will forgive their sin...If not, blot me, I pray, out of your book which you have written'. Even in the face of violent punishment against the people, Moses the hero casts his lot with the people. And the act wins concession from God. Moses' willingness to suffer violence with the people sets the hero where the hero belongs—with the people.

The tradition develops this heroic attribute to suffer with the people all the way to a description of vicarious suffering for the people. In Deut. 3.26, the storyteller assigns a speech to Moses that captures the vicarious element: 'But the Lord was angry with me on your account and would not listen to me'. Moses' petition, here rejected by God on the account of the people, was for permission to enter the land: 'Let me go over...and see the good land beyond the Jordan'. This Mosaic image of vicarious suffering catches an even more violent image of vicarious suffering in the poems about the suffering servant, a New Moses figure:

> His appearance was so marred beyond human semblance, and his form beyond that of the sons of men...He was despised and rejected by men, a man of sorrows and acquainted with grief. As one from whom men hide their faces, he was despised, and we esteemed him not. Surely he has borne our griefs and carried our sorrows. Yet, we esteemed him stricken, smitten by God, and afflicted. But he was wounded for our transgressions. He was bruised for our iniquities. Upon him was the chastisement that made us whole. And with his stripes we are healed.

It is a violent scene. It assumes that the people deserve violent judgment from the hand of God because of 'our transgressions...our iniquities'. But because the hero places himself before God in the place of the people, or at least like Moses, along with the people, God will place all of the violent judgment the people deserve on him. And because of that act, the violence the people deserve turns into compassion for the people. Because of the hero's intercession, because of the hero's vicarious substitution for the people, the violent judgment of God, the kind of violence suffered by enemies of God like the Egyptians and the Canaanites, becomes compassion. And in that compassion, the sickness of the world's people that leads to death becomes life. In the Kingdom of God, God heals every sickness, every violent attack of one human creature on any other creature in God's world. And the sign of that healing is the incredible compassion of God, the opposite of God's violence or the violence of any creature in God's world. Jesus admonished his disciples to participate in that conversion: 'You have heard that it was said, "You shall love your neighbor and hate your enemy." But I say to you, Love your enemies and pray for those who persecute you, so that you may be sons of your Father who is in heaven.'

Yet, violence is still a significant mark of human society. In Central America, in the Middle East, in the cities of the United States, people kill people. The administration of modern human society by violent means shrouds any administration of human relationships that depends on compassion. In what manner can violence become compassion in the human society of the modern world? 'Now after the Sabbath, toward the dawn of the first day of the week, Mary Magdalene and the other Mary went to see the sepulchre.'

Chapter 15

THE UNITY OF ISAIAH:
AN EXERCISE IN CANON CRITICISM

Modern critical scholarship has demonstrated clearly that the Isaiah of the Old Testament comprises at least three major units of prophetic literature, each derived from a distinctly different period of time in Israel's history. First Isaiah appears in Isaiah 1–35. Isaiah 36–39 is a section of the Deuteronomistic History taken word for word from 2 Kgs 18.13-20.19. Second Isaiah comprises chs. 40–55, and Third Isaiah appears in chs. 56–66. The critical discussion of these sections from the Isaiah text shows the periods of time for each to be as follows: Isaiah 1-35 comes from the Isaiah of Jerusalem who lived in Jerusalem during a relatively prosperous period, c. 742–700 BCE. Isaiah 36-39 comes from the Deuteronomistic History, a larger work tracing the history of both Israel and Judah, dating from c. 550 BCE. The work of the Isaiah of the Exile, the so called Second Isaiah, appears in Isaiah 40–55. The poetry of this section can be dated c. 540 BCE. The work labeled the Third Isaiah, Isaiah 56–66, is more amorphos in character, perhaps a collection of pieces from various origins. The date most likely reflected in the completed collection of the Third Isaiah is c. 520–515 BCE, the period of the construction of the second temple. Yet, it was a period marked with uncertainty and instability, perhaps also with class differences heightened by the poverty of the lowest class.

The distinctive content of each section heightens the sense of diversity in the collection. The First Isaiah addresses a relatively strong monarchy in a relatively strong and stable state. But the First Isaiah also knows the destabilizing power of the rising state in Mesopotamia, Assyria. During the career of the First Isaiah, the sister state of Israel, the northern territory of the originally unified kingdom under the Davidic monarchy, fell under the heel of the Assyrian imperialism.

The Unity of Isaiah

Among the critical items of content for the theology of this prophet are a special emphasis on the power and sovereign sanctity of Zion, Isa. 2.1-4, and the companion emphasis on the king in Zion, the messiah. It is significant that both points describe, not the current power structure in Jerusalem, but an anticipation of God's vindication over the enemies of Israel slated for some time in the future. Zion will be raised as a world mountain, the navel of the universe. And the king, the Son of God, will vanquish all enemies.

Three key texts set out the messianic dimension. One should note just here that 'messiah' refers to the anointed, the king. The messiah is distinctly a royal figure. So, Isa. 7.14-17 announces the birth of the Immanuel child, perhaps the king whose name promises God's presence for all who receive his position. But the prophecy is not just a proclamation of the birth of a king whose name promises God's presence. The Isaiah text announces that the child will be born to a 'young woman', or *'almâ*. The power of this text has been clouded in the history of the Christian Church, indeed, in recent discussion about the RSV translation of the term as 'young woman'. Part of the issue derives from the LXX translation of this text with παρθενος, virgin. From that text, the New Testament announces the birth of Jesus to a Virgin who conceives her son with the Holy Spirit. Much effort has been exerted in an argument designed to show that even though the Isaiah text does not use the more common Hebrew noun for virgin, *b^{e}tûlâ*, the noun, *'almâ* can refer to an unmarried woman, obviously virgin. So, in Exod. 2.8, the sister of Moses, obviously unmarried, is described as *hā'almâ*. Yet, to argue for a definition of the noun *'almâ* as virgin, an issue of importance for Christians, obscures the power of the word in the Isaiah prophecy. The word in its plural form, *'^{a}lāmôt*, describes a section of the royal harem. In the Song of Solomon, 6.8, the royal harem comprises three sections: (1) the queens, *m^{e}lakôt*, (2) the concubines, *pîlagšîm*, and (3) the maidens, *'^{a}lamôt*. The point of emphasis is that the *'alamôt* are third class citizens in the royal harem As a third class citizen, the *'almâ* is open to abuse, manipulation, and exploitation, not only from the king, but also from the upper classes in the harem. The remarkable thing about the Isaiah prophecy that an *'alma* would conceive is that an *'almâ* would ever have a chance to conceive. Yet, Isaiah observes that one from the *'^{a}lāmôt* will conceive and bear the royal son. The son who will carry the Immanuel name, the power of God as the messianic Son of God, will be born to a maiden who belongs to the third class of the harem population and thus to a maiden who knows the plight of submission to the power figures in the harem and the king himself. In the New Testament, the Magnificat catches this status: 'My soul magnifies the Lord, and my spirit rejoices in God, my Savior, for he has regarded the low estate of his handmaiden'. The key noun in the Magnificat is δούλης, an effective interpretation of the connotations of ^{a}lāmôt in Isa. 7.14. Moreover, in the same poem the poet confirms that in this relationship, God 'has filled the hungry with good things'. For the Isaiah text, the promise for the birth of the messiah, an event within the structure of the royal harem that effects the upper classes of power and wealth in Israel, promises an heir to the throne who will be sensitive to the problems of the lower classes of people, the exploited, the forgotten. A Davidic heir who also knows the plight of the hungry, the exploited, the third class of people in Israel's society can attend to the plight of the hungry since such social position marks the place of his birth. To emphasize the virginity of the ^{a}lmâ would mask the exploitation of the third-class citizens in the royal harem and everywhere else in the kingdom. It would emphasize the divine origin of the child. It would open the door for understanding heroes in Israelite tradition as heroic people, fully human, and people of God, fully divine. But it would risk obscuring the promise for an heir to the throne who would be sensitive to the problems of the lower classes of people, the exploited, the forgotten. A Davidic heir who also knows the third class of people in Israel's society can attend to the plight of the hungry since such social position marks the place of his birth. The Immanuel child, the child who symbolizes for Israel the promise of God's presence, makes it clear that God's promise does not come to royalty alone. It comes to those who cannot control their destiny by their wealth and power, by their position in the structure of the society.

The second messianic oracle, Isa. 9.1-6, announces the birth of a child, obviously to the royal family, for the government will be on his shoulder. The birth of the child is associated with light, a great light that corrects the darkness that had covered the people. In this oracle, the light is apparently simply the event of the birth that brings joy to the people. But the light also announces removal of oppression, the yoke of a burden, indeed, even the end of battle noise. The throne names in v. 6 associate the child with God, with strength and ability to direct the people, but perhaps of most importance, with peace.

'Wonderful Counselor, Mighty God, Everlasting Father, Prince of Peace.' Moreover, the government of this child will be eternal (cf. 2 Sam. 7.15-16). The power of this king will secure the dynasty of the king in power forever. But the king does not sit in that powerful throne for personal privilege. To the contrary, the throne elevates the messiah to a position of power that is secured by the administration of justice and righteousness. These terms direct the power of the throne beyond the king who administers the operation of the government to a consideration of the benefit of the people who live under the king's authority. Justice orders the society so that all within the structure of society can receive fair hearing. Righteousness orders all within the structure of society so that each returns the justice to the other and to the society at large. The power of the messiah will serve that just and righteous structure for all time to come.

A third poem, 11.1-9, defines the character of the messiah still one further step. From Jesse, that is, from David, the messiah will emerge marked by the mantle of the Spirit of the Lord. Key attributes for this messiah are wisdom, understanding, the spirit of counsel and strength, and especially knowledge and fear of the Lord. The last two attributes define the intimate relationship between this king, this messiah who can be called in the Jerusalem tradition the Son of God (Ps. 110.2), the God who rules from Zion, and the people who live under the messiah's administration. The description of this messianic warrior develops beyond personal attributes to the task of the messianic role. Again, justice and righteousness dominate the work of the messiah. But now, the messiah's clientele is defined—the meek and the poor. Both terms define not simply a social class of people, but particularly a class that calls for moral commitment. That commitment appears sharply in v. 5: 'Righteousness, faithfulness'. Both terms point to the integrity of the messiah.

But the ethical structure of the messianic kingdom moves beyond the messiah. In vv. 6-9, a description of peace in the kingdom depicts mutual enemies at rest with each other. Destruction by one element of society against the opposing element will end under the administration of the messiah's kingdom, the result of the knowledge of the Lord. But it should be clear that the focus of this peace is not passive, a peace imposed by God over the peaceable kingdom. It is active. It is the result of justice and righteousness. In that society, all creatures participate actively in the peace. No people, not the poor, not the hungry, not the exploited, the forgotten and ignored, will fall away unnoticed in the peaceable kingdom. The power of the king will secure the power of the Kingdom of God. And in that kingdom is righteousness and justice.

In contrast to the New David, the messiah, at the center of the First Isaiah, the Second Isaiah describes God's leader as a servant, a New Moses who will lead the people from their exile in Babylon through the wilderness to the land promised to the Fathers. Indeed, the imagery for the redemption of the people from their Babylonian captivity derives from the life and vocation of the shepherd. The four servant poems in the Second Isaiah demonstrate the point effectively. The first poem, 42.1-4, depicts the figure at the center of the power as God's servant, '*abdi (Ps.* 105.26), the one chosen by God, *b^{e}hîrî*. The task of this servant is to bring justice for all people, for the nations (vv. 1, 3, 4). And this justice derives from the Torah of the servant (v. 4), again an item explicitly at home in the Moses traditions (Exod. 12.49; 18.16, 20). But the important element in this Mosaic Torah is that with the servant, the Torah now offers the realm of God's grace to all the people, the coastlands and the nations.

In the second poem, the servant addresses the coastlands and the nations. The address establishes the authority of the servant by reference to the call of God, an element typical for prophetic tradition but characteristic for the Mosaic saga (Exodus 3). In this case, the authorizing event begins even before the prophet's birth. The typical reference to the prophet's mouth marks the commission to the task. But in this case, the servant's responsibility moves beyond a commission to deliver the people from exilic bondage to a universal role: 'I will give you as a light to the nations, that my salvation may reach to the end of the earth'. The light motif particularly relates the Moses tradition to the broader concerns of God's word for all people.

In the third poem, 50.4-11, the servant describes the burden of the task, a burden that involves suffering if the task should be properly fulfilled: 'I gave my back to the smiters, and my cheeks to those who pulled out the beard. I hid not my face from shame and spitting. For the Lord God helps me. Therefore, I have not been confounded'.

The fourth poem, 52.13–53.12, increases the image of the servant's suffering as a consequence of the servant's integrity in carrying out God's commission. But the new dimension in the presentation of the suffering is the vicarious quality. 'Surely he has borne our griefs and carried our sorrows. Yet we esteemed him stricken, smitten by God and afflicted. But he was wounded for our transgressions. He was bruised for our iniquities. Upon him was the chastisement that made us whole. With his stripes we are healed.' The vicarious quality of the servant's suffering that produces healing for the people is distinctly Mosaic (so, Ps. 106.32; Deut 4.21).

The Third Isaiah, Isaiah 56–66, also speaks of a special agent for God, an agent charged with a message for the people. Indeed, the special agent describes the authorizing moment with God. 'The Spirit of the Lord God is upon me because the Lord has anointed me to bring good tidings to the poor. He has sent me to bind up the brokenhearted, to proclaim liberty to the captives, and the opening of the prison for those who are bound...' Indeed, the proclamation of this messenger brings the promise of restoration. 'Instead of shame, you shall have a double portion. Instead of dishonor, you shall rejoice in your lot. Therefore in your land, you shall possess a double portion. Yours shall be everlasting joy.' But the restoration announced by this messenger is not a restoration to privilege. It is a restoration to responsibility. 'For I the Lord love justice.' Perhaps the sharpest description of that responsibility for the Third Isaiah comes in Isaiah 58, a depiction of the restoration of the cult with its liturgical festivals.

> Is not this the fast that I choose: to loose the bonds of wickedness, to undo the thongs of the yoke, to let the oppressed go free, and to break every yoke? Is it not to share your bread with the hungry and bring the homeless poor into your house, when you see the naked, to clothe him and not to hide yourself from your own flesh? Then shall your light break forth like the dawn, and your healing shall spring up speedily. Your righteousness shall go before you. The glory of the Lord shall be your rear guard. Then you shall call and the Lord will answer. You shall cry, and he will say 'Here I am'.

The servant images derive primarily from the Moses traditions. Indeed, the light motif, a part of the Moses traditions present also in the Second Isaiah, brings the rhapsody for ethics for the Third Isaiah to a close: 'Then shall your light rise in the darkness and your gloom be as the noon day'. And still another motif from the Moses traditions marks the second line: 'The Lord will guide you continually and satisfy your hunger with divine care'. The wilderness march with its manna and water shapes the promise for the life of an Israel who obeys, who 'takes delight in the Lord'.

In each of these sections of the Isaiah book, a figure appears who will serve the call of God to lead Israel in its task to deliver the word of God to the world. Each figure is distinct. In the First Isaiah, the figure is messianic, a new David who will deliver Israel by the power of his office in Zion. In the Second Isaiah, the figure is a servant, a new Moses who will deliver Israel by guiding the people through the wilderness to the new land, indeed, by the self-sacrifice that brings them to that goal. In the Third Isaiah, the figure is a messenger, but again a new Moses who will deliver God's hope for the new age to the people who languish in hopeless despair. The difference between the messianic figure with its Davidic lines and the servant figure with its Mosaic lines recalls, with sharp poignancy, the split in the fabric of Israel between the Davidic heir and the Mosaic heir, between the Jews and the Samaritans. And perhaps the split also recalls the division in Christianity between the hierarchical traditions of the Catholic community and the egalitarian tradition of the Protestant community. A dominant theme through the history of God's people is strife that breaks the community apart.

Yet, it is just at this point that the canonical unity of the book of Isaiah breaks through the classical critical discussion of Isaiah with its emphasis on the historical and traditional disunity to reveal the light of a remarkable unity, a reconciliation of the striving factions. What happens when the messiah of the First Isaiah and the servant of the Second Isaiah and the messenger of the Third Isaiah appear together, reconciled into one figure as the instrument of God's word? In the history of the tradition, has that canonical unity ever appeared in a single event in the stage of human history? Perhaps the event occurred with Josiah who sought to reconcile the North and the South under a common bond of loyalty and commitment to the Lord. But he died on top of a lonely mountain before the task was complete. Perhaps Ezra and Nehemiah together offered reconciliation for both poles in the exilic community of Jews and Samaritans. But reform and new law gave way to the despair of postexilic poverty. In the life and ministry of Jesus from Nazareth, both messiah and suffering servant come together specifically to call disciples to share their bread with the poor and hungry. And the call addresses both Jew and Samaritan. But he too died on a lonely hill, his gospel of reconciliation for rich and poor nailed to a cross of despair for human hope. Yet, the reconciled parts of the book of Isaiah remind the disciples of Isaiah that the honor and dignity of the messiah must combine with the integrity and commitment of the servant, even in the face of suffering and death. That unity reflected in the Book of Isaiah, that reconciliation stands at the center of the proclamation of a church created beyond the despair of disciples who followed their crucified Lord by the hope and vision of disciples called to reconciliation with all humankind by the Lord of the resurrection.

Chapter 16

SCOPE AND STRUCTURE FOR THE YAHWIST:
WHERE DOES IT END?

The Bible's first history, according to Coote and Ord, was written by the Yahwist, the author of the oldest strand in the Pentateuch.[1] Written as a defense of King David from within the court of the first king of the united monarchy, the Yahwist presents the history of the world from creation through the tradition about Balaam. The Yahwist, according to Coote and Ord, was a 'great tradition', a product of the urban court of the monarchy, in contrast to the 'little tradition', the perspective of the peasant shepherd class represented by the Moses tradition. 'The immediate occasion for the composition of J was the necessity of validating the establishment of the Davidic royal house, which replaced a much less centralized political arrangement in the highlands of Palestine.'[2]

Moreover, the entire scope of the Pentateuch is controlled by the Yahwist. The sources classically labeled E and P are supplemental revisions of J. J. reveals, according to the authors, no conception of the division between Judah and Israel.[3] One must ask just at this point about the significance of the murmuring tradition in the Yahwist.[4] That pattern shows a development in the history of the tradition that clearly reports rejection of the wilderness generation in favor of David and the citizens of the monarchy. Psalm 78 demonstrates that the rejection of the rebels in the wilderness occurs so that David and his court can assume their place as God's chosen people. Indeed, the

1. R.B. Coote and D.R. Ord, *The Bible's First History: From Eden to the Court of David with the Yahwist* (Philadelphia: Fortress Press, 1989).
2. Coote and Ord, *Bible's First History*, p. 6.
3. Coote and Ord, *Bible's First History*, p. 5.
4. G.W. Coats, *Rebellion in the Wilderness: The Murmuring Motif in the Wilderness Traditions of the Old Testament* (Nashville: Abingdon Press, 1968).

golden calf incident, Exodus 32–34, suggests the rejection of the northern political structures.[1] To treat these items simply as later supplements[2] obscures the complexity of the tradition.

Of even more importance in the Yahwist's construction is the role of Moses. According to Coote and Ord, 'J is a history of the world written by David's scribes with the Kingdom of David at its center...'[3] But J presents Moses as the hero of the story.[4] Does that construction imply that David is the New Moses?[5] Or does it suggest that for the Yahwist, the Mosaic leadership implies a critical judgment against David? David ought to have been the New Moses.

A vital element in the argument emerges from the quest by Coote and Ord for the end of the Yahwist. According to their conception, the Yahwist ends with a sharp focus on God's blessing for David, set out in the narrative about Balaam.[6] Balaam blesses Israel in the face of the challenge from Barak. That blessing sets the pattern for God's blessing on Israel through the kingship of David. Indeed, the allusion in the last of the Balaam oracles, Num. 24.15-24, to a 'star' that will come from Jacob, a 'scepter' from Israel, has commonly been interpreted as an allusion to David.[7] The Yahwist ends the story of Israel's emergence, according to Coote and Ord, with Israel still underway toward the land, yet nevertheless moving under the protection of the God Yahweh who will establish David as the instrument of divine authority over the people of Israel.

Yet, one major problem arises at just this point. The oracles of Balaam do not report that David's kingdom was established by God as the instrument for divine promotion for Israel. The oracle functions rather as a prolepsis. It anticipates an event that will establish the rule of God in Israel. But that event remains in the future. If the Yahwist writes from the context of the court of David, why does the J narrative leave Israel in the wilderness, merely anticipating God's action?

1. G.W. Coats, 'The Golden Calf in Psalm 22', *HBT* 9 (1987), pp. 1-12. See ch. 11 above.
2. Coote and Ord, *Bible's First History*, p. 6.
3. Coote and Ord, *Bible's First History*, p. 29.
4. G.W. Coats, *Moses: Heroic Man, Man of God* (JSOTSup, 57; Sheffield: JSOT Press, 1988).
5. Coote and Ord, *Bible's First History*, p. 234.
6. Coote and Ord, *Bible's First History*, p. 289.
7. M. Noth, *Numbers, a Commentary* (OTL; Philadelphia: Westminster Press, 1968), pp. 192-93.

Why does the narrative not report entry into the land that becomes the center for David's royal kingdom? Does the proleptic character of Balaam's blessing not anticipate some further act of God that will establish the kingdom that becomes the throne of David?

When one asks about the conclusion of the Yahwist, an answer to the question might be facilitated by a definition of conclusions as a typical genre element for narrative tradition. How does the storyteller typically bring a saga like the story of the Yahwist to a conclusion? In order to pose a point of comparison for the definition of the genre element, I suggest that a description of the final scene in the Gilgamesh Epic will suggest a typical pattern for a colophon in an ancient story. In the Babylonian form of the tradition, Gilgamesh plays a role similar to the character of Moses, then repeated by the character of Joshua in the Yahwist's narrative. A hero who defends the people against the enemy, Gilgamesh wins the day. The final scenes, set out by Pritchard from a difficult reconstruction. But the climax features the final moments of the hero. Despite the problematic character of the text, the point of focus seems quite clear. Lines 98 and 99 read:

(Gilgamesh) cried 'Woe!' and threw himself (in the dust).
'(hast thou seen)?' 'I have seen.'

Pritchard's translation suggests the following lines from the Akkadian tablet, repeating the leitmotif: 'I have seen'.

At no point in the Balaam legend does this particular motif appear. Certainly, the repetitious character of the motif does not appear in the Balaam material. This fact, coupled with the character of the allusions to the Davidic element as foreshadowing rather than climax, suggests that the Yahwistic narrative, clearly present in the Balaam legend, does not end with Balaam, but continues into the following sections of the canonical narrative.

The pressing question must then be posed. Where does the Yahwist's narrative end? The account of the death of Moses in Deuteronomy 34, with perhaps some elements of the priestly narrative intertwined, has traditionally been attributed to J.[1] The death tale for Moses, clearly the end of the Moses heroic saga in the Yahwist,[2] fits a part of the structural device paralleled by the Gilgamesh Epic. The final stages in

---

1. G.W. Coats, 'Legendary Motifs in the Moses Death Reports', *CBQ* 39 (1977), pp. 34-44. See ch. 6 above.
2. Coats, *Moses*, pp. 145-53.

Scope and Structure for the Yahwist 193

the Gilgamesh story mark the end of the narrative with a death report. Gilgamesh dies and is buried. Moses dies in the presence of the Lord. But the Moses death report leaves the people on the edge of the land. The ordination of Joshua, a part of the Yahwist's narrative, concludes the death report for Moses. But it does not conclude the epic structure of the Yahwist.

A text that offers a clear structural parallel with the conclusion of the Gilgamesh Epic and a fitting climax for the Yahwist's narrative appear in Joshua 24. Following the credo and the corresponding appeal to commitment in covenant with the Lord, the text reports that the people commit themselves to the Lord in a covenant bond. Joshua calls for a repetition of the commitment and the people respond again. The repetition, is similar to the repetition pattern at the end of the Gilgamesh narrative. But an even stronger element of repetition appears in the Joshua text. The concluding frame defines the people of the covenant as witnesses ('*ēdîm*) against themselves. The motif, '*ēdîm*, and its singular counterpart '*ēd*, is repeated in three different, critical elements of the scene. Indeed, a stone, '*eben*, v. 26, becomes the physical symbol for the witness. Then v. 27 asserts that the stone is the witness to the covenant because it has heard the process, the sensual process that parallels the appeal to seeing in the Gilgamesh narrative. On the basis of the event, sealed by the witness of the people, symbolized by the witness of the stone, the covenant is concluded, and Joshua can dismiss the people. The structural element that follows is the Joshua death report. The formal structure of the Joshua death report is not the same as the formal structure of the Moses death report in Deuteronomy 34. In effect, the Joshua account is simply a notice that Joshua died and was buried and that the people were faithful to the Lord for the period of Joshua's life and the lives of the leaders who followed him.

The Gilgamesh Epic also ends with a death report for Gilgamesh. But, as noted above, one of the most striking motifs in the death report is the repetition of the motif, 'I have seen'. Line 99 in tablet xii, a tablet that, according to Pritchard, might be labeled an inorganic appendage, calls for Gilgamesh to report what he has seen in the nether world. The affirmation of the report is marked by repetition of the motif. 'I have seen', a motif that marks the witness of Gilgamesh to the nether world. But it also marks the function of the narrative itself as a witness to the events in the narrative as the essence of reality. I suggest that the repetition of the character of Gilgamesh as a witness in the recurring phrase, 'I have seen', parallels the repetition in Joshua's address to the people calling them to be witnesses to the covenant, but, indeed, to the whole scope of God's acts that undergird the covenant and constitute the credo, thus to the whole scope of the Yahwist.

One of the most common narrative elements in the development of the Yahwist's plot is the depiction of the central figures in the tradition caught in the middle of various forms of violence, a tragedy in the human community depicted as broken intimacy.[1] From the opening scene of the Yahwist, that tragedy stands at center stage. But the consequence of that tragedy for the shape of the Yahwist's narrative is a sharp question—given the character of the human tragedy as broken intimacy, a tragedy that controls the shape of the Yahwist in depicting the human-God relationship, the human-human relationship, and the human-nature relationship, how does the Yahwist depict any resolution for the tragedy? The key element focused on broken intimacy runs the scope of the Yahwist's narrative. But the climax of the tension cannot be identified at the end of the Pentateuch, in Deuteronomy 34. The people depend on Moses for leadership, indeed, for mediating their relationship with the Lord. But Moses dies before entry into the land, before reconciliation with the Lord or with themselves. That tension, that focus on broken intimacy, sharpens in Joshua 22. The Reubenites, the Gadites, and the half tribe of Manasseh violate the system of unity at the basis of the people under Joshua's leadership by building an altar 'at the frontier of the land of Canaan' (v. 11). Joshua calls the people away from that act by demanding that the people 'pass over into the Lord's land where the Lord's tabernacle stands' (v. 19). The defense for the construction of the altar names the altar, not as a place for burnt offering, 'but to be a witness between us and you and between the generations after us...' The defense is repeated in v. 28 with the altar again named as a witness. Indeed, the conclusion in v. 34 observes that the Reubenites and the Gadites named the altar 'witness'. The institutional formula is in v. 34b: 'It is a witness between us that the Lord is God'. This act of construction parallels the covenant stone that serves as a witness to the words of the book of the law of God in Jos. 24.26. The ceremony with its recitation of the credo functions as a reconciliation between the people and God, an

---

1. G.W. Coats, *Genesis* (FOTL, 1; Grand Rapids: Eerdmans, 1983), pp. 49-53.

appeal caught explicitly in 23.8 by the reference to the intimate act, 'cleave' (*dābaq*) to the Lord your God...' (cf. Gen. 2.24).[1]

I propose, then, that the ending of the Yahwist appears in Jos. 24.1-32 (33). The central theme for the Yahwist, broken intimacy within the community of the people of God, is resolved in the cultic event at Shechem, highlighted by the credo. Moreover, the notation in v. 26 that Joshua should write these words in the book of the law of God must be an allusion to the integrity of 'these words' as a witness to the acts of God, indeed, as a 'book of the law of God'. The Yahwist thus covers the structure represented by the credo and developed in detail throughout the scope of the Hexateuch.

---

1. G.W. Coats, *Genesis*, pp. 49-60.

INDEXES

INDEX OF REFERENCES

OLD TESTAMENT

Genesis		1.27	155	14.19-20	162
1–11	153, 163	1.28	155	22	57
1.1-2	153	1.29-30	155	24.1-67	25
1–3	151, 153	1.30	155	24.11	106
1.3-31	153	1.31	155	27.1	78
1.3-5	153	2–3	168	29.1-30	25
1.6-8	153	2	159	29.2	106
1.6	153	2.1-4	155	31.25-32	27
1.7-8	153	2.1	155	32	58
1.7	153	2.2-3	155	39.1-6	91
1.8	153	2.2	155	39.3-4	80
1.9-13	154, 155	2.3	155	39.22	80
1.9-10	154	2.4–3.24	157	41.44	53
1.9	154	2.4	155	42.20	91
1.10	154	2.20	158	42.27	29
1.11-12	154	2.23	159	45.3-13	53
1.11	154	2.24	138, 159, 195	46.4	83
1.12	154			50.22-25	76
1.13	154	2.25	159		
1.14-19	154	3	160	*Exodus*	
1.14-15	154	3.1	135, 160	1–40	22, 28
1.16-18	154	3.8	161	1–14	26
1.19	154	3.14-15	161	1	41
1.20-23	154	3.16	161	1.6	28
1.20	154	3.17-19	161	1.8-12	24
1.21-22	154	3.22-24	161	1.15-22	24
1.21	154	3.22	161	1.22	171
1.22	154, 155	4	162	2	41
1.23	154	5.5	76	2.1-10	24, 25, 84
1.24-31	154	6–9	162	2.1-2	171
1.24-25	154	6.6	162	2.8	183
1.24	154	9.20-29	159	2.10	104
1.25	154	9.20-27	162	2.11–4.31	30
1.26-31	155	11	162	2.11-22	22, 24, 25, 28-30, 84,
1.26	155	12.1-3	21, 137		

Index of References

	104	3.14	17, 69	14.16	37, 39
2.11-15	22, 28, 105, 107, 172	3.16-18	27, 29	14.18	53, 54
		3.21-22	121	14.21	38, 45, 48
2.11-14	24	4.1-5	37	14.24-25	45
2.11-12	105, 107	4.18	23, 27-29	14.25	39
2.11	104, 108, 172	4.19-23	23, 28, 30	14.27	36, 45, 48
		4.19-20	28, 29	14.30	39
2.11	107, 110	4.19	28, 29	14.31	54, 74
2.12	107, 108, 172	4.20	25, 37, 38	15	44
		4.21-23	29	15.1-18	46
2.13-14	106, 107	4.24-26	23, 29, 30	15.4-5	46
2.13	107, 109	4.24	29	15.6-10	46
2.14-22	24	4.27-31	23, 30	15.8	46
2.14-17	24	4.27	26, 27	15.9	46
2.14-15	24, 107	4.31	74	15.10	46
2.14	105, 107, 109	5	116, 119, 121	15.14-16	54
				15.21b	45
2.15-22	28, 105-107, 173	5.1–6.1	23	15.22-27	59
		5.2	117	15.22-26	137
2.15-17	107, 109	5.7-9	117	15.24	59
2.15-16	107	5.10-14	118	15.25-26	137
2.16-20	22	5.14	118	16	168
2.16-17	107	5.15-19	118	16.3	137
2.17	107, 110	5.20	118	16.20	168
2.18-22	24, 107	5.22	119	16.22-23	168
2.18-19	107	6.2–7.6	22, 23	16.29-30	176
2.18	110	7–12	119	17	34, 37-39, 91
2.20	107	7–11	174		
2.21-22	25, 107	7.6	23	17.1-7	26, 38, 52, 59
2.21	25, 107	7.7–10.29			
2.22	25, 104, 106, 107	7.17	86	17.4	179
		7.19	37	17.8-16	26, 32, 77, 84, 91
2.23-25	25, 28	7.20-25	44		
2.23	28, 104	8.12	37	17.8-13	34, 35, 38, 40
2.24-25	28	10	121		
3–4	14	10.28-29	120, 176	17.8-11	37
3.1–4.18	22, 23, 25, 26, 30	10.29	119	17.8-9	43
		11.2-3	121	17.8	32, 35
3	26, 41, 186	12.10	122	17.9-12	35
3.1-6	16, 26, 27, 30	12.34	122	17.9	33, 35, 37
		12.35	121	17.10-12	35
3.1	26-28, 21	12.43-49	30	17.10	35
3.7-10	16	12.49	186	17.12	34, 37, 38, 40, 91
3.7-8	28, 136	13.1-16	30		
3.9-10	16	14	37-39, 44, 46, 49, 53	17.13	35
3.10	27			17.14-16	33
3.12-14	18	14.1–17.7	32, 40	17.14	33, 34
3.12	17	14.13-14	39	17.15-16	33, 34

17.16	34	32.25-29	177	25.2-7	168
17.18ff.	36	32.30-32	63, 96		
18	26, 28, 31, 32, 41, 43, 79	32.31-32	65, 96	*Numbers*	
		32.33-34	66, 67	11	89
		32.34	62, 65, 67	11.11-15	65
18.1-27	30	32.35	63, 66	11.16-17	79
18.1-12	31	33–34	66	11.17	80
18.1-7	25	33	66, 69	11.24-30	79
18.5	26	33.1-6	66	12	88, 93, 98, 179
18.7	25	33.1-3	17		
18.8	174	33.1	66, 68	12.1-16	138
18.12	31	33.2	66	12.1-15	91, 96
18.13-27	30	33.3	66, 67	12.1-3	96, 97
18.16	186	33.4-6	67	12.1-2	96, 97
18.20	186	33.5	67	12.1	88, 97
18.27	26	33.7-11	67	12.2b	89
19–24	26	33.11	67, 80	12.2	89, 97
19	26, 60	33.12-23	17	12.3	89, 90, 92, 94-96, 97, 138
19.1ff.	40	33.12-17	68		
19.1-2	26	33.12-13	67		
19.2	26	33.12	67	12.4-8	96, 97
19.5	57	33.12	67	12.4-5	96
19.6	57	33.13	68	12.4	89, 97
24.13	26, 27	33.14	68	12.5	95
31.12-17	156	33.15	68	12.6-8	78, 94, 95
31.13	156	33.16	17, 69	12.6	97
31.14-17	156	33.17-23	69	12.7-8	97
31.16	156	33.17	69	12.7	80, 91, 92, 95
32–34	57, 61, 71, 72, 191	33.18	69		
		33.19	17	12.8	96, 97
32	63, 65-67, 125, 129, 180	34	69-71	12.9-15	96
		34.2-3	69	12.9-14	95, 97
		34.7	69	12.9-10	96, 97
32.1-6	60	34.8-9	69	12.10	88
32.1	60, 61, 125, 126	34.9	69	12.11-12	97, 139
		34.10	70	12.11a	96
32.4	60	34.11	174	12.11b	96
32.7-35	62	34.27-28	70	12.12	96
32.8	62, 132	34.29-35	70, 80	12.13	92, 97
32.10	62, 63	34.29-30	70	12.14	97
32.11-13	63	34.33-34	70	12.15	97
32.11	63	35	70	13–14	179
32.12	64			14.13-25	65
32.13	68	*Leviticus*		14.13-19	64
32.14	65	13.37	144	14.20	65
32.18	128	14.3	144	14.21	65
32.21-24	96	14.48	144	14.35	138
32.21	128	18.1ff.	54	15.32-36	147

16	89, 176	34.7	77, 78	*1 Kings*	
16.29-30	176	34.9	79	3.9	158
20.2-13	81	34.10	80	12	165
20.22-29	80, 82	34.11-12	80, 81	12.25-33	128
21.4-9	139			12.26-33	60
21.6	139	*Joshua*		12.28	61
21.9	140	1–24	133	17.23	140
21.21-31	39	2.10	46, 50, 54	19.8-12	127
21.33-35	42	6.1-21	39	19.8	26, 27
21.34	39	22	194	19.11-14	69
23.22	129, 130	22.1-6	163		
24.7-9	142	22.11	194	*2 Kings*	
24.8	129	22.17	142	2.9	80
24.15-24	191	22.19	39, 194	2.13	80
24.17	142	22.28	194	12.16	40
27.12-23	77	22.34	194	13.14-21	83
27.13-14	81	23.8	195	18.4	133, 139, 140
27.18-21	79	24	193		
27.20	79	24.1-32	195	18.6	159
		24.1-28	142	18.13–20.19	182
Deuteronomy		24.2-13	152	20.5	144
1–34	18	24.12	122	22–23	142
1.37	82	24.14-15	52	22.7	40
3.26	82, 180	24.26	193, 194, 195		
3.27	82			*1 Chronicles*	
3.28	79	24.27	193	9.22	40
4.21	82, 100, 187				
25.17-19	33, 34, 39	*Judges*		*2 Chronicles*	
26.5-11	142	6.11-24	16	7.14	145
26.5-9	151			34.12	40
28.60	138	*1 Samuel*			
28.61	138	2.35	91	*Ezra*	
28.63	138	3.20	91	10.3	177
31	78	14.6-15	35, 36		
31.1-23	77	15.2-3	33	*Job*	
31.2	78	15.2	39	1–42	17, 18
31.7	79	22.14	91		
31.14	79	31.1-7	36	*Psalms*	
31.23	79			18.36	94
32.39	141	*2 Samuel*		21.6	79
32.48-52	77, 81	7.15-16	185	22	125, 130, 132
32.51-52	81	11.2-5	159		
33.17	130	12.1-7a	112, 123, 172	22.2	130
34	41, 83, 193, 194			22.4-5	130
		20	101	22.6	130
34.1-12	77, 82	20.2	159	22.7	130
34.4	81, 82	22.36	94	22.11	130
34.6	42			22.12	130

22.13-20	130	19.22	145	33.5	141
22.20-22	130	29.19	92	33.6	141
22.22	130, 131	32.7	92	42.10	146
22.23	131	36–39	182		
30.3-4	141	40–55	147, 182	*Ezekiel*	
45.4	79	42.1-4	186	13.10	143
45.5	94	42.1	186	13.16	143
78	164, 190	42.3	186	34	114
78.67-72	164	42.4	78, 186		
89.20	158	43.10	54	*Hosea*	
92.11	130	43.16-17	46	6.1	145
105.26	186	45.9	58	8.5	167
105.37	121	49.6	133	12.13	146
106.32	82, 187	49.13	92	13.4	174
110.2	185	50.4-11	186	14.1-8	145
149.4	93	51.9-10	46	14.1-3	145
		52.13–53.12	186	14.1-2	145
Proverbs		53.4-9	82	14.2-3	145
15.33	92	53.8	141	14.3	145
18.12	92	56–66	182, 187	14.4-8	145
18.24	157	57.14-21	146	14.4	145
		57.14-15	146	14.5	145
		57.14	146	14.8	146
Song of Solomon		57.15b	146		
6.8	181	57.16	146	*Amos*	
		57.17	146, 147	2.7	93
		57.18	147	5.21-24	135
Sirach		57.20	147	5.24	167
1.27	91	57.21	147	8.4	92
		58.1-14	147, 187		
		58.1-5	147	*Micah*	
Isaiah		58.2	147	1.9	144
1–66	19, 182	58.3-4	148	3.5	143
1–35	182	58.4	148	6.8	167
2.1-4	183	58.6-7	148		
6.10	145	58.8-9	148	*Nahum*	
6.19	145			3.19	144
7.9	91	*Jeremiah*			
7.14-17	183	3.22	145	*Habakkuk*	
7.14	184	6.14	137, 143, 144	3.4	70, 71
9.1-6	144, 184				
9.2-7	166	8.11	137, 143, 144	*Zechariah*	
9.6	184			11.17	78
11.1-9	123, 164, 185	12.1	58		
		12.2	58	*Malachi*	
11.5	185	15.8	144	1.4	146
11.6-9	144, 185	30.12	144		

NEW TESTAMENT

Matthew		17.5	71	3.14	140, 141
1–28	19, 20	27.45-50	83	17	142
9.1-8	144, 149				
12.9-14	148	*John*		*1 Corinthians*	
16.15	71	2.13	178	11.17-26	149
17.1-7	71	3.14-15	149		

INDEX OF AUTHORS

Aberbach, M., 125, 128
Albright, W. F. 78, 178
Andersen, F. I. 128
Anderson, B. W. 84
Auerbach, E. 78, 81, 85

Baentsch, B. 89, 95
Bailey, L. R. 132
Barr, J. 50
Barth, K. 43
Barzel, H. 82
Beegle, D. M. 84-86
Begrich, J. 131
Bentzen, A. 136, 141
Boecker, H. J. 118, 173
Brekelmans, C. H. W. 31
Bright, J. 48, 49
Brown, R. E. 142
Brueggemann. W. 43, 44, 60, 86, 87
Buber, M., 17, 173

Campbell, J. 84, 170
Carlson, R. A. 80
Chadwick, H. M. 40, 84
Chadwick, N. K. 40, 84
Childs, B. S. 24, 29, 32, 34, 35, 38, 39, 60, 61-63, 65, 67-70, 84, 97, 106, 108, 109, 127, 136, 138, 171, 178
Coats, G. W. 28, 30, 32, 41, 57, 59, 77, 81, 82, 91, 107, 110-13, 116, 118, 122, 123, 126, 133, 135, 137, 138, 142, 169, 171, 172, 176-78, 190-92, 194, 195
Cody, A. 31
Coote, R. B. 190, 191
Cross, F. M. 48

Dahood, M. 131
Delekat, L. 93, 94
Davenport, J. W. 125, 128-30
Dunlop, L. 59, 73
Dus, J. 61

Edelmann, R. 128

Ford, L. S. 57, 74, 75

Gelin, A. 93
Gerbrandt, G. E. 123
Gray, G. B. 92
Greenberg, M. 85
Gressmann, H. 24, 26, 37, 41
Gronbaek, J. H. 32, 36, 37-39
Gunneweg, H. J. 23, 28

Habel, N. 16
Hals, R. M. 40, 79, 90, 94
Hay, L. S. 49
Hyatt, J. P. 33, 34, 37

Jirku, A. 70
Jolles, A. 94

Knierim, R. 28, 31, 52, 55, 112
Kraus, H. J. 131
Kutsch, E. 16

Lind, M. C. 55
Lindblom, J. 143
Lohfink, N. 59
Long, B. O. 35, 140

Mann, C. S. 178
Martin-Achard, R. 93

Index of Authors

McCarthy, D. J. 120, 174
Möhlenbrink, J. 33, 34, 36, 37
Muilenburg, J. 68

Newman, M. 61
Noth, M. 15, 22-25, 28, 29, 32-34, 36-38, 41, 42, 49, 51, 56, 77, 81-83, 86-90, 92, 97, 110, 125, 128, 138, 191

Ord, D. R. 190, 191
Osswald, E. 76

Perrin, N. 58
Porter, J. R. 97
Preuss, H. D. 16

Quelle, G. 143

Rad, G. von 18, 26, 42, 43, 80, 82, 83, 85-87, 169
Raglan, L. 83
Rahlfs, A. 93
Richter, W. 14, 16, 17, 23, 26
Rowley, H. H. 149

Sanders, J. A. 114
Sasson, J. M. 61, 70, 71, 125
Schildenberger, J. 92, 93, 95
Schmid, H. 29, 76, 112
Schmidt, W. H. 111
Schnutenhaus, F. 76
Smend, R. 34, 37, 39, 76
Smolar, L. 125, 128
Steck, O. H. 141

Tomes, R. 53
Tucker, G. M. 104

Van Seters, J. 112
Vater, A. M. 174
Vaulx, J. de 89
Vaux, R. de 122
Vries, J. de 36, 40, 42, 47, 55, 77, 79, 83, 85, 171, 173

Weiser, A. 131
Westermann, C. 58, 59, 141, 146
Whybray, R., N. 128
Wolff, H. W. 145

Zimmerli, W. 42, 52

JOURNAL FOR THE STUDY OF THE OLD TESTAMENT

Supplement Series

82 RHETORIC AND BIBLICAL INTERPRETATION
    Dale Patrick & Allen Scult
83 THE EARTH AND THE WATERS IN GENESIS 1 AND 2:
    A LINGUISTIC INVESTIGATION
    David Toshio Tsumura
84 INTO THE HANDS OF THE LIVING GOD
    Lyle Eslinger
85 FROM CARMEL TO HOREB:
    ELIJAH IN CRISIS
    Alan J. Hauser & Russell Gregory
86 THE SYNTAX OF THE VERB IN CLASSICAL HEBREW PROSE
    Alviero Niccacci
    Translated by W.G.E. Watson
87 THE BIBLE IN THREE DIMENSIONS:
    ESSAYS IN CELEBRATION OF FORTY YEARS OF BIBLICAL STUDIES
    IN THE UNIVERSITY OF SHEFFIELD
    Edited by David J.A. Clines, Stephen E. Fowl & Stanley E. Porter
88 THE PERSUASIVE APPEAL OF THE CHRONICLER:
    A RHETORICAL ANALYSIS
    Rodney K. Duke
89 THE PROBLEM OF THE PROCESS OF TRANSMISSION
    IN THE PENTATEUCH
    Rolf Rendtorff
    Translated by John J. Scullion
90 BIBLICAL HEBREW IN TRANSITION:
    THE LANGUAGE OF THE BOOK OF EZEKIEL
    Mark F. Rooker
91 THE IDEOLOGY OF RITUAL:
    SPACE, TIME AND STATUS IN THE PRIESTLY THEOLOGY
    Frank H. Gorman, Jr
92 ON HUMOUR AND THE COMIC IN THE HEBREW BIBLE
    Edited by Yehuda T. Radday & Athalya Brenner
93 JOSHUA 24 AS POETIC NARRATIVE
    William T. Koopmans
94 WHAT DOES EVE DO TO HELP? AND OTHER READERLY QUESTIONS
    TO THE OLD TESTAMENT
    David J.A. Clines
95 GOD SAVES:
    LESSONS FROM THE ELISHA STORIES
    Rick Dale Moore

96 ANNOUNCEMENTS OF PLOT IN GENESIS
   Laurence A. Turner
97 THE UNITY OF THE TWELVE
   Paul R. House
98 ANCIENT CONQUEST ACCOUNTS:
   A STUDY IN ANCIENT NEAR EASTERN AND BIBLICAL HISTORY WRITING
   K. Lawson Younger, Jr
99 WEALTH AND POVERTY IN THE BOOK OF PROVERBS
   R.N. Whybray
100 A TRIBUTE TO GEZA VERMES:
    ESSAYS ON JEWISH AND CHRISTIAN
    LITERATURE AND HISTORY
    Edited by Philip R. Davies & Richard T. White
101 THE CHRONICLER IN HIS AGE
    Peter R. Ackroyd
102 THE PRAYERS OF DAVID (PSALMS 51–72):
    STUDIES IN THE PSALTER, II
    Michael Goulder
103 THE SOCIOLOGY OF POTTERY IN ANCIENT PALESTINE:
    THE CERAMIC INDUSTRY AND THE DIFFUSION OF CERAMIC STYLE
    IN THE BRONZE AND IRON AGES
    Bryant G. Wood
104 PSALM STRUCTURES:
    A STUDY OF PSALMS WITH REFRAINS
    Paul R. Raabe
105 ESTABLISHING JUSTICE
    Pietro Bovati
106 GRADED HOLINESS:
    A KEY TO THE PRIESTLY CONCEPTION OF THE WORLD
    Philip Jenson
107 THE ALIEN IN THE PENTATEUCH
    Christiana van Houten
108 THE FORGING OF ISRAEL:
    IRON TECHNOLOGY, SYMBOLISM AND TRADITION IN ANCIENT SOCIETY
    Paula M. McNutt
109 SCRIBES AND SCHOOLS IN MONARCHIC JUDAH:
    A SOCIO-ARCHAEOLOGICAL APPROACH
    David Jamieson-Drake
110 THE CANAANITES AND THEIR LAND:
    THE TRADITION OF THE CANAANITES
    Niels Peter Lemche
111 YAHWEH AND THE SUN:
    THE BIBLICAL AND ARCHAEOLOGICAL EVIDENCE
    J. Glen Taylor
112 WISDOM IN REVOLT:

METAPHORICAL THEOLOGY IN THE BOOK OF JOB
Leo G. Perdue
113 PROPERTY AND THE FAMILY IN BIBLICAL LAW
Raymond Westbrook
114 A TRADITIONAL QUEST:
ESSAYS IN HONOUR OF LOUIS JACOBS
Edited by Dan Cohn-Sherbok
115 I HAVE BUILT YOU AN EXALTED HOUSE:
TEMPLE BUILDING IN THE BIBLE IN THE LIGHT OF MESOPOTAMIAN
AND NORTH-WEST SEMITIC WRITINGS
Victor Hurowitz
116 NARRATIVE AND NOVELLA IN SAMUEL:
STUDIES BY HUGO GRESSMANN AND OTHER SCHOLARS 1906–1923
Translated by David E. Orton
Edited by David M. Gunn
117 SECOND TEMPLE STUDIES:
1. PERSIAN PERIOD
Edited by Philip R. Davies
118 SEEING AND HEARING GOD WITH THE PSALMS:
THE PROPHETIC LITURGY FROM THE SECOND TEMPLE IN JERUSALEM
Raymond Jacques Tournay
Translated by J. Edward Crowley
119 TELLING QUEEN MICHAL'S STORY:
AN EXPERIMENT IN COMPARATIVE INTERPRETATION
Edited by David J.A. Clines & Tamara C. Eskenazi
120 THE REFORMING KINGS:
CULT AND SOCIETY IN FIRST TEMPLE JUDAH
Richard H. Lowery
121 KING SAUL IN THE HISTORIOGRAPHY OF JUDAH
Diana Vikander Edelman
122 IMAGES OF EMPIRE
Edited by Loveday Alexander
123 JUDAHITE BURIAL PRACTICES AND BELIEFS ABOUT THE DEAD
Elizabeth Bloch-Smith
124 LAW AND IDEOLOGY IN MONARCHIC ISRAEL
Edited by Baruch Halpern and Deborah W. Hobson
125 PRIESTHOOD AND CULT IN ANCIENT ISRAEL
Edited by Gary A. Anderson and Saul M. Olyan
126 W.M.L. DE WETTE, FOUNDER OF MODERN BIBLICAL CRITICISM:
AN INTELLECTUAL BIOGRAPHY
John W. Rogerson
127 THE FABRIC OF HISTORY:
TEXT, ARTIFACT AND ISRAEL'S PAST
Edited by Diana Vikander Edelman

128 BIBLICAL SOUND AND SENSE:
     POETIC SOUND PATTERNS IN PROVERBS 10–29
     Thomas P. McCreesh, OP
129 THE ARAMAIC OF DANIEL IN THE LIGHT OF OLD ARAMAIC
     Zdravko Stefanovic
130 STRUCTURE AND THE BOOK OF ZECHARIAH
     Michael Butterworth
131 FORMS OF DEFORMITY:
     A MOTIF-INDEX OF ABNORMALITIES, DEFORMITIES AND DISABILITIES
     IN TRADITIONAL JEWISH LITERATURE
     Lynn Holden
132 CONTEXTS FOR AMOS:
     PROPHETIC POETICS IN LATIN AMERICAN PERSPECTIVE
     Mark Daniel Carroll R.
133 THE FORSAKEN FIRSTBORN:
     A STUDY OF A RECURRENT MOTIF IN THE PATRIARCHAL NARRATIVES
     R. Syrén
135 ISRAEL IN EGYPT:
     A READING OF EXODUS 1–2
     G.F. Davies
136 A WALK THROUGH THE GARDEN:
     BIBLICAL, ICONOGRAPHICAL AND LITERARY IMAGES OF EDEN
     Edited by P. Morris and D. Sawyer
137 JUSTICE AND RIGHTEOUSNESS:
     BIBLICAL THEMES AND THEIR INFLUENCE
     Edited by H. Graf Reventlow & Y. Hoffman
138 TEXT AS PRETEXT:
     ESSAYS IN HONOUR OF ROBERT DAVIDSON
     Edited by R.P. Carroll
139 PSALM AND STORY:
     INSET HYMNS IN HEBREW NARRATIVE
     J.W. Watts
140 PURITY AND MONOTHEISM:
     CLEAN AND UNCLEAN ANIMALS IN BIBLICAL LAW
     Walter Houston
141 DEBT SLAVERY IN ISRAEL AND THE ANCIENT NEAR EAST
     Gregory C. Chirichigno
142 DIVINATION IN ANCIENT ISRAEL AND ITS NEAR EASTERN ENVIRONMENT:
     A SOCIO-HISTORICAL INVESTIGATION
     Frederick H. Cryer
143 HOUSES AND THEIR FURNISHINGS IN BRONZE AGE PALESTINE:
     DOMESTIC ACTIVITY AREAS AND ARTIFACT DISTRIBUTION
     IN THE MIDDLE AND LATE BRONZE AGES
     P.M. Michèle Daviau

144 AMONG THE PROPHETS:
    ESSAYS ON PROPHETIC TOPICS
    Edited by P.R. Davies and D.J.A Clines
145 THE SPEECHES OF MICAH:
    A RHETORICAL-HISTORICAL ANALYSIS
    Charles S. Shaw
146 THE HISTORY OF ANCIENT PALESTINE FROM THE PALAEOLITHIC PERIOD
    TO ALEXANDER'S CONQUEST
    Gösta W. Ahlström
147 VOWS IN THE HEBREW BIBLE AND THE ANCIENT NEAR EAST
    Tony W. Cartledge
148 IN SEARCH OF 'ANCIENT ISRAEL'
    P.R. Davies
149 PRIESTS, PROPHETS AND SCRIBES:
    ESSAYS ON THE FORMATION AND HERITAGE OF SECOND TEMPLE
    JUDAISM IN HONOUR OF JOSEPH BLENKINSOPP
    Edited by E. Ulrich, J. Wright, R.P. Carroll & P.R. Davies
150 TRADITION AND INNOVATION IN HAGGAI AND ZECHARIAH
    J.A. Tollington
151 THE CITIZEN-TEMPLE COMMUNITY
    J.P. Weinberg
152 UNDERSTANDING POETS AND PROPHETS:
    ESSAYS IN HONOUR OF GEORGE WISHART ANDERSON
    A.G. Auld
153 THE PSALMS AND THEIR READERS:
    INTERPRETIVE STRATEGIES FOR PSALM 18
    D.K. Berry
154 MINHAH LE-NAHUM: BIBLICAL AND OTHER STUDIES PRESENTED TO
    NAHUM M. SARNA IN HONOUR OF HIS 70TH BIRTHDAY
    Edited by M. Fishbane & M. Brettler
155 LAND TENURE AND BIBLICAL JUBILEE: DISCOVERING A MORAL
    WORLD-VIEW THROUGH THE SOCIOLOGY OF KNOWLEDGE
    J.A. Fager
156 THE LORD'S SONG: THE BASIS, FUNCTION AND SIGNIFICANCE
    OF CHORAL MUSIC IN CHRONICLES
    J.W. Kleinig
157 THE WORD *HESED* IN THE BIBLE
    G.R. Clark
158 THE SOCIOLOGY OF SACRED TEXTS
    Edited by J. Davies & I. Wollaston
159 THE SHAPE AND SHAPING OF THE PSALTER
    Edited by J.C. McCann
160 KING AND CULTUS IN CHRONICLES:
    WORSHIP AND THE REINTERPRETATION OF HISTORY
    G.W. Coats